FROM GENERATION TO GENERATION

How to Trace Your Jewish
Genealogy and Personal History

ARTHUR KURZWEIL

WILLIAM MORROW AND COMPANY, INC.
New York   1980

Grateful acknowledgment is made for permission to reprint from the following works:

"Sueños," reprinted by permission; © 1975 *The New Yorker Magazine, Inc.* "Unto the Fourth Generation," copyright © 1959 by Mercury Press, Inc., from *Nightfall and Other Stories* by Isaac Asimov. Reprinted by permission of Doubleday & Co., Inc. "A Worker Reads History" from *Selected Poems of Bertolt Brecht*, translated by H. R. Hays, copyright © 1947 by Bertolt Brecht and H. R. Hays; renewed, 1975, by Stefan S. Brecht and H. R. Hays. Reprinted by permission of Harcourt Brace Jovanovich, Inc. "Family Reunion" reprinted from *Lying, Despair, Jealousy, Envy, Sex, Suicide, Drugs, and the Good Life* by Leslie H. Farber, copyright © 1976 by Basic Books, Inc., reprinted by permission of Leslie H. Farber and *Commentary*, copyright © 1974 by the American Jewish Committee. "My Grandmother Had Yichus," copyright © 1949 by May Natalie Tabak; reprinted by permission by May Natalie Tabak and *Commentary*, copyright © 1949 by the American Jewish Committee. "Testament of a Jew from Saragossa" from *Legends of Our Time* by Elie Wiesel. Copyright © 1968 by Elie Wiesel; reprinted by permission of Holt, Rinehart & Winston, Publishers. "The Crippler," from *And God Braided Eve's Hair* by Danny Siegel. Copyright © 1976 by Danny Siegel; reprinted by permission.

Library of Congress Cataloging in Publication Data

Kurzweil, Arthur.
   From generation to generation.

   Includes index.
   1. Jews—Genealogy—Handbooks, manuals, etc.   2. Kurzweil family.   I. Title.
CS21.K87   929'.1'02403924   79-26466
ISBN 0-688-03600-7

Printed in the United States of America

   2   3   4   5   6   7   8   9   10

Book Design by Michael Mauceri

For
Richard Carlow,
Ed Rothfarb,
and
Robin Kahn.

Since childhood,
a special kind of family.

"There is no treasure like friends."
אֵין מִכְמָן כַּחֲבֵרִים
Mivhar Hâ-Peninim

Special Foreword* by Elie Wiesel

הסכמה

What is a name? A mask for some, a vantage point, a reminder for others. Sometimes it signifies danger. Often: support.

For Paul Valery, nothing is as alien to man as his name. Understandably so. Imposed from without, the name dominates the person and invades him, ultimately taking his place. So why then not rid oneself of it along the way?

In the Jewish tradition, a name evokes a deeper and more respectful attitude. We are Semites because we are the descendants of Shem, which signifies: name. We call God, who has no name, "Hashem," the Name. In other words, our relationship with the name is of a mystical nature; it suggests an imperceptible, mysterious element. Its roots go deep into the unknown.

In the era of night, a name was a source of danger and death. But at the time of the first exile, in Egypt, it brought salvation. The Talmud affirms it: it is because our ancestors did not change their name that they knew deliverance.

For in Jewish history a name has its own history and its own memory. It connects beings with their origins. To retrace its path is thus to embark on an adventure in which the destiny of a single word becomes one with that of a community; it is to undertake a passionate and enriching quest for all those who may live in your name.

Therein lies the value and the appeal of Arthur Kurzweil's book: it shows us that each name is a call transmitted from generation to generation in order to force themselves to question the meaning of their survival.

Let us listen to this call.

---

* This "Special Foreword" is actually a Haskamah. Since the fifteenth century, it has been a Jewish custom for an author to seek, from a great scholar or rabbi, a "Haskamah" or approbation, which approves or recommends the work to its readers.

I have asked my teacher, Elie Wiesel, May his light shine, to continue this Jewish tradition. He has consented with this generous and moving Haskamah.

A.K.

Acknowledgments

Thanking people for their contributions and assistance while I was writing and researching this book is much like the process of family history itself: The list doesn't seem to end. There are those who helped me twenty years ago, before I ever imagined I'd write a book on Jewish family history and genealogy and there are others who helped me yesterday. Yet while the list is long, there are those who were crucial, and it is they who I wish to acknowledge here. Each of them can share with me in any kind remarks which this book receives. As for any criticism, I'll accept that myself.

At the top of the list is Ed Rothfarb, great friend and talented artist, whose comment in passing served as the inspiration for this book—in much the same way that his comment to me years ago was the inspiration for my first published article at age sixteen.

There are some friends who become your teachers and some teachers who become your friends. I am blessed with several wonderful friendships such as these: Lucjan Dobroszycki, Danny Siegel, Avery Corman, and Alida Roochvarg. All were vital to the writing of this book in ways they are probably not aware of.

There are family members who become your teachers as well. Maurice Gottlieb, Michelle Zoltan, and Sam and Rose Kurzweil have been supportive and instructive from the very beginning. I would also like to thank the Kurzweil Family Circle, which has been generous in its love and encouragement through the kindness of each of its members. In addition, I will be forever grateful to my aunt, Hilda Kurzweil, who, through her thoughtfulness and efforts on my behalf, has changed the entire course of my career.

Two friends who always serve as my personal life raft, and who are forever there with their love and support are Robin Kahn and Richard Carlow. Everyone should have two friends as these.

In my school career I was fortunate to encounter two master teachers whose influence permeates this book. Dr. Robert Sobel, professor of history at New College at Hofstra University, and David Christman, Dean of New College, were those profoundly important people. Dr. Sobel taught me to love history and Dean

Christman encouraged my writing—specifically my writing on Jewish subjects. To them I will be forever grateful.

The following institutions and their staffs were helpful, patient, and encouraging while I wrote this book and for years before as well: The New York Public Library Jewish Division, The New York Public Library Local History and Genealogy Division, The Leo Baeck Institute, and the YIVO Institute for Jewish Research. YIVO should be visited and supported by every Jew who cares anything about preserving our history. At YIVO, I would specifically like to thank Dina Abramowicz, Zachary Baker, and Lucjan Dobroszycki.

A friendship based on the shared love for a subject—in this case Jewish family history and genealogy—is an important friendship. Steven W. Siegel, my co-editor at *Toledot: The Journal of Jewish Genealogy*, deserves my thanks for the thousands of times I have consulted his expertise and for much more. He read the entire manuscript with care and sincere interest, and offered many, many suggestions, each of which was valuable.

My love and thanks go to Zsuzsa Barta, one of my cousins living in Budapest, and Jozef Schlaf, one of my cousins living in Warsaw, for the love and affection they have given to me, and for helping me to discover the mysteries of Eastern Europe. More than anyone, they have proven to me that family history is more than finding ancestors long gone: It is finding living relatives and sharing a life with them.

My brother, Ken Kurzweil, is a talented, creative teacher who serves as an inspiration to me for his professional abilities, and whom I value as a brother I can come to for almost everything. I thank him for that, and for much more.

This book would never have been published had it not been for the help of Sally Wendkos Olds. She introduced me to my agent, Julian Bach, who was excited about my work from the very beginning. Infinite thanks go to him for believing in what I am doing and for his efforts on my behalf.

Every author should have an editor like Bob Bender at William Morrow. When I think of our relationship, I think of the process of flying a kite: An author must be held tightly enough to be directed, loose enough to fly freely. It is a delicate balance which Bob achieves masterfully. I thank him for that and for his friendship.

Special thanks are also due to Maris Engel and Sharon Fliegel, who assisted me at one stage of my research, and Dr. Jeffrey Kahn, formerly with the Genealogical Society of Utah, who was always available for any help he could give. Maris Engel, a special and loving friend, also deserves more than I could ever give in return for her genuine friendship.

To Irving Adelman and the Reference Department of the East Meadow Public Library I owe my gratitude for teaching me how to use a library and, more importantly, how to love a library.

More than any other individual, Elie Wiesel has influenced and inspired my growing involvement in Jewish life. For this inspiration, and for the *haskama* which he has given to this book, no amount of thanks will ever be enough.

I also want to thank Lisa Kurzweil for her contribution to the writing of this book. I often have wondered if I could have done it without her.

If all the above-mentioned people were put on one side of a scale, I would need just two more people to create a balance on the other side—in terms of their importance to my life and work. My parents, Saul and Evelyn Kurzweil, are those people. They have given me my sense of love for family and Jewish life—which is just what this book is about.

As I complete this book, Jewish tradition urges me to pause and say:

בָּרוּךְ אַתָּה, יְיָ אֱלֹהֵינוּ, מֶלֶךְ הָעוֹלָם, שֶׁהֶחֱיָנוּ וְקִיְּמָנוּ וְהִגִּיעָנוּ לַזְּמַן הַזֶּה.

Baruch ata adonai elohainu melech ha-olam sheheheyanu v'kee-y'manu v'hee-gee-anu lazman hazeh.

Blessed art Thou, Lord our God, King of the universe who has kept us in life and sustained us and enabled us to reach this season.

ARTHUR KURZWEIL
August, 1979

Contents

*I do not wish anything
to happen in Jewish history
without it happening to me.*
—ELIE WIESEL

PART I

WHY?

Chapter 1

These Are My Generations:
Climbing up My Family Tree

In the spring of 1970, I wandered into the Jewish Division of the New York Public Library for the first time in my life. The cross section of Jews who sat at the long tables in that room spread over many decades and many worlds. There were young Chassidic men leaning over rare rabbinic texts, and middle-aged Reform rabbis preparing for a future sermon. There were college women writing term papers on history, and scholars writing books on obscure topics.

Standing near the doorway, I looked around at the faces and the books they were reading and I wondered where I fit into this peculiar congregation of Jews. Some of them were reading Yiddish, a language barely known to me, and others were strict observers of the Law, a way of life which I have never known. I was unlike them all, I concluded, and yet there I found myself, nonetheless, approaching the card catalog, looking for my own way, my own Jewishness.

Walking toward the drawer of the library card catalog for a portion of the "D" titles and authors, I knew I was wasting my time. Why would this library—or any library—have information on the town of Dobromil, the town in which my father was born, the town I learned of as a child through the dozens of stories my father told me?

I have told many people this: that my father told me dozens of stories about the little shtetl in Galicia, the town of his birth, of his mother's birth and his father's birth, of their marriage, and of their life "on the other side." Yet it is not true. While I feel that it was dozens of stories, it was just a few, though the few had more power than any collection of wondrous tales that could ever enchant a child. There was the story of the day my father was brought to the shul by his mother to change his name. He was gravely ill, his father was in America saving money to send for his wife and three children. My father was dying. His mother carried him to the shul and renamed her son. He was born Saul; now he was Chaim—for "life." Surely the Angel of Death would be fooled.

19

And, of course, the Angel was fooled, and I thought of this as my father told and retold the story to me, whenever I asked him to recite the tale again. Vividly I imagined my father being carried by his mother. Vividly I imagined the Angel of Death searching for a little sick boy named Saul who was nowhere to be found. I knew, as my father told me the story with pure seriousness, that I was born because many years before the Angel of Death was fooled.

Or the story of my grandmother's milk business in Dobromil. My grandfather was in New York, sending whatever money he could, but it was not enough. So my grandmother went into the milk business. She would go to the Christian peasants out in the fields and buy milk from them to bring back to the towns nearby and then resell it. My grandmother was a strong and healthy woman, but she could not carry all of the milk cans at once. So she would carry what she could as far as she could, and then she would return for the remaining cans. She would walk back to the point where she had left the first batch and then stop to rest. After this she would begin again, carrying what she could to the next point, and then returning for the remaining milk jugs. All by herself, she sold milk to the people in the nearby villages.

This story, too, did I imagine in minute detail. I walked, in my dreams, with my grandmother as she struggled with the heavy cans of milk. I stood with her as she poured the milk from her larger containers into the small jars and bottles of the people to whom she sold the raw milk. And I asked to hear the story over and over, visualizing the field which we walked across together.

There may have been other stories, but just a few. Not nearly the dozens I thought I had been told. But I dreamed about the shtetl of Dobromil a lot, and though I grew up in a suburban town in New York, I considered Dobromil home.

How can a young man, graduating college, raised in the most modern country in the world, near the city of New York, having (at that time) never stepped outside the borders of this country, consider a shtetl on the Russian-Polish border which today hasn't a Jew in it, to be "home"? It was a question I had yet to solve, but I felt it nevertheless. Every time I sat and had daydreams about the little town, I felt warm and at home. Throughout my childhood my imagination ran wild with the few stories I was told, so by the time I had reached the card catalog of the library, I already had faces of townspeople, visions of dirt roads, corners of brittle shuls, and Shabbas candles on freshly laid tablecloths all crystal clear in my mind.

Expecting to find nothing as I flipped through the cards in the drawer in the library, I came across an item which startled me. The top of the card read DOBROMIL, and the description of the item indicated a book.

A book on Dobromil? Impossible, I thought. As clear as my dream of Dobromil was, as warm as my love for the town which was my father's for only eight years after which he came to America, I didn't think the town deserved a book. By its importance in my life it deserved much more, but how could such a small town take up the pages of a book, in the New York Public Library no less?

I filled out the form required for the librarian to retrieve the book as I sat at a table among the Chassidim and the scholars and the casual readers of the latest Jewish magazines. As I waited, I stared at faces around me. As I looked at the deep lines on the older faces, I wondered where these people were from, what they were reading, how they lived. Did they believe in God? Did they survive death camps? Who were they? What were their stories? As was a habit of mine, I began to create stories about the people around me. I invented histories for them. I gave men wives and women husbands. I gave them houses and apartments, pasts and tragedies. That man over there was a widower for years. That one was a rabbi who hasn't "believed" in years, but would never admit it to a soul. His face was plagued with guilt. The man across from me was a scholar, having manuscripts in his desk, waiting for the world to discover his brilliance.

And then the book arrived.

I looked at the cover for a long moment, reading the words *Memorial Book—Dobromil* several times as I held the book and felt its weight of more than 500 pages. Flipping through the book I saw the Hebrew letters, English letters, and photographs pass quickly before my eyes. Several times I flipped the pages rapidly, almost not wanting to stop to examine the detail, mostly because I was too excited to look at one page while I wondered impatiently what was on the next.

Turning to the first page, a full-page photograph, I read the caption: "Main Street in Dobromil." There is no way for me to know how many minutes I sat staring at the picture. The photograph showed an unpaved road, several small buildings with slanted roofs, and a few people on the street. I expect no one to believe me when I say that the picture was familiar to me. I had imagined it just this way.

With this photograph, my dreams of years were confirmed. There

Dobromil, Galicia, ca. 1938, home town of the author's father, grand-parents, and great-grandparents. (Courtesy Jozef Schlaf)

was a Dobromil, it *did* have dirt roads, and little houses, and people who stood at the shul while the Angel of Death was being plotted against. As I came out of the trance which had me reliving each of the stories in all of the detail which I had filled in for years, I was able to begin to examine the book more closely. I continued to have a sense of disbelief, not fully realizing that in my hands was a book on a subject as profoundly important to me as this. A book on the shtetl of Dobromil was for me what a walk on the moon would be for a boy who grew up wanting to be an astronaut.

The book was in three languages: Hebrew, Yiddish, and English. Turning to the English section, I read the titles of the chapters including "Destruction of Dobromil," "Historic Dobromil," and "Personalities." One was called "Dobromiler Grandparents." My grandparents were Dobromiler grandparents, so I turned to the chapter to see what it said. It was a story written by a woman whose grandparents were from Dobromil. It was then that I looked at the front of the book to see when it was printed. The date was 1963. This confused me, because I could not understand how a book could be published so recently about a town which was such ancient history to me—regardless of the nature of my fantasies.

I decided to look through the book page by page, in order to examine the photographs which were scattered in plentiful quanti-ties throughout. As I turned the pages I looked at the photos, glanc-ing at the faces in each of the shots. It did not even cross my mind that I would see a face that I would recognize. My father was just a boy when he left Dobromil and his father was a simple tinsmith. My father's mother was in the milk business, and the only other person whom I could think of at the time was my great-grandfather, the man whom I was named after, who also was a tinsmith. The possibility that they would be in this book was too remote to even have considered.

It was for this reason that I was absolutely stunned when I saw a picture of Avrahum Abusch, my great-grandfather, as I looked at a group photo which took up an entire page.

Jewish trade organization from Dobromil, Poland.

Had the man across from me not been engrossed in the Talmudic text in front of him, he would have seen me shake. As a person to whom the New York Public Library was the center of the modern world, I was overcome by the just-discovered fact that my great-grandfather had his picture in a book in that very place. A picture of my great-grandfather. I could say it over and over and it would still sound unbelievable to me.

I could sit still no longer. I ran to the librarian at the desk in the front of the room to share my discovery. To the best of my recollection, she took the matter quite casually. What was at the time the most exciting thing that had ever happened to me was taken in stride by the woman at the desk before me. I didn't understand why she couldn't appreciate the importance of my discovery. Part of me still doesn't. Because that discovery opened up the door to a search which has taken me many years and which, I am happy to say, offers no end in sight. The discovery of that photograph said one thing to me—one thing which changed my life: "You have a past," it said, "a past and a history, and you can discover it if you want."

The reason I recognized the photograph of my great-grandfather, Abusch, is because I had taken a great interest in him for years. Ever since I first heard the story of my father's name change from Saul to Chaim I wondered about my name as well. I was told that it was my great-grandfather after whom I was named, so I have always asked questions about him, collected pictures of him, and I became his imaginary friend. Actually, he became my imaginary conscience. For the longest time I have envisioned him in heaven, watching me. This didn't upset me, nor did it frighten me, but I have to admit that there have been many times when I would base choices of mine on what my great-grandfather in heaven would think. Even during the periods of my life when I rejected the notions of God, heaven, and anything supernatural, I still remained in the state of mind which had me think of how my great-grandfather would feel if I did what I knew to be wrong. In those times, I did not believe that he was watching and judging, but rather that being named after him I had a responsibility to maintain his "good name." To this day I am convinced that this is a positive effect of learning about history and, in particular, family history. We have a responsibility to the past.

In the library, I took the book on Dobromil to the photocopy services and had a few pages duplicated. One was the picture of my great-grandfather. Another was the title page of the book. And a third was a street map of the shtetl, Dobromil, complete with little squares representing houses, and captions of many of the houses in Yiddish which I would have to get translated. I took the photocopies and went to visit my parents.

My father was amazed at the discovery I had made and was most excited by the map of the shtetl. Glancing at the map for no more than a few seconds, he unhesitingly pointed to a spot on the map and said, "We lived here."

The spot he pointed to had a number, and we looked at the number guide to the map where my father read the Yiddish caption. It said, "The Glazier Ennis." We looked at each other and smiled. Ennis was my grandmother's maiden name and her family were glaziers. So, not only did the book have a picture of my great-grandfather on my grandfather's side of the family, but it also had a map with the house of my grandmother's family.

How many times I had been in that house in my dreams. How many times I imagined eating at the table, playing outside, walking through the fields with my grandmother, helping her carry the milk cans back to the house. That house came to represent to me an entire world that I often longed for but knew I'd never find. It was a world which I knew was destroyed; a world which only my dreams could capture. I would never know if I was nearly correct in the way I imagined it. But now I had it on a map. Now I could place it at the exact point on earth where it still might be standing.

Where it still might be standing. This was another part of my daydreams. Often I wondered what happened to the house where my father grew up. Who lived there now? Who sat in the doorway that I have wanted to sit in? It was years later that I spoke to a man who went back to Dobromil shortly after the war. The town, which was once almost completely Jewish, was already occupied by the Ukrainians as if it had always been theirs. They lived in our houses, ate at our tables, and slept in our beds.

As my father and I looked at the map, he remembered more stories about his childhood and the town. I was delighted. I was also impressed by my father's memory. He had left Dobromil as a child of eight, and he had often been told by other family members that he could not remember much, probably because they themselves could not recall much, though they were older. But as my father looked at the map of the town where he spent the first eight years of his life, he proved them wrong time and again. He began to identify many places on the map with ease and finally turned to me and said, "See, I remember the place well."

I returned often to the New York Public Library Jewish Division to look at the Dobromil book. I was like a little child who asked for the same picture book from the librarian and sat with it, reliving the same fairy tale. It was not much different for me. I relived the fairy tale over and over again. Each time I returned to the book, I became more familiar with the faces in the photographs and they became my neighbors. The only section of the book which I avoided with each visit was "The Destruction of Dobromil." I would not read it or look at those pictures. Not yet. I was not ready. I was still building the town. There was no way that I would let it be destroyed so quickly.

One day I decided to use the photocopy of the title page which I had made the first day I discovered the book. It included the names of a few men who had apparently put the book together. They were identified as the Book Committee. The organization of which they were a committee was the Dobromiler Society, which was a landsmannschaft. At that time I had no idea what a landsmannschaft was. Landsmannschaften are organizations consisting of people from a town in Europe. In other words, people from Dobromil, and their families, joined together to form an organization when they arrived in America. (There are also landsmannschaften in Israel and other countries.) These organizations were homes away from home for new immigrants. People were able to associate with familiar faces, reminisce about the Old Country, and be of emotional and financial support to each other. Often the first thing a landsmannschaft did was to raise money to buy a burial plot for members.

The title page of the Dobromil book indicated that the Dobromiler Society was located in New York, so I deduced that the men on the Book Committee were also New Yorkers. I decided to call them.

I searched through the several New York City area phone books for the names and finally came across one that matched. They were all uncommon names which made my search easier. The man whose phone number I found was a Philip Frucht. I dialed his number and a man answered.

"Is this Philip Frucht?" I asked.

"Yes."

"Are you the man who helped to put the book on Dobromil together?"

"Yes. Who are you?"

"My name is Arthur Kurzweil," I answered. "You might have known my family. There was a picture of my great-grandfather in the book."

"What did you say your name was?" he asked.

"Kurzweil."

"I'm sorry," he said. "I knew most of the people in Dobromil, but this family I must not have known."

"But you must have known them. There was a picture in the book," I pleaded.

Again I repeated my name, but it did not help. It was then that an idea struck me. Though I knew my grandfather to be named Julius, his name in Yiddish—and therefore in Dobromil—was Yudl. I also knew that though my grandfather was a roofer in Brooklyn, he was a tinsmith in Dobromil. So I asked Mr. Frucht, "Did you know Yudl the tinsmith?"

Frucht's voice perked up. "Who are you to Yudl?" he demanded.

"I'm his grandson," I said.

The next thing I knew, Frucht was shouting into the next room to his wife, telling her that he was speaking to Yudl's grandson. He sounded as excited as I was.

"What did you say your name was?" he asked me again.

"Kurzweil," I said, pronouncing it the way I was always taught to say it. "Kerzwhile."

"You mean 'Koortzvile,'" Frucht pronounced it. "No wonder I didn't recognize it."

Inside myself, I was a bit ashamed. Though it was the way I was taught since childhood, it was not the way my grandparents said our name, or my great-grandparents, or their parents, or any of the people in Dobromil. I must have spoken my name incorrectly a hundred thousand times. I robbed it of its Jewishness and made it American.

It has been difficult to change that habit. Still, I am not as bad off as those people who do not even know the spelling of their name because of some episode which occurred at Ellis Island. I have come to believe that names are terribly important. I have already mentioned the significance of the knowledge that I had of being named for my great-grandfather Abusch. Actually, the importance of that went farther. Several times I have been told that I resembled Abusch, in personality as well as in looks—from old photographs of him. Psychologically, this had an impact, the same way that it would if I was told that I was a "bad boy." Children who are labeled "bad" often live up to the name. I too wanted to "live up" to the name of my great-grandfather. He was a kind man, I was told, so I wanted to be a kind man. He always had a good sense of humor, so I wanted to have a good sense of humor. He was religious yet modern and I wanted to be religious yet modern. He was a role model which I took very seriously because of our shared name. How I would love to know whom *he* was named for!

Surnames are equally important. I could never understand how a person could change his last name. Of course, I know the history of it: it was often a survival tactic in response to anti-Semitism. But for me, changing one's name is like cutting off an arm. It is part of you. How can you bear to lose it?

After Mr. Frucht gave me a lesson in pronouncing my own name, I asked him if he knew my family. He did, indeed, and quite well. I learned many things from the conversation which followed, including the fact that my grandfather Yudl had once been a president of the Dobromiler Society himself. Frucht proceeded to tell me many stories about Dobromil and his relationship to my family and finally suggested other people who would be equally able to fill me in on further details. After completing my talk with Mr. Frucht, I was elated and mystified. Perhaps it was the quality of Frucht's stories. He spoke about Dobromil as if it still existed as a shtetl. The affection he had for his town was inspiring, and it brought the town that much closer to me. But one of his comments made the biggest impact of all. After we spoke about Dobromil, the conversation turned to me. "What do you do?" he asked. I told him that I was a librarian, the head of a department, with a staff of people working with me. Mr. Frucht replied, "That's wonderful. It's always nice to hear about the success of a Dobromiler."

It was all that he needed to say to make my day, or perhaps my year! Here was a man, born and raised in Dobromil, calling me a Dobromiler, calling me a member of the shtetl. He didn't know that I have walked the streets of the shtetl in my dreams, that I imagined the town to be mine for years, or that I longed so often to go there. He didn't know that I have relived so many times the stories told to me by my father. Yet he called me a Dobromiler. My wish had been realized.

Often I have wondered how many people would think all of this crazy. I still wonder. There is a touch of madness to all of this dreaming and feelings. Why in the year 1970 would a young man in his twenties, born and raised in New York suburbs, be elated at being called a member of a shtetl? What is the point? What does it mean? Who really cares? I have no answer for it, except to say that the more I learn about the shtetlach of my ancestors, the more at home I feel. It was in these places that my ancestors struggled to survive, and something within me drives my body and soul to visit the streets of my families' past. I visit them in photographs, in stories, in names, and in dreams. And Mr. Frucht merely said out loud what I had been unable to say myself. I am a Dobromiler; I was born in New York but come out of a shtetl. In fact, as I reach farther and farther back in my past, I have come out of Egypt as an Israelite. This is what the Passover Hagaddah says and it is true. My experience with Dobromil teaches me this.

I am a child of America, but I am a Dobromiler.

Finding the Dobromil book and speaking to Philip Frucht launched my casual interest about family history into an obsession. Often I wonder when it really began. For a while I thought it was with the discovery of the Dobromil book, but something had to have brought me to the library. Then I thought it was the stories

Wedding portrait of Abusch and Hinde Ruchel Kurzweil, ca. 1890, in Przemysl, Poland. (Courtesy of Saul Kurzweil)

which my father told me, but something made me ask to have them told over and over again. Most recently I have come to recall an incident which occurred early in my childhood. I was in my father's synagogue on Rosh Ha-shonah and I can recall sitting next to my father listening to the rabbi's sermon—which I did not understand. I must have been eight years old or so. But at one point in the sermon, the rabbi said that at this time of year God opens the book of life, a book with everyone's name in it, and decides who will live and who will die.

I remember wondering as the rabbi made that statement how God organized his book. Was it alphabetically, or by family? I imagined it to be by family, and to this day I visualize it in that way. In fact, I hope someday to be God's librarian for those books.

Obviously, my interest in family relationships had an early beginning, and more obviously as time went on, I saw it become, as I said, an obsession.

I began to contact people in my family on a random basis, taking trains and buses (and making phone calls to people too far to visit) to gather information about the family. Each conversation led me to more people, and in very little time I had more than a hundred names of cousins and ancestors. I was particularly interested in talking to the oldest members of the family, asking them to reach back in their memories to the earliest people and stories that they could recall. The family tree grew with amazing speed, and I was admittedly surprised by the cooperation I had gotten. Everyone was interested in telling me what he knew. I even received letters from people who had heard of my interest and had decided not to wait for me to get around to them. I found that I had gathered names, dates, towns, and stories about a huge number of people. The family, which I never knew to be that large, became enormous. Of course, many of the names which I had gathered were of people who were no longer living, but the family was still quite large. One factor became very helpful to my research; there is a Kurzweil Family Circle which has been in existence for more than thirty-five years. While the organization did not have any historical information to hand me, it did have a membership list as well as a cemetery plot. I visited the cemetery and sent questionnaires to the members of the Family Circle.

The questionnaires asked for information about each person's immediate family and his own ancestors. I included return envelopes and in a short period of time my mailbox was overflowing with filled-in questionnaires. I spread them all out on the floor and began to build a sizable family tree stretching back several generations. I also received more names and addresses of people who were not members of the Kurzweil Family Circle and I wrote to them as well. Then I sent additional letters out to people asking for stories and I received more history about the family. In the course of my research I discovered a branch of the family who have lived in Israel for a few generations, branches of the family in cities around the United States, and most surprising of all, I found the name of a cousin who still lives in Poland. At that time, he was

Family Circles and Cousins Clubs have formed among Jewish families for the past 100 years in the United States.

just a strange name on a piece of paper, but today he is my cousin Joseph, with a wife Daniele and a daughter Anna. They live in Warsaw, and Joseph is the only member of the Kurzweil family who survived the war and still lives in Poland. He is a writer of Jewish history, which is surely a rare thing for anyone in Poland today. We write to each other regularly.

In time, I had accumulated a lot of information and was becoming quite familiar with the history of the family. My questions to older relatives surprised them. I asked them about things that they themselves hadn't thought about for decades. A crucial point came when I felt as if I was living in a different place at a different time. Again, my dreams at night took place far away in time and space. It was becoming unusual for me *not* to have a dream about some ancestor or other. I entered the world of my ancestors in my conscious and subconscious lives. At times I felt it unhealthy. Newspapers interested me less than historical accounts of Galicia which I borrowed from the library.

My picture collection grew as well, helping my dreams, undoubtedly, to create vivid images of the shtetl and the past. Some people loaned me photographs, others gave them to me. I also discovered a large box of pictures which my parents had, filled with old photos of family members and street scenes. Eventually, I had just about exhausted every possible lead that I had on people who could contribute information about the family.

The process of meeting these people was wonderful. In effect, I was doing two things at once: building a family history and making new friends and acquaintances. Both were rewarding and priceless. It was fascinating to learn what paths my cousins' lives had taken. We all descended from the same people, but because of the different kinds of choices our closer ancestors made, we went in varied directions. Remarkable was the physical resemblance between people who had never seen each other before. My cousin Joseph from Warsaw, for example, looks remarkably like my father.

When I completed the stage of my research which dealt with people I had known or was referred to, I began searching through phone books. Since Kurzweil is an uncommon name, it was a rather easy task—at least compared with a name such as Schwartz or Cohen. The New York Public Library has a collection of just about every available phone book in the world, so I spent hours combing them, looking for Kurzweils to call or write. Again I was met with remarkable success. I came up with people who were definitely related to me but who knew nothing about my family. Several generations back, their ancestors and mine went in different directions, and sooner or later lost contact. Now, for the first time, cousins were getting to know one another. It was relatively easy for me to figure out if someone was a cousin. I had accumulated enough names and places to be able to discover the link in a rather short time. My family tree was organized well enough for me to have easy access to the material within it.

One phone call to an unknown Kurzweil met with an unusual series of circumstances. I called a man whose name was Arthur Kurzweil, just like me. I identified myself on the phone and told him what I was doing. He voiced disinterest and told me that he'd call me back if he became interested. I was upset by this, having experienced nothing like it in the months that I was pursuing my family history. But I decided, some weeks later, to call again and try my luck. I asked him politely what his grandparents' names were, and when he told me I immediately knew who he was. His grandparents came to America long before most Kurzweils and because of this they grew apart from the rest of the family, most of whom came to the U.S. rather late, historically. So it was obvious why we would not have known about him.

When he told me their names, I proceeded to tell him the names of some of his aunts and uncles.

"Your aunts and uncles must be Bessie, Morris, Pauline . . ."

"Who told you this?" he asked.

"And your parents must be Harry and . . ." I continued.

"Are we related?" he asked.

We certainly were, and I explained exactly what the relationship was. He still wasn't convinced. The phone conversation ended shortly after that, and there was still doubt in his voice. Later on, months later, he told me that he thought I was representing a business which does family-tree research for a fee.

His disbelief troubled me, as did his unwillingness to cooperate, since he could have been the link between me and many other people in his "missing" branch of the family. I wanted to make the family tree as complete as possible, and he was a source for quite a bit of information. Rather than give up, I decided to tackle the problem with even more energy than usual. It brought me to examining public records.

Until this point, I had very little experience with the use of public records. Actually, the only time I ever used them for my family-tree research was to get the death certificate of my great-grandfather, Abusch. Death certificates often provide the names of the deceased's parents, including the mother's maiden name. In this case, I was able to verify what I was already told by relatives as to my great-great-grandparents' first names, and I also learned the maiden name of Abusch's mother. This was important for two reasons. First, it added another major branch to my family tree. Second, it led me to the knowledge that my great-grandparents were first cousins.

So, I began to do research into this unknown branch of the family. I used census records which gave me information about household members in 1900. I sent for immigration records which provided still more information, and I went to the Surrogate's Court and looked up the wills of several people. It all added up to a lot of facts, though it was the difficult way of doing what could probably have been done in a conversation. But it was a fortunate thing also because in the process of looking for the items I was after, I discovered things about other branches of the family. In the end, I had a thick file of data on my entire family, provided by public documents in the United States. This included the names of towns in Europe where people originated, dates of immigration, names of steamships taken to this country, and even copies of the passenger lists of the ships. I have in my possession the passenger list of the ship which took my father and his brother, sister, and mother to America in 1929. It is an important document to me, for obvious reasons.

Over the years, many people have asked me if I was related to Professor Baruch Kurzweil of Israel. Recently, Professor Kurzweil died. I had no idea if he and I were related, though I knew quite a bit about him, because of the fact that I am in the habit of looking for the name "Kurzweil" in just about every book I pick up. Since Baruch is perhaps the most famous Kurzweil in the world, his name has shown up often. Baruch Kurzweil was a leading literary critic in Israel. He was an Agnon expert and was also known for his critique of the work of Gershom Scholem. His criticism of Scholem made him quite a controversial figure (as did many other of his points of view) since Scholem is seen as almost untouchable when it comes to his field of research.

But though my knowledge of the work of Professor Kurzweil grew, I still did not have an answer to the question, Were we related? No one in my family, immediate or more distant, knew the answer, though many of us had been asked the very same question. Then one day I received a reply to one of the many letters I sent to Kurzweils around the world. I went through scores of telephone directories of this country and around the world at the New York Public Library, and wrote to as many Kurzweils as I could find. While many people are in the habit of checking phone books for their last name whenever they are out of town, I do the same— and write to them. The letter I received on one particular day was from Israel. It was from an Amram Kurzweil who began his letter with a warm message of support for what I was doing regardless (he said) of whether we were related or not. He then drew for me a family tree of his family, listing descendants as well as ancestors. At the top of his tree was the following sentence: "My grandfather's father (whose name I do not know) came from the town of Przemysl." It was the same town that I knew to be my great-great-grandfather's! As I examined the family tree further, I discovered the name Baruch Kurzweil.

This discovery had two pieces of significance to it. In the first place, it answered my question about Professor Kurzweil. Secondly, it taught me something about family history research. From all of my research on Baruch Kurzweil, I was led to believe that his family came from an altogether different part of Europe than my family. Items about Professor Kurzweil, provided in many different sources, included his biography and even some family background. Again, the region of his ancestry was given as a different part of Eastern Europe. Ordinarily, I would have drawn the conclusion that we were not related. The fact of the matter is that the accounts that I read never went back far enough. But Amram Kurzweil, who is Professor Kurzweil's uncle, knew an earlier town of origin than any of the encyclopedic items I had found, and so I was able to discover that our families were from the same place originally. Of course, this still does not prove that we are related, but if two Kurzweils come from the same town in Eastern Europe, it is likely that we are.

Another letter from a Kurzweil in Israel brought more interesting results: One day I received a detailed piece of correspondence from a man named Dov Kurzweil. While he was eager to exchange notes of the histories of our families, it was clear from his letter that we would not be able to establish any family links—at least not from what he knew. While Kurzweil is not a common name, it is not altogether rare in Europe, so it is quite possible that many Kurzweils are not related (though I must add that I am beginning to doubt that since I continue to discover more originally unknown cousins all of the time). I wrote Dov back, thanking him for his letter, but adding that there appeared to be no relation.

Months later, a letter arrived from a man in California, also a Kurzweil. He responded to one of my many inquiries to Kurzweils around the country and world. Again, as I read his letter it became clear that he was not related. His letter, however, was quite enthusiastic, and he indicated that he would love to hear from me and share information regardless of whether we were cousins. He said this because I told him in my letter that I had collected a mass of material on Kurzweil families around the world. One comment in his letter was odd. Near the end he wrote, "My father was an atheist, but I always assumed that we were Protestant."

As I reread his letter, I had the feeling that some of the details he provided were familiar. Though it was obvious that his family and mine were unrelated—at least for the past several generations— I was sure that I knew some of what he had written. Then I remembered: The information that he gave and the information given by the Kurzweil in Israel matched! They were not related to me, but they were related to each other. I wrote him back, explaining this to him, and adding that it appeared as if his family was originally Jewish. I waited for a reply from him, sure that I would get one based on the enthusiasm which he registered in his letter, but he never answered me.

After seven years of research on one of the many branches of my family, I realized that I had made a mistake: I had neglected all of the other branches. In large part, it was the fact that my last name is Kurzweil which subconsciously made me think that I was more a Kurzweil than a Gottlieb, which is my mother's maiden name. For that matter, I was equally an Ennis, which is my father's mother's maiden name. I am also just as much a Klein, a Loventhal, a Rath, a Grünberger, and countless other names as well. But the fact that we generally take the names of our father, added to the stronger family ties in my father's family, resulted in my becoming singularly obsessed with the Kurzweil family for, as I said, seven years.

There were some worthwhile results of this obsession, however. I would have never gotten as far as I did, had I spread myself thinly over a few families. On the other hand, the worst enemy of the genealogist is time, and I am yet to learn, I am sure, of people in other branches who have recently died and who would have told me much had I begun earlier. The results of my Kurzweil research are dramatic: I have a nearly complete genealogy of my great-great-great-grandparents and all of their descendants—nearly 500 of them. I have dozens of early photographs of the family, countless stories about individuals, and a wealth of information about the history of my ancestors. The one thing which I did not forget to do is to obey a cardinal rule of family history research: *share your findings.*

I deeply wanted to let everyone know what I had found. I wanted children in the family to be able to look at my family tree and see who their ancestors were. The family tree included seven generations, and it would be important for family members to be able to glance at the tree and see their ancestors as well as to understand how large the family was, and the paths they traveled. Another important part of my research which I felt especially bound to share was my Holocaust findings. More than 100 members of the Kurzweil family were killed in the Holocaust. I collected their names, their relationships to the rest of the family, their ages, and in many cases their specific fates. There are no graves for these cousins of mine; and no memorials. My family tree was their memorial. I wanted the family to know them and to remember them.

I decided to write a book. It would be a modest undertaking, privately printed as inexpensively as possible, which I would sell at cost to the family. It took me two years to finish the book, and it finally came to 140 pages, complete with all seven generations of the family, pages of photographs, history of the family, and an index so that anyone could easily find himself (or others) on the tree. The book was a labor of love and a grand success. Kurzweils from all over the world asked for copies. More than 100 books are on book-

shelves in the homes of Kurzweils that I know. While I was putting
the book together I became somewhat obsessed with it. I worked
on it every spare moment at a frantic pace. But I loved doing it. And
the result of it is this: I now know that as long as those books exist,
future generations of my family will know from where they came.
They will know what tradition brought them to the point at which
they are. They will know the names of the people who struggled to
live and to bring up children. They will also know of those ancestors who were murdered by the Nazis. Most of all, they will know
who they themselves are.

There is just one last chapter to the story of the Kurzweil family
research. After I printed the family books, I helped to organize a
party. To that party, which was a celebration of Chanukah, I invited everyone whom I had contacted during the years of my research.
On the day of the party, more than 100 people came to celebrate.
It was the largest gathering of Kurzweils—perhaps ever. Great-great-
grandchildren of the same people saw each other for the first time.
Friendships were made. Others were renewed (some people who
hadn't seen each other for forty years were there). It was everything
that a family reunion should be. Most importantly, it provided us
with the opportunity to understand firsthand what the Talmudic
passage means when it says that if a human life is killed, it is as if
a world is killed and if a human life is saved, it is as if a whole
world has been saved. Each of us at that party were cousins, descended from the same two people. Had my great-great-great-grandparents not lived to marry and have children, none of us would have
been there.

For seven years, as I said, I neglected the history of my mother's
family. My mother, saint that she is, listened patiently to the un-
folding story of my father's family, never expressing confusion over
my apparent lack of interest in her history. In part, there was an
obvious difference between families. While my father was born in
Europe and remembered a significant amount for an immigrant
who arrived here at age eight, my mother was born in New York
and knew almost nothing about her European background. She
had never met her father's parents, and just met briefly with her
mother's parents. She had very little to say when I asked her about
the history of either side of her family.

In addition, her family was small. While my father's family—
both sides in fact—had large Family Circles (family organizations
with regular meetings, a cemetery plot, and a history), my mother
hardly knew more than just the immediate family. On superficial

view, her family seemed not to have had much of a history that could be discovered. There were no older members of the family in America alive to speak about the family. Generally, my mother could understand quite well why I did not pursue her family and its history.

One final factor in the situation is that my mother's family was significantly different from my father's in terms of Jewishness. My mother's father arrived in the United States by himself as a teenager and adapted to the American way of life rather quickly. While retaining an internal sense of himself as a Jew, he was mostly assimilated. My mother's mother also arrived in this country at a young age, with her sister, and she too assimilated quickly. My mother grew up in a different kind of home from my father's home. His was the home of Orthodox immigrants. Hers was the home of assimilated Jews.

Despite all of this, I had the desire to learn about my mother's family, and decided to begin. When I asked my mother who would be the best source, she instantly said that her cousin Maurice Gottlieb would be the person to see. Maurice, her first cousin, is an intelligent, quick-witted man who was born in Europe and who my mother thought would remember some things. Though he lived in New York, I decided to write to him. Many people find it easier to talk than to write, but I knew that Maurice had once wanted to be a writer. I always try to get people to write about their history. Their letters become documents to save forever.

Maurice wrote back a lovely letter detailing what he knew about the family and its history. He named the towns in Europe where the family originated, and the people who made up the family tree. He mentioned some occupations and a few other details. The most surprising item was that his grandfather—who was my great-grand-father—was a rabbi. I was shocked. Could it be that my grandfather, the assimilated American, was the son of a rabbi? On closer reading, I understood that while the man was a rabbi, he worked, at times, as a slaughterer (a shochet), and that he did not function in the way that I know rabbis to function. He had smichah (was "ordained") but did not have a congregation. It was fairly common for a man to have smichah. Nevertheless, it was startling to learn that this branch of my family was so religious.

I telephoned my mother and asked her if she knew that her own grandfather was a rabbi. She admitted that while she recalled that her father told her this, she never believed him. It just didn't seem likely.

Also in the letter from Maurice was the fact that the family name was not Gottlieb, but was changed from the original name of Rosenvasser. This interested my mother. Imagine spending your life thinking that your name is your own, only to find out that it was originally something else—Rosenvasser in fact!

Weeks passed and I did little more to pursue the history of my mother's father's family. The discovery that the family name was Rosenvasser and not Gottlieb became something of a family joke. My father began to call my mother Miss Rosenvasser, and I too made reference to the name on many occasions—perhaps to the point of being obnoxious. I checked the name "Rosenvasser" in several Jewish encyclopedias but found nothing. I looked through a few New York phone books and found the name spelled two different ways: Rosenvasser and Rosenwasser. But despite this, I did not call these people or write to them. What would I say—"My family name used to be Rosenvasser and I wonder if we are related"? While I did do this in my Kurzweil research, it was when I had more to offer. Usually when I call or get a call from someone named Kurzweil, I immediately know how the person is related after he tells me the name of his grandparents. But I had far too little to go on to begin to make telephone inquiries. In addition, the news that our name was Rosenvasser was still too recent a discovery for me to fully believe it.

After a while it happened that my grandparents (my mother's parents) moved out of their apartment, which they had lived in for several decades, and went to live with my parents. My grandparents were in their mid-eighties and my grandfather had been held up at gunpoint. Their move was an opportunity for me to find things in their apartment which might give me additional leads concerning their family history. Both of my grandparents had denied for years that they had any photographs, letters, or anything which would help me in my search. They both told me their parents' names and that was all. They claimed that there was nothing else to know.

I was far from convinced. It is impossible to save nothing of family interest during a lifetime of more than eighty years. When my mother and I went to their apartment on Dyckman Street in upper Manhattan to put things in boxes and pack up the place, my belief was confirmed. Not only was it untrue that my grandparents saved nothing, but the drawers, closets, and hidden compartments of their apartment were a virtual museum of family history. I found a huge box of photographs, some dating back to the early 1900's in Europe. I found a large bundle of letters received by both of my grandparents from their families in Europe who stayed and were killed in the Holocaust. I found nearly every birthday card that my grandmother had ever received. I found scraps of paper with the names and birthdates of all of my grandmother's brothers and sisters, some of whom I would never have discovered had it not been for these papers. I found receipts for tickets on cross-Atlantic steamships. I found copies of letters of inquiry regarding Holocaust victims in my family. I found tefillin of my grandfather and members of his family. I found old, valueless European money saved from Europe. And finally, I found two framed pictures, each containing the images of married couples, one being my grandmother's parents and one being my grandfather's parents.

I showed the photos to my mother immediately. "Of course," she said, "I haven't seen them for years. Those are my grandparents."

The contrast between the two couples was, as they say, like night and day. My grandmother's parents appeared to be a fairly modern, well-dressed, cosmopolitan couple. Her father was wearing a three-piece suit, cufflinks on the shirt, a ring on his finger, and pince-nez glasses. His wife wore a fancy dress, her hair appeared to be styled, and she wore a large brooch on her dress. They posed for the picture standing against each other, and the photo was taken indoors, a flowing curtain appearing in the background.

I describe the picture in detail to contrast it with my grandfather's parents. His mother wore a peasant dress and a kerchief around her head. No hair was visible. His father wore a long black coat from neck to foot and a broad-rimmed hat. He had a long white beard and side-curls of a few inches. They posed for the picture outside, an old fence in the background. They were both sitting down, at least a foot apart.

While I was fascinated by the contrast between these two couples whose children married each other several thousand miles away from where these photographs were taken, my attention quickly was drawn to my grandfather's parents, who were obviously Chassidic. His father was the rabbi, the shochet! I could not take my eyes off the photograph. I stood staring into my great-grandfather's eyes which stared back at me. I looked at his side-curls, his long coat, his hands folded gently on his lap and I wondered who this man was. I was his great-grandson, and yet the distance between us, not only in miles and years, but in ways of life was startling. My own great-grandfather was a Chassid. If not for this photograph I might have never known.

It was shocking that I had never been told about this. It was

Chassidic couple, Asher and Bliema Gottlieb, of Borgo Prund, Transylvania. (Courtesy Samuel L. Gottlieb)

always my belief that my father's family was the religious side of the family, but here before me was the photograph of just a few generations ago, of my great-grandfather, a Chassidic man. The progression of history began to come clear. My grandfather, as a teenager, left Europe and his family and traveled to America, land of opportunity. He cut his side-curls, said goodbye to his rural Chassidic community, and went in search of a "better" life. Upon arrival in America he discovered a different world and rapidly became a part of it. I have to admit that I was always troubled by this. My Jewish involvement has, over the years, become more and more traditional and it has been largely an uphill battle for me. I was not raised in a very traditional home, and this was partly because of my family history: My mother's parents were not traditional and this affected my upbringing. Had my grandparents been, I too might have had a different kind of life. But this feeling was dramatically resolved when I brought the newly discovered photograph of my great-grandparents to their son—my grandfather. I also showed my grandfather another photograph I had found of him as a young man. In it, he was dressed in a modern suit with spats, a stylish hat and was holding a cane!

My grandfather was excited by the sight of both pictures. He repeated over and over that those were his parents, and also enjoyed seeing this picture of himself as a young man. He then told me that the picture of him was taken in Europe. I was confused because I knew that he came to America as a teenager and this was a later picture. He told me that he went back to visit his parents twenty years after he had left them. It was an incredible thing to imagine. Here was a picture of a fully Americanized man, the son of a Chassid, returning to see his parents and family. One could just imagine the scene when he arrived in town looking the way he did as compared to the way his father looked. And I was right! My grandfather told me that his own father was upset by how his son had changed. His father wanted him to stay there and not to return to America, the country that made him leave the old ways. My grandfather refused, of course, and returned to America. The rest of the story is obvious: Had my grandfather stayed and returned to the religious ways of his family, he would have shared their fate —the Death Camps. Yet he returned, continued to assimilate, and I, his grandson, was born years later. *And today, I connect once again with the tradition of my great-grandfather, through my family history research.*

I remembered that the letter from my mother's cousin, Maurice, who had originally written to me telling me about the family and what towns we had come from, also contained his regret that he could not find a picture of his grandparents. Now that I found one, I wanted to call him and share with him what I had found. I arranged to visit with him and show him the photograph. I also hoped to get more information from him. I suspected that he knew much more than he wrote in his letter. When I arrived at his home, it became quickly apparent that Maurice knew quite a bit about the family history. He identified many photographs for me, told me stories about members of the family, and taught me a lot. But one item, which he mentioned to me in passing, became a clue which became the key to centuries of family history. Maurice told me that as a child he was scolded for playing a childhood prank. The way in which he was scolded was memorable, because he was told, "That's no way to behave, especially since you are an 'ainicle' of the Stropkover Rebbe." At the time I did not know that the term "ainicle," while it means "grandson," means "descendant" in that context. In any case, my genealogical ears perked up and I knew that I may have hit upon a major find.

That night was somewhat sleepless for me. I couldn't wait to go to the library the next day and find out about "the Stropkover Rebbe." If my mother's first cousin was his descendant, then I was too, and it would be an important and meaningful discovery for me. The following morning I went to YIVO—The Institute for Jewish Research in Manhattan—and began to search for anything I could find about the Stropkover Rebbe.

YIVO, with one of the finest (if not the finest) collections of material on Eastern European Jewry, had a book with biographical material on Chassidic Rebbes, with an index by town. It was just what I needed. I looked up Stropkov and found that there were several rebbes who were known to have been connected with the town of Stropkov at one time or another. I struggled with each entry written in Hebrew and one by one I rejected each as possible ancestors. When I finally got to the last entry I was startled to see the name of Chaim Joseph Gottlieb. My mother's name was Gottlieb. He must be my ancestor! I was terribly excited for about one minute until I remembered that Maurice wrote me that the name of our family was not originally Gottlieb but Rosenvasser. Suddenly, I was afraid that this was not my ancestor at all, but that we had simply taken his name because of his reputation as a rebbe. I knew that people named children after their teachers, and perhaps this was a similar case.

Still, there was something within me that said that he was my direct ancestor. I had a feeling about it, and knew that eventually I would understand how the name Rosenvasser came into the picture. It seemed rather likely that Chaim Joseph Gottlieb was an ancestor since the names matched and since it also confirmed the story by Maurice about being scolded as a child. Another possibility was that the name Rosenvasser was the original name and that it predated the rebbe.

What I found myself doing from that point on was breaking just about every genealogical rule in the book, especially the following two: Never make claims that you aren't sure of, and do research from the known to the unknown. You start with what you know and you see how far back you can go, step by step. You should go backward, one generation at a time. This rule is to discourage people from picking out a famous individual from history and trying to make a connection. It has been shown often enough that people who set out to prove that they descend from an illustrious figure do it—regardless of how accurate their findings are. In other words, it is not respectable genealogy research to pick King David and then try to establish descent from him. Except for the fact that I had some good clues to go on, I was doing just that. It is not advisable methodology.

The other rule that I broke was telling everybody I knew that I was a descendant of the Stropkover Rebbe, Chaim Joseph Gottlieb. At the time it was just circumstantial evidence, but it was such an exciting possibility to be a descendant of a Chassidic Rebbe that I couldn't help it. The only good part about it was that it pressured me to get to work immediately and to find out the truth.

The short biography of the rebbe which I found included the fact that he wrote a book called *Teev Gitten v'Kiddushin*. YIVO did not have the book, but the New York Public Library Jewish Division did, so I went to examine it. I was amazed to see that the book contained a brief genealogy including the names of the rebbe's grandfather (which would take me back to the 1600's!), and the rebbe's sons, one of whom was named Usher. My great-grandfather was named Usher, and for a minute I thought I had solved the whole problem, until I realized that the dates were wrong. There would have to be at least one generation between the rebbe's sons and my great-grandfather. I still hadn't established a link. It occurred to me that my great-grandfather, Usher, might have been named after the rebbe's son Usher. But it was still speculation.

After examining the rebbe's book in the library, I wondered if there were any disciples of his alive and in New York. I discussed the question with a librarian in the Jewish Division, and when she noticed that the "approbation" (seal of approval) for the book was written by Chaim Halberstamm, the Sanzer Rebbe, who was a contemporary of Chaim Joseph Gottlieb and whose descendants live in New York, she suggested that I contact them. I made a few phone calls, but no one seemed to be able to help me. A few days later a Jewish newspaper in New York, *The Jewish Week*, called me for an interview. I was going to be interviewed on radio station WEVD the following week to talk about some of my genealogy research, and the newspaper wanted to make a feature story out of it. In the interview I mentioned my belief that I was a descendant of the Stropkover Rebbe, well aware of the fact that it was still speculation. The newspaper ran the story, and it was the best thing that could have happened at the time.

In response to the article, I began to get phone calls from people who also claimed descent from the rebbe. The first call, in fact, was from someone whose name sounded familiar. I recalled that my mother's cousin, Maurice, had suggested I call him for more information about the family. I never did, although I did file his name and number away for future use. It is significant that I mention this because while it is true that my interview with the newspaper offered me an opportunity that few people get, it is equally true that had I followed the advice of my mother's cousin, I would have discovered the same thing. It is important to track down the most obscure leads because they might very well bring you to a pot of genealogical gold.

The man told me that he too was a descendant of the Stropkover Rebbe, and we proceeded to compare notes. Within a few minutes the man realized that he knew who I was and that we were definitely related. He knew my mother and her brother and her parents from years ago. When I asked him how we were related he said, "We're cousins," but he knew little more than that. It was an answer I had learned to expect. So many times in my research I encountered people who were sure we were related, but knew nothing more than that. Although he wasn't able to provide any more information about our relationship, just the fact that he felt we were related and that he also knew that he was a descendant of the Stropkover Rebbe permitted me to be more at ease about my claim of descent. But, of course, I was not satisfied and wouldn't be until I was able to document my relationship to Chaim Joseph Gottlieb with names and dates and each generation between us carefully spelled out.

What the man on the phone was able to do, however, was to give me the name of another man who might be able to help. His last name was also Gottlieb and he was a cantor. I called him and I was spared the need to make introductions since he had heard me on the radio the night before which was when the tape was broadcast. He asked me to hold the wire and came back a minute later with a copy of the rebbe's book. He had a more recent edition though. It was a reprint of the original with an added preface which was a biography of the rebbe! On the phone I told the man everything I knew about my family including all the names I knew, but he was unable to match me up with the genealogical information provided in the biography. I was disappointed but not discouraged. A final piece of information that he told me was that the man who wrote the biography lived in Brooklyn. He gave me his phone number.

The biographer's name was Rabbi Israel, and when I called him he was nice enough to suggest that we meet to pursue the question. He also told me where I could get a copy of his book. The next morning I went to Williamsburg to purchase the book from the source suggested by Rabbi Israel.

It was the first time I had ever gone to Williamsburg. Though I have been a New Yorker all my life, I was always a bit afraid to go there. I had heard too many stories about the Chassidim in Williamsburg who do not like outsiders. I felt hostile toward them, wondering why they thought they had the right to look down upon other Jews who were not like them. But my experience that first time was just the opposite. I found the people on the street and in the shops to be quite friendly and I realized that I had only heard the sensational stories. I liked everyone I met.

When I arrived at the address given to me by Rabbi Israel, a young girl answered the door and asked me to wait a minute. She returned soon afterward and brought me down the street to a grocery store and a young man who appeared to be her brother. They spoke in Yiddish for a few seconds, after which she left. The young man, who appeared to be about my age, was dressed in traditional Chassidic street clothes with an apron for while he worked. He brought me down the block to a storage room. It was there that the books were kept. He looked for a clear copy, brushed off the dust, and sold it to me. Together we walked back to his store. Before we said goodbye I asked him why it was that he had these books to sell. He told me that his father printed them. So I asked him why his father printed them. He answered me by saying that he was "an ainicle of the Stropkover Rebbe." He used the very same words that my mother's cousin Maurice had used when I first began this journey.

It then dawned on me that I was standing in Chassidic Williamsburg with a young man, a Satmar Chassid I later found out, who was a cousin of mine. He and I both were descendants of the same Chassidic Rebbe! (Assuming that my belief was correct.) To be honest, I must admit that I did not tell him that I was also a descendant of the rebbe. I was afraid that he would wonder why I was obviously not Chassidic. In some ways, I wondered myself—though I knew. Yet it was startling to see how strange fate is. There we were, both of us the same age, both of us stemming from the same family tree, and yet we were in two different worlds. His line took him to Williamsburg, and mine took me elsewhere. It was confusing and fascinating.

It was then that I remembered from one of the many conversations that I had, that there was a Gottlieb's restaurant in Brooklyn and that the owners of this restaurant were descendants of the same rebbe. I located the address and decided to go there for lunch. The owner of the restaurant wasn't there, but his son-in-law was, and we had a conversation, briefly, about the rebbe. Yes, he said, it was true that they were from that family and the owner would be back the next day. I was disappointed, but I was also excited by my new possession—the book by the rebbe and the biography within it. I called Rabbi Israel, the biographer, and made an appointment for Sunday, just a few days away.

Those next few days were a blur to me. I was so preoccupied by the whole experience that I couldn't think about anything else. I simply counted the hours until I could see Rabbi Israel, who would surely be able to link my branch of the family with the rebbe. Finally, Sunday came and I went to Rabbi Israel's home. The rabbi was a pleasant and kind gentleman who made me feel quite at home. He asked me if we could speak in Yiddish and I was sorry to have to tell him that I could not. He took me down to his basement where his library was and we discussed my family. Again I repeated everything that I knew, but nothing seemed to match. Again the name Usher was the same, but the dates were obviously wrong. I felt that I had reached a dead end. It appeared that with all of the circumstantial evidence that I had gathered, it was nothing more than that. If the rabbi who wrote the biography of the rebbe could not help me, then who could? I began to feel that I was wrong from the beginning: I shouldn't have made any claims, even to myself, without knowing for sure. Now it seemed as if there was nothing more to do but go back to thinking that my mother's family was a small one, that they may have known the rebbe's family in Europe and may have even taken his name, but other than that there was no relationship. I would have to be satisfied with the truth, and with a genealogy which went back no farther than my great-grandfather.

I looked dejectedly at Rabbi Israel, but continued a general conversation about my research. He, too, had the hobby of genealogy, and he showed me some of the material he had collected on Chassidic families. Since he was showing his collection, I decided to show him what I had brought with me. I had gathered whatever I had concerning the Gottlieb family and showed him pictures and other documents. One piece of paper in particular interested him. It was a piece of stationery, with a letterhead that read, "Bistritz and Vicinity Aid Society." It also had my grandfather's name on it listed as financial secretary. I had found the stationery in my grand-parents' apartment.

Rabbi Israel looked at it and told me that there was a man in the neighborhood who was from Bistritz. He was known as the Bistritzer Rebbe. Rabbi Israel suggested that he might be able to help me. Handing me his phone, Rabbi Israel looked up the rebbe's phone number and told me to call him. Thinking back on that morning, I'm glad I was forced into it. I doubt very much that I'd have the courage to call a rebbe by myself. It's just not some-thing that I'm accustomed to doing. When I dialed the number from Rabbi Israel's home, a man answered the phone. He asked me if I could speak Hungarian and I said no. I asked him if he could speak English and he said "A little." I told him that I was a grand-son of Zalmen Lieb Gottlieb from Bistritz, and I asked him if he might have known him. He told me that he knew Pinchas Gottlieb. Pinchas was a brother of my grandfather and I was excited to hear that I was speaking to a man, a rebbe, who knew a great-uncle of mine. I also knew that Pinchas had been killed in the Holocaust.

The rebbe asked me to come to his address which was just a few blocks from where Rabbi Israel lived. I quickly left Rabbi Israel after thanking him for his help. While I was still disappointed by what had happened, I was distracted by my imminent visit with a rebbe.

When I arrived at the address, I was surprised to be at a syna-gogue. I expected an apartment or a house, but there I was standing at the steps of a synagogue with a sign in Yiddish announcing it to be the Bistritzer synagogue. The rebbe came to the door and asked me to come in.

At that moment, what I entered was not just another synagogue run by another rabbi, but a different world from the one that I had known. The shul was a room, a square room, crowded by benches and long tables, books spread upon them. The room was dimly lit, tallisim hung in several spots around the place, and I stood there for a few moments taking it all in. It was unlike anything I had ever seen, except in photographs of shtiebles in Europe. And then I knew that I was in a shtieble, just like the ones my ancestors prayed in, and that the fact that this one was in Brooklyn and that my ancestors were in Europe made no difference once the door was closed. The rebbe was an elderly man, bearded of course, and slightly bent from age. Yet he was very quick and his eyes were bright. His face was serious, but friendliness came through. He asked me to sit down, and I did, at one of the long benches in front of one of the long tables. The rebbe said that he would be back in a moment. I examined the room from every angle, imagining the activity which must occur each day at prayer times and each Shabbas. What was then a silent room must burst with religious energy, the same kind which my great-grandfather, with his long coat, wide-rimmed hat, and beard with side-curls must have had just three generations ago. I was truly in another world and delighted by this opportunity.

The rebbe returned and we spoke briefly about my family. He did know my grandfather's brother, and knew that he was killed in the Death Camps. He told me that they studied together. After he had run out of things to tell me, in his broken English, about my family in Europe, I decided to tell him the story of my search for a connection with Chaim Joseph Gottlieb, the Stropkover Rebbe. I told him every detail, like a fool, as if he cared. But he listened with intense interest, asking questions along the way. I concluded by saying that Rabbi Israel was unable to help me, and I wondered if he remembered whether my family descended from the rebbe.

One of the most intriguing aspects of this whole encounter was the seriousness with which he took what I was saying. He communicated to me, by his questions and his comments, that what I was doing was very important. He never explained why, but continued to indicate this to me. I, on the other hand, wondered if I was taking up too much of his time by talking to him about what I thought must be dead ends. But he never once seemed impatient, and on the contrary he was eager to spend as much time as I wanted in discussing the matter.

One of the additional pieces of information which I had discovered along the way was that my great-grandfather's father was named Shlomo. I knew this from the inside cover of my grandfather's Bible where many years ago he wrote brief genealogies of his mother and father. Rabbi Israel was unable to use this additional name for my purposes, but the rebbe seemed interested. He looked through the biography of the Stropkover Rebbe that Rabbi Israel had written, and while flipping through the pages he kept repeating "Usher ben Shlomo, Usher ben Shlomo, Usher ben Shlomo." The rebbe just repeated those names, the names of my great-grandfather and his father, over and over to himself as he looked through the biography. It was obvious that he was looking for the names but I was sure he would not find them there. A few times while he was examining and reading the biography, a phone in a back room rang. The rebbe was so involved in the biography that it was not until the fifth or sixth ring that he stood up and walked to the back to answer it. Each time the phone rang, the rebbe took too much time to answer it and it stopped before he got there. When he returned to look through the biography again, he seemed happy that he didn't have to talk on the phone so that he could get back to his reading.

In the meantime I just sat there, watching the rebbe continue to read the book and repeat the names, "Usher ben Shlomo, Usher ben Shlomo." I sat there staring and looking around the room. My imagination was active during those minutes, wondering what it was like when the room was filled with praying Chassids. Suddenly, the rebbe spotted something on a page. He brought it to the window since the light in the room was rather poor. He then came back and sat down and said, "Shlomo was the son of the rebbe."

I didn't know what to do. I knew that he was wrong since Rabbi Israel told me each of the names of the rebbe's sons. But I was not comfortable telling this rebbe that he was incorrect. Somehow it just didn't seem right to contradict a rebbe. I decided to say, "Really?" in a confused and somewhat doubting voice.

He looked again and said, "No, no, no, no, no." He shook his head in apparent disappointment in himself and sat in silence for a few minutes staring at the book. He then looked up and told me that where he was from it was a custom to take a mother's last name rather than a father's. In fact, he said, this was so in almost 50 percent of the cases in his community in Europe. Then he said, "The rebbe Gottlieb had a daughter Gittel. Her husband was Shlomo Zalke." He paused and then in a deep, confident tone as if he were making a proclamation said, "This is your Shlomo. You come from them and take her last name. This is my opinion."

His remarks sounded final, and he ushered me to the door. There was something unreal about the whole thing, especially the way it ended, but the rebbe seemed absolutely convinced that his opinion was right. When I left, I looked at the biography and reread where it said that the rebbe's son-in-law was named Shlomo Zalke, not just Shlomo. For some reason, the name Zalke sounded familiar. I rushed home and looked again at the genealogy written by my grandfather in his Bible. There it was. He did not just write the name Shlomo, but Shlomo Zalke! I had forgotten about this! It was now obvious. And it was obvious that I was, in fact, a descendant of the Stropkover Rebbe. Everything matched: the names, the dates, and even the story about the name not originally being Gottlieb.

We had taken the name of the rebbe's daughter rather than his son-in-law. I had finally found the link.

The rebbe in Brooklyn was able to solve the entire issue for me. The fact that my great-great-grandfather, Shlomo Zalke, took the name of his wife, Gittel Gottlieb, explains the fact that Maurice was told the name was not originally Gottlieb. I couldn't wait to call my mother and share the news with her. When I did she was delighted to hear all of my stories. My father, whose family I had researched for seven years, stood by with a smile on his face, as I detailed the generations of my mother's family back farther than I was ever able to get with the Kurzweil family.

There is a postscript to this story which I must add, though it is not nearly complete. In fact, the very day before I wrote this I discovered additional information which brings my family history to even earlier beginnings. In response to the article in the newspaper, *The Jewish Week*, which ran the story about my research, I received a letter from a delightful young woman whose husband is a descendant of the Stropkover Rebbe. This makes us cousins, of course. Her name is Michelle Zoltan, and we have established a nice friendship based on our mutual interest in the history of this family. Michelle offered to translate the biography of the Stropkover Rebbe for me from the Hebrew. I have just recently received the first chapter.

The chapter speaks about the rebbe and his lineage and indicates that his mother is a descendant of Rabbi Isaiah Horowitz, a renowned rabbi of the 1500's and early 1600's. After doing a little bit of checking, I was able, in a short time, to trace Rabbi Horowitz's family back several generations to the 1400's. In other words, I am a descendant of Rabbi Isaiah Horowitz (known as "the Holy Shela'h"), and consequently I am a descendant of his ancestors as well.

From the tiny, assimilated family of my mother, I am now able to document descent back through some of the most illustrious rabbis of the past several centuries to the Middle Ages in the 1500's. And I do not intend to stop here.

After having celebrated, for dozens of paragraphs, the discoveries that I have made about my ancestors, I feel compelled to remind all of us that the Talmud warns: "A learned bastard takes precedence over an ignorant High Priest." In other words, all the illustrious ancestors possible are meaningless if we, ourselves, are not learned and worthy on our own. The crucial question that arises when genealogical discoveries are made is this: "What do we do with the knowledge of who our ancestors were?

For myself, I have found that learning about my family history had drawn me farther and farther into Jewish Tradition. The more I learn about my ancestors, the more I learn about Jewish history and therefore, Jewish learning. The more facts I have about the lives of my ancestors, the more I learn to respect them and feel grateful to them for their decisions. It matters little, on one level, whether they were religious or not. I respect them for surviving as Jews and for being able to live and raise children, who eventually raised me. I have learned much about courage when I begin to understand what it was like to make the decision to journey to America. I continue to learn about faith and belief as I discover the obstacles set before my ancestors in Jewish history.

A special kind of awe comes over me when I learn about an ancestor of mine such as Isaiah Horowitz who lived around 1600. Here was a man whose life and works are known until today for their greatness. The energy and power that this man had can be described by comparing it to ripples in water: A small force pushed into a body of water will create small ripples which will last a few seconds. The more powerful the force, the greater the ripples and the longer the duration of the vibrations. Such a powerful force was this direct ancestor of mine. There is no question in my mind that he is in large part responsible for the religiosity of his descendants. As I examine those descendants I can see how devoted they were to learning and Torah, and like strong ripples in water, he was one of the forces behind them. So powerful were the vibrations which he sent that they have reached me here in the 1970's. His message has traveled a great distance, not in space but in time. Nearly 400 years has his influence spread.

I certainly do not claim to lead a life on a par with his, but I am influenced by him. Just the fact that I am able to document my descent from him indicates how powerful an influence he has been. As I make this kind of discovery about an ancestor, I am forced (delightedly so) to encounter his life and teachings and to learn from them. This is the purpose of family history within the Jewish Tradition. It is not to make boastful claims about ancestors. It is not to take credit for the achievements of others, nor is it to take responsibility for the actions of others. But it is to continue to receive a message, first given at Mount Sinai, and still transmitted today. The message of Sinai is handed down through generations, and as a famous Midrash says, the Torah is given at Sinai every

Portrait of Ruchal Ennis in Galicia, ca. 1920.

moment if we will only listen for it and hear. I do not accept to accept every letter of its message, but I do try to receive the message nonetheless. My family history helps me to connect with that event, and with the history of the Jewish people. In this way, I celebrate my ancestors and the lives that they led.

Chapter 2

In the Beginning: From Adam and Eve to You and Me

Even a person who is generally unfamiliar with the Bible knows something of the famous "begat" verses in various places throughout the text. One might think it odd that a document such as the Bible, which is supposed to offer the central teachings of Judaism and which is supposed to be the word of God Himself, would contain such a vast quantity of genealogical material. If, in fact, God wrote the Bible, or spoke the words to Moses at Mount Sinai, one can hardly imagine the encounter including so many instances when God had to recite for Moses the family trees of literally hundreds of people.

In the first place, the lists of names often *appear* to be extraneous. When one is interested in getting to the heart of the matter, to the teachings of God, one hardly wants to be interrupted by the fact that Meshullam is the son of Azaliah who is the son of Shaphan (II Kings 22:3). Secondly, what in the world do all of these names have to do with anything important?

One has to wonder what God had in mind. Or traveling the route of many scientific Biblical scholars, one has to question the motives of those individuals who wrote and edited and canonized the text. Couldn't they have spared us the lists of names? Or are those names, those genealogies and census lists, of some value that we cannot see on the surface?

Genealogy has been an interest of Jews since the very beginnings of history. The Bible is filled with genealogies, listing the ancestors and descendants of famous Biblical figures as well as more obscure characters in the Biblical drama.

In the Bible, three different types of genealogies can be found. There are the census records which document the tribal clans found in the Book of Numbers. There are the genealogies in Genesis which include the line of humankind from Adam, as well as the "Table of Nations" in Genesis 10. A third type of genealogy found in the Bible are the background genealogies used to introduce individuals and families throughout the text.

The fact that genealogies appear so frequently in the Scriptures prompts us to question the reasons for it and to ask what importance genealogy played in the lives of the people who were connected with the beginnings of Jewish history. The Bible records the history of the Jewish People as stemming from a tribal society as well as a patriarchal tradition. It is understandable, therefore, that a consciousness of one's genealogy would exist in order to document and affirm membership in a particular clan.

Prior to the establishment of clans and tribes, however, we find in the earliest chapters of Genesis intriguing genealogies which deserve careful inspection. When God caused the Great Flood to destroy all of humankind except for Noah and his family, He created the situation where everyone who would be born from that point on would be a direct descendant of Noah and his wife. No longer would the human race possibly stem from the children of Cain and his wife, or from anyone but Adam and Eve's grandson Enosh (a direct ancestor of Noah). The many other children born from Adam and Eve as indicated in Genesis 5:4 ("After the birth of Seth, Adam lived 800 years and begot sons and daughters") died in the Flood. Along with Noah and his wife on the Ark were their three sons, Shem, Ham, and Japheth, and their wives. According to the narrative, it is these three couples who began what would become the future generations of the world.

The point here is a most simple yet profound one. With all of the "group consciousness" which is illustrated in great detail throughout the Bible, the point remains that our source is the same for each and every one of us. A creation story based on several simultaneous creations of humans would obviously have had different ramifications. But when the source of all people is so carefully spelled out for the reader, more humble conclusions have to be drawn.

In fact, Chapter 10 of Genesis, which we have already mentioned as being the "Table of Nations," is a detailed description of our common roots. This chapter is to be found directly after the story of the Flood. The chapter lists, in detail, the descendants of the three sons of Noah. Each of the descendants represents not only an individual but also the founder of a future nation, hence the term "Table of Nations." What this succeeds in doing is to explain the sources of nearly every nation known to the region whose story is told throughout the Bible. As the many books of the Bible unfold and nations, tribes, and individuals appear, most of them find their source back in Chapter 10 of Genesis.

As you can see from the genealogical chart, the following list of names appears as descendants of the three sons of Noah. Based on early beliefs as well as recent Biblical scholarship, the list indicates which groups and countries each name represents:

Gomer: People of Asia Minor known as Cimmerians
Magog: The Scythians, located on the border of the Caucasus
Ashkenaz: From Armenia and the upper Euphrates (not to be confused with Ashkenazim—Jews from Germanic countries)
Madai: People of Indo-Iranian origin known as the Medes
Javan: From Greece
Elishah: From Cyprus
Tarshitth: Tartessians
Kittim: From Cyprus
Dodanim: From Rhodes
Tubal: Tibareni
Meshech: From Asia Minor, identified with Assyrian sources
Tiras: Etruscans
Elam: Elamites, identified with Iran
Ashur: Assyrians
Lud: Lydians of Asia Minor
Aram: Arameans
Joktan: South Arabian tribes
Cush: Ancient kingdom of Northeast Africa
Put: Region of Libya
Canaan: Canaanites and various other groups.
Mizraim: Egypt
Casluhim: Philistines
Caphtorim: Crete

The Table of Nations is not complete, nor does it claim to be. Genesis 10:5 states, for example, "From these the maritime nations branched out." This implies that while the narrative is certainly explaining the origins of many nations of the world, it is not supplying a complete inventory. Again, however, most of the known ancient world is represented.

In the episode directly after this chapter of Genesis, the nations of the world are divided even more radically. This is the famous Tower of Babel incident, when the peoples of the world are punished, apparently for attempting to build a tower to heaven. God's choice of punishment is to create different languages which prevents people from communicating with one another. At the same time, God "scattered them from there over the face of the whole earth" (Gen. 11:8). This radically changes the world situa-

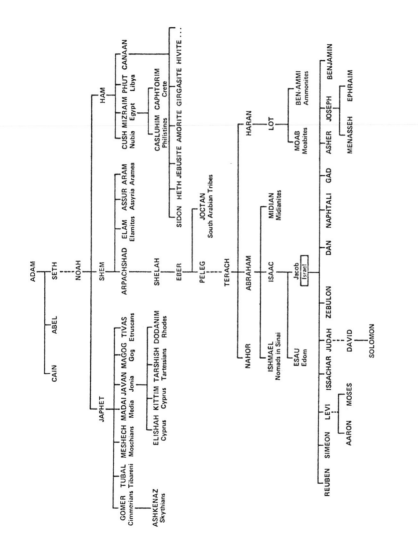

Biblical genealogy including the "Table of Nations."

tion and a new phase of human history begins. Suddenly, we have many languages, many nations or groups, and many more locations. In short, we have the basis for the rest of human history with its coming conflicts, customs, and beliefs. But beneath it all are the genealogies which tie all people together.

As the Bible continues, leaving Genesis behind, other genealogies and references to ancestry appear. In the Book of Numbers of the Five Books of Moses, two extensive census rolls are presented, one dealing with apparent military activities, and the other concerning itself with the division of the land of Canaan by the Tribes.

The Book of Chronicles, like Genesis and Numbers, is well known for its genealogies and tribal lists. The Hebrew name of the Book of Chronicles is *Divrei ha-Yamim* which means "the events of the times." The first chapter in the Book of Chronicles is a collection of genealogical lists taken from Genesis but presented in an abridged form. Chapters 2 through 8 of Chronicles list the Tribes by families and appear to be extensive genealogies. Within Chronicles, the genealogies contain three different elements. One is the simple relationships of the numerous clans within the Tribes by descent, a second is the establishment of names of specific settlements taken from the name of the father of the settlement, and third is the establishment of names of families.

In addition to Genesis, Numbers, and Chronicles, genealogies and references to them can be found in many places as we have said. The Book of Ezra contains references to genealogies and, in fact, both Ezra and Chronicles together have been popularly called *Sefer Hayuhasin*, meaning "Book of Descent." In Ezra 2:62, we find the statement, "These sought their registry among those that were reckoned by genealogy, but they were not found," indicating that the genealogies kept before the exile to Babylonia were missing on return. Also in the book of the prophet Nehemiah we read (7:5), "And my God put into mine heart to gather together the nobles, and the rulers, and the people that they might be reckoned by genealogy. And I found a register of the genealogy." The text continues by offering a lengthy genealogy and list of those who were exiled to Babylon.

After the return to Zion, that is, after the destruction of the First Temple and the Babylonian exile, genealogies acquired a special significance. Before the destruction of the Temple, the Priests and the Levites kept careful track of their lineage for obvious reasons: they had to prove their descent in order to serve as Temple functionaries. The problem arose that when they returned to Zion, they looked for their genealogies, as the passage from Ezra 2:62 indicated, but could not find them. Needless to say, this caused something of a crisis, as well as an increased interest in genealogy. Not only did the Priests and the Levites want to establish descent, but others who were interested in reclaiming family property also found that they now had taken a keen interest in documenting their ancestry.

After the Second Temple was established, Jewish concern with genealogy ran high. The reason was simple: verification of "family purity" was required for many marriages. A Kohan, for example, cannot marry an unchaste woman, proselyte, a divorcee, or a widow under certain circumstances. The laws surrounding this subject are quite complex, and the interest in genealogy in the days of the Second Temple surrounded this issue.

In order to remain "pure," marriages involving Kohanim were carefully arranged as not to introduce any impurity to the line. Families who were able to make claims such as these were careful to document their lineage so as to offer proof of their contention. One must keep in mind that this seemingly unusual preoccupation with "purity of descent" makes a lot of sense when viewed within the context of the times. The Priests, or Kohanim, were direct descendants of Aaron from the House of Levi, and through Biblical command were responsible for many important religious functions which are set forth in considerable detail throughout the Bible. It is clear that the distinction between Kohanim and Israelites created a "class system," but recognition of this social system in light of it being a directive of God allows us to understand the importance that the designation had for the people.

The documentation of genealogical information was quite important in the time of the Second Temple and we know there was a special room where the genealogical lists were maintained and updated. Even many Kohanim who did not reside in the vicinity of the Temple, in other words who already lived in the Diaspora, were recorded in this room in the Temple.

There was an entire body of law restricting certain marriages which made genealogies essential. The Mishnah lists ten social classes who returned from the exile in Babylonia. These included Kohanim, Levites, Israelites, Mamzerim (bastards), Asufim (foundlings), and others. Along with these social classes there were laws prohibiting certain combinations of marriages. Because of this, genealogies were an important consideration for the entire population.

The notions of social classes, restricted marriages, and purity of descent are obvious invitations for corruption and fraud, and Jewish experience has been no exception. The Talmud, for example, records an incident concerning someone who attempted to imitate a Babylonian accent in order to claim Babylonian descent. The motive for this was the notion that Babylonian purity was greater than that of people in Israel, based on the belief that those people whose purity was in doubt went to Israel with Ezra. It is not difficult to imagine that individuals and families often made claims of descent which they were pressed to substantiate. While it is true that settling questions of priestly genealogy was handled by the Great Sanhedrin (Mid. 5:4; Tosef., Sanh. loc. cit.), Johanan b. Zakkai decreed that no rabbinical court would deal with matters concerning genealogy (Eduy. 8:3).

There was certainly an undue preoccupation with genealogy during the period of the Second Temple. Abuse must have been widespread, since we find in the Talmud such statements as, "When men quarrel among themselves, they quarrel over birth" (Kid. 76a), and a striking criticism of ancestor "worshipers" which reads, "A learned bastard takes precedence over an uneducated high priest" (Hor. 3:8).

It is refreshing though to see the seemingly intentional traditions and legends which offset genealogical abuse. Some of the greatest sages in Jewish history have legends attached to their family background providing them with questionable or even infamous lineage. In addition, Rabbis Meir and Akiva are said to have both come from families of converts. These legends are of great importance because they attempt to reverse the evils of a class system and the abuse of genealogical information.

When the Second Temple was destroyed, the Priests lost their function, but this did not bring a halt to the interest in genealogy for the purpose of documentation of one's status. To the contrary, the possession of proof of priestly descent became even more valuable since there was no longer a Temple where a Priest could derive status. This behavior continued for quite some time, but eventually ended when it became almost impossible to document pure descent. In modern times, Orthodox and Conservative synagogues still recognize the classes of Kohan, Levite, and Israelite during certain rituals, while Reform congregations generally ignore the designation. On the one hand, for a present-day individual to claim descent from the House of Aaron seems rather questionable. On the other hand, to imagine that this family tradition has possibly been passed down generation to generation is an intriguing one.

In addition to the specific genealogies set forth in the Bible, a more general concept related to the subject of ancestors and descendants appears both in Biblical as well as Talmudic sources. This is the doctrine of *Zekhut Avot* meaning "merit of the fathers." The idea behind the concept is that descendants of righteous individuals will be rewarded and, conversely, descendants of wicked people will not reap any benefits, or perhaps will even be punished. The concept is certainly one which gives pause for thought since the implications are far reaching. As a motivation for righteous living, the idea appears to be a powerful one. If we thought that our good deeds will benefit our descendants or that our bad deeds will live after us, we might be much more conscious of our actions.

However, even the religious validity of this concept is in serious question. While the Bible reads, "For I the Lord your God am an impassioned God, visiting the guilt of the fathers upon the children, upon the third and fourth generations of those who reject Me, but showing kindness to the thousandth generation of those who love Me and keep My commandments" (Ex. 20:5-6), it also reads, "Parents shall not be put to death for children, nor children be put to death for parents: a person shall be put to death only for his own crime" (Deut. 24:16). There is an apparent contradiction here, a resolution of which is attempted several times by different sources. The Talmud, for example, states that the sins of the father cause suffering by the children and descendants only when the same sin is repeated by the descendants themselves (Ber. 7a; Sanh. 27b). While this may appear to be an attempt at "getting around" the contradiction, there is something to be said for the wisdom of the explanation. If the Biblical passage noted above from Exodus 20:5-6 is not taken literally but rather as a metaphor for the impact of education and upbringing, a profound idea may be derived. The actions and therefore the influence of a parent on a child as well as future generations can be vast. In fact, the decisions of our parents can easily be seen to have lasting effects not only on us as their children but also on our own children. Family habits, customs, and ideas stay with people for generations. Furthermore, referring once more to the Exodus passage, one can hardly deny that bad or negative habits often appear to have more lasting effects than positive habits.

The Bible contains many references to the general notion of "merit of the fathers." The passage "And because He loved your fathers, He chose their offspring after them" (Deut. 4:37) is one of the clearest. In a conversation between God and Moses, when God is expressing His anger over the Golden Calf incident and is threatening to destroy the people, Moses says, "Remember Your servants, Abraham, Isaac, and Jacob" (Ex. 32:13). This was an effort by Moses to evoke the name of his ancestors for the purpose of calming God's anger.

The Talmud, as well, contains the recording of incidents when ancestors affected current events. In Yoma 87a, descendants of Aaron are not killed because of their ancestor. Many other similar cases are to be found in the Talmud. Again, however, the scale is balanced. Abuse of this concept can surely happen, and the Talmud records, "R. Kahana taught, let not a man say for the sake of my righteous brother or father I shall be saved, for Abraham could not save his son Ishmael, nor Jacob save his brother Esau . . . as it is written 'no man can by any means redeem his brother'" (Ps. 49:8) (Yal. Ps. 46).

Among the uses and abuses of genealogy and ancestor-consciousness in the Bible and Talmud, we find the unifying principle that knowledge of one's ancestors has been important since the beginning of our people. We find that hardly a character is introduced into the Biblical drama who is not accompanied by, at least, a genealogy of a generation or two. One is not identified by one's name alone, but rather by one's name and then the name of one's father. Again, often much more than just the name of one generation is provided. We also find cases where the female side of the genealogy is offered, though there is no question that in the rather male-oriented society represented by Jewish history, the male line is far more plentiful than the female line.

It is instructive to note how God reveals Himself for the first time both to Jacob (Gen. 28:13) and to Moses (Ex. 3:6). To Jacob, God says, "I am the Lord, the God of Abraham thy father, and the God of Isaac. . . ." To Moses, God says, "I am the God of thy father, the God of Abraham, the God of Isaac, and the God of Jacob." In both cases, the revelation is generational, indeed genealogical. The first revelation to Moses is the more remarkable of the two when one remembers that the years of slavery, deprivation, and assimilation which were experienced during the bondage in Egypt still did not wipe out the memory of the ancestors of Moses and the children of Israel.

Throughout the Scriptures and likewise in the Siddur, the designation of God is expressed as "God of our Fathers" or "God of Abraham, Isaac, and Jacob." I was once told a Midrash by a rabbi concerning the notion of "God and God of our Fathers." The question is asked, "Why must we say both 'God' as well as 'God of our Fathers'?" The explanation is this: "If our belief in God is based solely on our own thinking, it is likely that someone could convince us to change our own thinking; if our belief in God is based only on the belief of our ancestors, then it would not involve us the way that it involved our ancestors. But if our belief in God is based on a combination of our own belief and the belief of our ancestors, then our faith will be strong.

A somewhat unusual genealogy to be found in the Bible is at the very end of the Book of Ruth. The last verses of this book indicate that Ruth was the great-grandmother of King David. According to the Soncino edition of the Bible, "Everything leads up, in the last instance, to David, and so the whole purpose of the Book is achieved in the final verse of this chapter." The impact of this is great when one knows that Ruth, a Moabite woman, converted to Judaism. Considering the illustrious reputation of King David coupled with the prophecy of Isaiah that the Messiah will be David's descendant, we can understand the message springing from these final verses in Ruth.

Underlying all of the many different issues raised by Biblical and post-Biblical genealogies is the belief that to know one's family is important. Regardless of the fact that we can document the abuse of this as we have just discussed, the benefits of such a consciousness certainly outweigh the disadvantages. Needless to say, anything can be used or abused, just as the same objects can be either tools or weapons, depending upon one's use of the object. The exact same thing holds true in the case of genealogies. As we have seen, the genealogies kept during the period before the destruction of the Second Temple were often used as weapons. High status was derived from them and too often this status was not deserved. But this does not mean at all that if there were no genealogies there would be no social competition, no status seekers, and no class division. In our own time, when we do not have such exacting interest in genealogical documentation, we still have an overabundance of status seekers and social competition.

As we have shown, the rabbis were aware of the abuses of genealogies and took steps to counterbalance this. But let us look at the other side of the coin regarding genealogies in the Bible and therefore in the very beginning of Jewish history and tradition. What merits did genealogies bring?

Already we have discussed the message behind the "Table of Nations" in Genesis, Chapter 10. To state briefly, the Bible teaches that all people come from one source, that of Noah and his wife, who in turn stem from Adam and Eve. But as we continue in the

Biblical narrative and come to accept the mentions of family genealogies as something common, we have to step back and wonder what it is all about.

Most importantly, the genealogies offer a perspective oriented toward family lines. There is no question that within the Jewish Tradition, the central institution is the family. One cannot escape (nor should one want to) the fact that Judaism, from its beginnings, placed a heavy emphasis upon the family, keeping it together, and using it as an instrument for righteous living. Since teaching was basically a process between parent and child, the importance of the family becomes vital. The line from the most well-known and perhaps important prayer in Jewish liturgy, the Shema, reads, "Thou shalt teach them diligently unto thy children . . ." This prayer, recited several times during the day, is a constant reminder that the relationship between parents and children is a vital one according to Jewish Tradition. One of the obvious implications of the concept of the family is that of responsibility. Membership within a family is a demand for respect and responsibility among individuals where mutual respect as well as love ought to be found. Since we are not just for ourselves, but rather are part of a group, we must be more responsible for our actions. Responsibility for one's actions is a cornerstone of Jewish belief. A constant reference to the genealogies of Biblical characters is also a constant reminder that we are a part of families, with all that comes with it.

This is not the place for a full-length celebration of the family as an institution. Libraries can be filled with volumes on the subject. But it is appropriate to observe that the Jewish Tradition has always participated in this celebration of family life, rejecting celibacy and monasticism, and extolling the idea of marriage and family. As Job 5:24 says, "and thou shalt know that thy tent is peace." The word for marriage in Hebrew is *kiddushin* which means "sanctification." While there are a vast amount of opportunities to sanctify events, the supreme act of sanctification is marriage. It is not the theory of just a few observers that the survival of the Jews as a people is the result of, in large part, the importance of the family.

One of the most dramatic episodes in the Biblical drama is that of the binding of Isaac, when God commands Abraham to slaughter his son. Just as Abraham, out of his faith in God, is about to obey the command, God stops him, announcing that no more will there be human sacrifice. It is a high point dramatically, so one has to wonder why, in the Biblical text, the narrative of the event is followed immediately by a seemingly meaningless genealogy. (Gen. 22:20-24). Apparently, Rashi, the great Biblical commentator, wondered about this same juxtaposition of texts. He wrote that the genealogies presented at this point in the Bible were written to introduce one very significant person into the story: Rebekah, who appears in the genealogy.

One might ask whether it is necessary to introduce Rebekah in this way. Why not just wait until she appears in the story? Consideration of this question might lead one to draw a more general conclusion about the genealogies throughout the Bible. The genealogies serve the function of continually bringing the story forward, closer to the present-day reader. While a story or novel being read could be far removed from the reader, it is hardly possible for a reader of the Bible to avoid the fact that this is not a story to be considered at long distance, but rather that each incident brings Jewish history closer to the present moment.

While the events recorded in the Bible certainly do follow a chronology, there is still room for the reader of a history to disassociate himself from that history, but this is all the more difficult when a genealogical approach is taken—as it is in the Bible. Page by page, the Bible offers a history via the generations of the people in the story. Each generation is connected by a family tree, linking everyone together to a family of humankind. The Biblical narrative serves to connect us with the text, and there seems to be no more effective means possible than to say: This is your family.

Though humankind can be seen as a family, based upon the "Table of Nations," so too can the Jewish People be seen as a family, for, in fact, the Jewish People are a family. When we make reference to Abraham as, "Our Father, Abraham," we are not simply speaking in metaphor. Abraham and Sarah are at the top of the genealogy of the Jews. When we see ourselves and our people as a family, how much more powerful a conception that is than to view our community as a random group of individuals. We have an obligation to our family, whether this is seen on a small scale or a larger one, that of the family of Jews.

Again, by using this kind of perspective, we run the risk of abusing the concept. By viewing the Jewish People as a family, we are also excluding the rest of the world. The risk involved in seeing people in groups, be it a family, a nation, a club, or a religion, is that rather than building bridges between groups, walls could be built. Once again, however, when the situation is weighed, the advantages and benefits of membership *can* be greater than the problems created.

The Bible, then, is the beginning of the story of the family known as the Jewish People. The genealogical consciousness of that people helps to maintain itself as a group, to bind individuals closely in family units, and to be instructive. Knowledge of one's ancestors is knowledge of their way of life. Because of this, the concept of "generations," of "Abraham begat Isaac," becomes a vital part of our lives as Jews.

PART II

HOW?

Chapter 1

How to Begin Your Search

The most current event in Jewish history is happening right this moment—with you. Surely there are things happening now which will be remembered in the future whereas your life and mine will be forgotten. But in a real sense, you are a part of Jewish history. In the twenty-first century, Jews will look back and see you—and your life—as Jewish history in much the same way that we look back on the lives of our grandparents and great-grandparents as fitting into a special chapter of history.

It is in this spirit that Jewish genealogy ought to be first approached: You are a part of Jewish history and you must explore the rest of Jewish history by beginning at home with yourself. Jewish genealogy begins at home. Throughout this book we will discuss the many documents, books, photographs, and other material which will help to make your family history a rich one. But before we can go any further, we have to start now, with this very moment.

So, we begin with a question which is simple enough, but whose answer is actually the key to the entire pursuit of genealogy. The question is this: How did you get to where you are this very minute?

By this, I do not mean how did you travel to the spot on which you are sitting or standing, but rather what were the circumstances under which you arrived where you are?

There is another way to approach this question and that is by describing a game which we often play. Have you ever thought to yourself, "If I never met you, I would never have met. . . ." Or, "If it weren't for my meeting you by chance, then this and that would not have happened to me." For example, had I not skipped a grade in elementary school most of my friends would not be my friends today. This is because I would have had a completely different set of friends and my life would have been very different!

Every action we take sets off a chain reaction of events which affects the future. I am sure that we can all think of dozens of things that would or would not have happened if it were not for something else.

So it is with genealogy and family history.

One of my grandmothers came to America with her older sister when they were the ages of fifteen and seventeen respectively. In other words, two young girls, all by themselves, set off for America in a steamship seventy-two years ago! Had they not been on that boat, I would probably never have existed.

This is a perfect illustration of our "game." Decisions made by our ancestors had significant (if not vital) effects on our lives.

Mathematically speaking, each of us has 1,024 direct ancestors in just the last ten generations. This is not aunts, uncles, or cousins. Just *direct* ancestors (parents, grandparents, great-grandparents, etc.). Again, in just ten generations, we've had 1,024 direct ancestors. We each have two parents, four grandparents, eight great-grandparents, sixteen great-great-grandparents, and so on. If we imagine any *one* of those people—let us say one of our several great-great-great-great-grandmothers—and imagine that she was killed as a child in a pogrom, we would not be here today. If any one of those 1,024 direct ancestors had been killed as a child before being able to marry and have children, we would not be here. Likewise, if of the 512 married couples in the last ten generations in our families, one couple decided to marry someone else instead, you would not be here.

What this illustrates is how clearly the decisions and fate of our ancestors affected all of us. Even more dramatic perhaps is the fact that if any one of your ancestors had converted or married outside of Judaism, you might not be here as a Jew reading this book on Jewish genealogy.

Therefore, we begin our journey into our family history with ourselves and we repeat the question: How did you get to where you are this very minute?

To answer this question, you have to begin to explore the recent history of your family. Actually, you have to ask the same question of your parents: How did *they* get to where they were all their lives? And of course, to answer this question of them, you must ask the question of *their* parents and so on.

1. Where do I start? I've always wanted to trace my family but I don't know how to begin.

Since everyone has a different family, there is no perfect system for every family historian. There is no chart for all families to use by filling in the blanks since we each have different-sized families. There is no step-by-step order to your research since each of us will find different problems and successes when climbing our family trees.

But there is a place where each of us can begin—and that is with ourselves. Get a big, looseleaf notebook to use exclusively for your family history. Begin by writing down everything that you know. Your name. Your parents' names. Their parents (your grandparents). Aunts, uncles, cousins. Dates of birth, marriage, death. Places. In other words, take inventory of what you already know. If you know a lot—great! If not, that is why you are beginning your family history research.

2. But how do I keep track of what I write down? Is there a system or format that I should use?

Some people have devised elaborate coding and filing systems to keep track of their family history notes. Others have made simple and useful systems which serve the same purpose. In the "workbook" appendix of this book, you will find some simple forms and charts which you can use to keep track of the information you compile. Don't worry too much about your system. Just make sure you *write down everything.* Don't rely on your memory for anything. If something is written down you will find it. If not, you might lose it forever. And write clearly; inability to read one's own handwriting is a common problem among researchers.

3. After I write down everything I know, where do I go from there? Do I just trace one branch of my family or do I trace all branches at once?

When you are just beginning, your first priority is talking to relatives. Your first priority among the relatives is the oldest of them. Therefore, you ought to begin by phoning, visiting, or writing the oldest living relatives on *all* branches of your family. Otherwise, you might get very involved with one branch of your family while other branches, quite frankly, are dying off! I would bet that there is not one genealogist who has been able to avoid saying, "If only I had spoken to him a long time ago."

After you have spoken to your oldest relatives on all sides of the family, you can zero in on one branch. Remember: The books, archives, and libraries will wait. The people will not.

4. Do you mean to say that I must research all branches of my family? What if I am just interested in one particular branch?

Of course, you can do what you like. But consider two things. One, that while you are just interested in one branch today, your interest may broaden in the future. By then, it may be too late to interview important family members. Secondly, keep in mind that if you don't become the family historian, chances are that nobody will. You have the opportunity to capture and save your family story. Don't let it disappear.

5. What's next? After I have interviewed all of my relatives, where do I go from there? I'm anxious to trace back as far as I can and most of my relatives don't remember too far back. Aren't there books or vital records that I can check to trace back through the generations?

One of the two great misconceptions held by beginning family historians is that they can quickly go to a reference book and find out all about their family. Of course, the other great misconception is that no records exist and that tracing Jewish families is impossible. Both notions are wrong. There are plenty of excellent and effective sources (as you will learn by reading this book), but if you are just beginning, you are not ready for them *yet*. Be patient. You do not discover your family history overnight. Like any other hobby—stamp-collecting, for example—you slowly build on your collection. Watching it grow and then suddenly, months later, seeing that you have really built something to be proud of is what it is all about.

6. That still doesn't answer the question. What's next?

Again, there is no system for everyone. This book is not a simple step-by-step guide. I would suggest that you read through the book and see the *possibilities*. Learn what sources exist. This will give you a better idea what information you *need*. Genealogy and family history is always a detective process. Your new discoveries will be based on information you already know. One fact will lead to another and another. By reading through this book, you will get a good idea of what you need to know in order to discover new information. In fact, it would be a good idea to read over the entire book before even talking to your oldest relatives. In this way you will learn what kinds of questions to ask and what kinds of information you ought to be looking for.

7. Do you mean to say that from this point on, I'm on my own? Isn't there a checklist of things to do? I feel lost.

Research isn't easy. But don't be afraid of it either. Just get involved with it. Decide what you'd like to know (with this book helping you to crystalize those ideas) and go after it.

But if you really want a next step, I will at least share with you the mistake of *most* beginners: Most of us *never* interview enough relatives! We are so eager to "begin the research and the discoveries" that we fail to understand how it is the *people* in your family who can offer you the most information.

So, your next step, after contacting your oldest living relatives, is to contact other relatives as well. *The best leads, the best information, and the best stories I have gathered for my family history have come from relatives.* While I have discovered a great deal in record books and libraries, none of that would have been possible without information provided by people.

If you *ever* wonder what to do next, always ask yourself: Whom have I not yet interviewed?

8. Isn't it true that Jews cannot trace their family histories because of name changes and the destruction of records?

Not at all! In my own case, I've traced back to the 1500's on one side of my family, and the late 1700's on another. In the latter case, I have traced 500 descendants of my great-great-great-grandparents to places all over the world. On another branch of my family I have located copies of my great-grandparents' marriage record in Hungary from the mid-1800's which includes information about my great-great-grandparents. I have also located information on 103 members of one branch of my family—all 103 of whom were killed in the Holocaust.

Jews *can* trace their genealogies and family histories, and that is what this book is all about. By the way, genealogy has been a part of our tradition ever since the first chapters of Genesis.

9. Is there any special equipment needed for all of this?

While there will be more detailed discussion of this throughout the book, I will briefly mention some standard items which will come in handy throughout your search.

A cassette tape recorder. When you interview family members, tape them. How much I would love to have a recording of my great-grandfather—but I can't. What I *can* do is provide the same kind of thing for my descendants.

File folders, paper, notebook, etc. Be generous with these items. The better your note keeping and record keeping are, the better off you'll be when you need to record or find something.

Envelopes, stationery, postage stamps. Family history depends heavily upon writing letters. Keep a supply of these things at all times so that mailing letters and other requests for information does not get held up because you haven't had a chance to go to the post office.

10. Am I aiming for any specific goal in my family history? Do I try to go back as far as possible or to find as many living relatives as I can? Where does it end?

Don't worry about it ending; you're just beginning. As far as your "goal" is concerned, that's up to you. You might want to specialize in one subject—let's say, "What happened to your family during the Holocaust." Or you might want to go as far back as you can on one branch. Genealogy and family history is open-ended. People often ask me if I have finished my research. No, I haven't. I have been researching my family history for ten years and I have no intention of stopping. It hasn't been ten years full time; it's like any other hobby: Sometimes I work on the family history like a madman for a week or two. Other times I neglect it for a few months. The only difference between it and other hobbies I have had is that this one has affected me in profound ways. I feel a great sense of connection with my family and with Jewish history. And I feel a responsibility to that history—to continue as a link on an ancient chain of Jewish Tradition.

On the other hand, I could have stopped at any point with the knowledge that I had gathered a lot of material about the history of my family and that it was now saved from disappearing. It was now a part of the history of my family that would not be forgotten.

As you enter your family history, you will find that it will take you in many directions. You will develop your own special interest

Three-generation genealogy, in Hebrew, found in front cover of old family Bible. First line reads, "Zalmen Lieb Gottlieb, son of Asher Yeshia, son of Shlomo Zalka."

within it as you proceed. If you want to trace back as far as you can, go in that direction. If you want to trace living members of your family, do that. If you have other interests within your family history, then pursue them.

The most important advice is this: Begin now. Don't wait until tomorrow.

GATHERING YOUR HISTORY

Collecting Stories

Your family tree is only the bare framework of your family history. Without the stories, legends, tales, and episodes of your cousins and ancestors, all you will have is a dry collection of names and dates.

When you interview or correspond with relatives and others, encourage them to tell stories, and be sure to record these stories either by writing them down or by taping them. A cassette tape recorder is one of the finest tools that a family historian can have. In future years, when your descendants listen to the family history which you have recorded, they will have the priceless experience of hearing the voices which you have heard, and they will be able to listen, firsthand, to the same tales which you received from the many people with whom you have spoken. Imagine what it would be like for you to be able to hear stories told by your great-grandparents. By recording stories yourself, you will be able to offer this precious gift for future generations of your family.

Cassette tape recorders are small enough and silent enough to be inconspicuous. Rarely do they inhibit the person whom you are recording. Nonetheless, it is important that you tell people when you are recording them, for ethical reasons. In addition, you can purchase, for a few dollars, an attachment for your telephone so that you can record phone conversations. But again, you must tell people what you are doing.

> The stories that I most like to tell are the the ones I heard from my grandfather.
>
> —ELIE WIESEL, *A Jew Today*

Family Legends: Are They True?

I once had a conversation with Elie Wiesel about my family history research. At one point in our exchange, he said to me, "Are you getting stories?"

I told him I was.

"Are you writing them down?" he asked.

"Yes, I'm writing them all down."

"Very good," Wiesel said. "This is very important. You should collect as many stories as you can. Write them down. Save them. You should have a file. Label the folders by name and save the stories. This is very important."

I was well aware of Elie Wiesel's interest in stories, but I was also taken by the personal concern that he expressed and the detail with which he explained a file system for me to use. In fact, I was maintaining just the kind of file system he had suggested.

After a pause, I said, "Of course, I don't think that all of the stories I've been told are true."

"What does it matter if they are true?" Wiesel replied.

I mention this conversation with Elie Wiesel because a discussion regarding the "truth" behind family legends is an important one. Genealogists who are serious about their work have tried to be strict for a long time in accepting only that which can be documented and verified. This is a reaction to the many people who have made false claims about who their ancestors were and what they did. I, too, want to underline the notion that claiming things that are false is the worst family history "sin" possible. On the other hand, there is something to say for recording and even investigating family tales which have dubious origins.

The rule of thumb which I use is this: I record everything. Even the wildest stories (and I've heard some good ones!) are saved. The stories become an important part of the family history—not as fact, but as legend. I am careful to record not only the tale, but its source. And even if it's not true that my great-great-grandfather once offered a plate of food to a hungry man who happened to be Franz Josef, who in turn made my great-great-grandfather his personal guard, I still think it's important that the story has survived and has come down to me.

Don't perpetuate a fraud, but don't rob your family history of its richness by being "scientific." A tale which is not "true" in fact, can be quite "true" in its message. In the case of my great-great-grandfather, the story says that he offered food to a stranger and did not know he was the Emperor. He also did not think he would be rewarded for his act of charity. It's a good lesson.

R. Joshua ben Levi said: He who teaches his grandson

Torah, the Writ regards him as though he had received it direct from Mount Sinai.

—Talmud, Kiddushin, 30A

Ten Common Family Myths—or Truths!

During the past several years, I have had the great opportunity to speak on the subject of Jewish family history on genealogy to more than 200 groups. In addition, I have received letters from hundreds of readers of my articles on the same subject. I am constantly hearing family stories from people who have heard the same tales from their relatives. These people are often quite eager to share their stories with me and believe wholeheartedly that their stories are true.

After hearing scores of stories by so many different people, I began to realize that many of the same legends kept popping up. Over and over again I would hear variations of the same stories. Here are the bare outlines of the ten tales I have heard most often:

1) "We descend from the Baal Shem Tov."

The Baal Shem Tov, founder of Chassidism, is the subject of a great number of legends, and family legends are included. He is claimed as an ancestor by large numbers of people, and is in competition with the next two individuals as "The Most-Often-Claimed Jewish Ancestor."

2) "We descend from the Vilna Gaon."

The Vilna Gaon, one of history's great Talmudists, was an eighteenth-century Lithuanian luminary.

3) "We descend from King David."

To descend from King David, of course, is to open the possibility that the Messiah will come from your family. Jewish Tradition states that the Messiah will spring from the House of David. In fact, a lengthy genealogy in the New Testament attempts to document this connection between King David and Jesus.

4) "We are related to the Rothschild family."

I do not know whether it is to claim heir to the fortune, or simply to say that once they brushed shoulders with the richest Jewish family in modern history, but a huge number of people seem to claim this relationship.

5) *"My ancestors were rabbis."*

It's very possible, but often I have the sense that someone remembers an old man with a long beard and therefore assumed he must be a rabbi.

6) *"There is a fortune of money buried under our house in Eastern Europe."*

If I were to add up the amount of money each of the tellers of this tale has claimed is in a box below his old home, I'm sure it would be greater than the contents of Fort Knox.

7) *"My family left Spain during the Inquisition."*

For me, this is a fascinating story. Certainly many of us do indeed descend from Jews who left Spain centuries ago. But there is little documentation of individual families who left or were expelled. This means that either many families are adopting these stories as their own, or that the story has in fact been handed down from generation to generation since that time. Of course, both reasons could be true for different people!

8) *"My ancestors were horse thieves."*

Frequently this is said as a joke. Often people will speculate and say, "If I trace my family, I'm sure we'll find horse thieves," as if to say that "the truth will finally come out!" But the fascinating thing is that this claim is also made in dead seriousness by so many people.

9) *"Everything in our town was destroyed in the Holocaust. Not a house or person was left. Nothing was saved."*

I am often deeply moved when people say this, not because it is true, but because they believe it. I am certainly not disputing the fact that these people have these awful events in their memories. But I have visited many towns in Eastern Europe which were at one time Jewish towns. The vast majority of the Jewish populations of these towns as well as the buildings were destroyed, but the towns were not—in many cases—as completely obliterated as people say. I have found Jewish cemeteries in places where people report that they were leveled. I have found surviving Jews in places where people say every last Jew was killed.

My point is not to lessen the damage done or to belittle the person who tells of this, but rather to point out the psychological as well as physical effect of the Holocaust. I also mention this to encourage the researcher *not* to give up his or her research simply because something like this is reported.

10) "My family knew Emperor Franz Josef I personally."

A great folk-hero to the Jews in recent years is Franz Josef I of Hapsburg who lived from 1830 to 1916. Friendly to the Jews of his empire, he became a popular figure among the Jewish population. Often he would be spoken of by Jews as "the Emperor, may his majesty be exalted." It was not uncommon to find a picture of Franz Josef on the wall in the homes of Jews. He was a friend to the Jews, at least when compared with almost every other European leader in history, and it is probably for this reason that so many Jewish families claim that they knew him personally. My family has a Franz Josef story as part of its history.

Each of these ten stories has got to be true in some cases. Some of us do descend from King David, the Baal Shem Tov, or the Vilna Gaon. Some of us do come from Spain originally and some of us are related to the Rothschilds. Many of us do have rabbis in our past, and some of us must have been horse thieves.

But it is striking how often these claims are made. The purpose of discussing these stories is not to say that if you have a similar story in your family to automatically dismiss it. On the contrary, record the story, remember it, and even pass it along to the next generation. It is my belief that there is a germ of truth in each story. It is our job to learn the stories, enjoy them, and perhaps speculate as to how or why the story originated.

> The study of history will never become obsolete, and a knowledge of one's grandfathers is an excellent introduction to history.
>
> —Maurice Samuel

What Questions Should You Ask?

When you interview a relative or any other individual for your family history research, it is important that you prepare yourself in advance for the meeting. Effective oral history cannot occur if you just ask questions off the top of your head with little or no thought about what you want to know, what is important to ask, and what the best ways of asking are.

While you will want to be thorough, it is my own personal opinion that you should strike a balance between your own specific interests, and more general topics. In other words, try to cover a broad range of areas but don't avoid focusing on the areas of greatest interest to you. In my own case, I have little interest in politics but a large interest in religion. I try to ask questions concerning politics when it is relevant, but my interviews with relatives have a decided slant toward the religious. I am most interested in the religious thought, activities, and evolution of my family.

The following questions should serve as a guide to your oral history interviews. Do not simply go down the lists of questions and ask them one by one. Rather, pick the questions which interest you, and use them to begin a conversation. Rely on the questions and on your notes to get you started, but know when to put them aside in order to engage in a free-flowing dialogue. If you simply go down the lists asking questions, the oral history will be dull and stiff. Each of these questions has the potential to begin a long, in-depth discussion about the topic at hand.

Oral History Questions and Topics

EUROPEAN ROOTS

1. What towns did your family come from in Europe? Where were those towns located?
2. Who were the immigrants to America? Did you come here, or was it your parents, grandparents, etc.?
3. Do you know the specific reasons for your family coming to America?
4. If you came to America, who came with you?
5. Describe the trip.
6. Did you experience anti-Semitism in Europe?
7. In what port did your ship dock? Do you know the name of the ship and the date it arrived?
8. What was life in Europe like? What are some of your early childhood memories?
9. Did your family live in one town in Europe, or did various branches of the family live in different places? Did your own family move from one place to another?
10. Who was the first person in the entire family to come to America?
11. What contact continued with the Old Country? Did you receive letters from relatives who remained in Europe? Were those letters saved?

PERSONAL AND FAMILY LIFE

1. What were your parents' names? Your mother's maiden name?

2. Where were they from?
3. How many brothers and sisters do you have? What are their names? What was the order of their birth?
4. Did they marry? Have children? What are their names?
5. What are their occupations? What was your father's occupation?
6. Did your mother work?
7. What do you remember about your grandparents? Do you know their names, including maiden names? Where were they from? What were their occupations?
8. Do you remember your great-grandparents? Their names and anything about them?
9. Where were they from?
10. Whom were you named after? What do you know about that person?
11. What is your spouse's name? Your children's names?
12. Where did your family live in the U.S.? Did they live elsewhere?
13. What memories are especially vivid from your childhood?
14. Do you remember your first job and how old you were?
15. What were the living conditions in your home as a child?

RELIGIOUS LIFE
1. Was your family religious?
2. In Europe, were they Orthodox or Chassidic?
3. If they were Chassidic, did they follow any particular rebbe?
4. Did the religious life in your family change when you came to America—or over the years?
5. Was there any resistance to coming to America on the part of anyone in your family for religious reasons?
6. Did your family belong to a synagogue in America?
7. Is there a family cemetery plot? Where is it? Who bought or organized it?
8. Do you remember your childhood during holidays such as Passover or the High Holidays? Others?
9. Is there a family Bible?
10. Did you have a Bar/Bas Mitzvah?
11. Do you remember the shul in Europe? What was it like?

ARTIFACTS
1. Do you have your ketubah (marriage document)?
2. Is there a family photo album?

3. Do you have old photographs?
4. Are there any family heirlooms which have been passed down from generation to generation? Do you know through whom they have been passed down?
5. Do you have any old candlesticks, kiddish cups, or tefillin? (Do not give the impression that you want them—just that you'd like to *see* them.)
6. Do you have your passport? Your parents' passports?
7. Do you have your citizenship papers? Your "first papers"?
8. Do you have your birth certificate?
9. Do you have any old letters written by family members?
10. Are there any recipes that have been in the family for a long time?
11. Are there any other old family-history items, such as diaries, Bibles, books, etc.?
12. Is there a written genealogy in the family?
13. Do you know anyone else in the family who would have old family documents?

> Tell ye your children of it, and let your children tell their children, and their children another generation.
>
> Joel   1:3

Follow Leads Like a Detective

Family history is not a simple matter. You will not be able to find out everything you want to know from any one book, relative, library, archive, or photograph. Like a detective, you will have to listen carefully for "leads" which will help you to discover more and more. When you interview a second cousin of your mother who suggests that "Aunt Bertha could tell you more," you must get in touch with Aunt Bertha. If someone mentions, in passing, that a branch of the family once lived in Omaha, Nebraska, you should check it out. If a family legend says that an ancestor of yours was in the Civil War, do the research to find out if it's true.

In my own particular case, one tiny clue, mentioned once, was able to send me on the road to trace my family back to the 1500's! In another case, a small lead helped me to discover my cousin and his family who survived the Holocaust and still live in Warsaw. I can tell countless stories of dramatic family history discoveries that I have made due simply to the fact that I investigate the most obscure clues I hear. In almost every case, the effort paid off.

Our past is not behind us, it is in our very being.

—BEN-GURION, "Call of the Spirit"

Taking Notes

An important part of your family history research will be taking notes. If you are in a library checking out a book source, or in an archive examining public records, or visiting a relative for oral history, note taking will be vital. Many amateur researchers make the dangerous mistake of thinking that they will remember what they have been told during an interview or what they have seen in a book. Caution: You will forget! If you are like most people, you will, very shortly into your research, begin to get sources and places confused.

It is much like the vacation you have taken. After a while you begin to forget where you saw what. When you return home and tell your friends about your trip, you are unsure if it was Rome or Florence where you ate at that fabulous restaurant.

Take notes. While good note taking is a skill which develops over a time, it is generally best to write down as much as possible. It is also advisable to type up your notes after a session of note taking. Type your notes as soon as possible to avoid being unable to read your own handwriting (which so often happens!). Also, if you type your notes the same day that you have taken them, it will be fresh in your mind and you will be able to be accurate.

Many people feel that note taking is a waste of time. But if you plan to do a good job on your family history it is essential—and you will discover it yourself after very little time as a researcher.

Often the question arises, "How do I keep track of my information? Should I set up a file system? An index card file? How do I make sense out of all my little notes and papers?" These are difficult questions to answer. There are two approaches I can suggest. The first is to invent a system which works for you. Don't worry about whether it's "right" or the best system. If it works for you, it's the best. My second suggestion—and this is only for those of you who cannot or would not invent your own system—is to go to the library and consult the many "how-to-do-it" genealogy books which explain some simple and some elaborate systems for keeping records. Also ask your librarian if your library has some privately published family histories and genealogies (most libraries have some, having received them as gifts). These will help you set up a system of your own based on the experience of others.

There are many books on the market which offer charts and forms which you can fill in to keep track of your family's history. While I have yet to see a book I am perfectly happy with, almost all of them are useful. I suggest you consult or buy one and adapt it to your own interests and to your own family. For example, many books have charts in them which ask for "date of baptism." This clearly does not apply to the Jewish researcher. On the other hand, the general format of these "fill-in" books can help a great deal when you try to put your gathered information into some order.

> I, Ahimaaz, the son of Paltiel ben Samuel ben Hananel ben Amittai, sought God's aid and guidance in order to find the lineage of my family and He bountifully granted my request. I concentrated my mind and soul upon this work; I put the family documents and traditions in order, and I narrated the story in rhymed form. I began with the earliest tradition during the time of the destruction of Jerusalem and of the Temple by the Romans; then I traced it through the settlement of the exiles in the city of Oria in Italy (where I am now living) and the arrival of my ancestors in Capua; and finally, I have concluded with my own generation. I have written it all in this book for the use of future generations.
>
> —AHIMAAZ BEN PALTIEL, Jewish poet, born in 1017.

Visiting Relatives and Others

One of the most rewarding yet time-consuming aspects of family history research is visiting people. Yet, however much time is required, the investment invariably pays off.

Do not expect or desire that all your information will come to you. Often people do not write letters, or do not write them well. In addition, a story told by a relative will almost always be better in person than on a page. Think of yourself: If you had to write a story on paper, you would probably not embellish it the way you would if you had the opportunity to tell it aloud.

Family history is also not simply the collection of names, dates, and stories. The process of meeting new people, sharing discoveries and experiences, and making new friends is a fringe benefit (if not a reason in itself) of your family history project.

Another fascinating phenomenon has happened to me many

times. I will establish a correspondence with a relative and will acquire a lot of new information. On occasion I will call the person and will receive even more family history over the phone. Then the information source will "run dry," but I will visit the same person who had no more to tell me and discover that there is much more to hear and see. Photographs will be found, old passports and documents will appear, additional stories will be remembered, and I will regret not having visited sooner.

It is a particular mitzvah to visit an elderly person. So often I have been given the opportunity to bring a little bit of joy into someone's life by visiting with a person who was delighted to share information with me. One strong suggestion concerning the visiting of older relatives in particular: Don't just visit once and forget about them. An occasional phone call, a note, or even additional visits are important. Otherwise you have just "used" them. After you have made an acquaintance or have reestablished a family relationship, it is incumbent upon you to take responsibility for it. It takes very little effort to call and say hello, or write a short letter to someone who has shared with you a part of his life.

> A people's memory is history; and as a man without a memory, so a people without a history cannot grow wiser, better.
>
> —I. L. PERETZ

Family Photographs

Something that you must ask of each person whom you interview for your family history is to see his old photographs. Family photographs are an important and exciting part of your family history pursuit, and it is a special experience to be able to see pictures of your ancestors, of your ancestors' siblings, and of Holocaust victims whose photographs may exist.

As I visit people and see their photographs, I know that I want to have copies of many of them. Yet, I am certainly not going to ask for them (old photographs are among people's most precious possessions), and I even hesitate borrowing them. In the first place, I do not want to risk losing them, and secondly it becomes quite expensive to have them reproduced. But there is a solution to that problem. It is relatively easy to duplicate them yourself.

What you need is a 35mm camera and a set of three close-up lenses which can be bought, presently, for between $15.00 and

$20.00. That is all the equipment you need. In other words, if you already have the camera, your investment is $15.00 or so. You will break even after duplicating just a few photographs when you compare this process to the usual lab fees.

When you visit people who have old photographs, bring your camera and the lenses. If you use a close-up lens, all you have to do is set the photograph down on a table, make sure that there is enough light, and take a photograph of the photograph. It is necessary to use a tripod to make sure the camera does not move. The cost of tripods varies.

With this process, you can build a collection of old photographs for a small investment, and you also will have negatives of the photographs which can be made into prints for pennies. You can then make prints for people who might like copies of some photographs from your collection. Often I have photographs of people which other family members would love to have. Giving copies of photographs to people is a nice gift, and is also an incentive for them to share more with you.

This is only one way to duplicate photographs. With a little time and patience it works quite well. However there are other ways to do the same thing, and I would suggest that you visit a good camera shop and ask about equipment available to make copies of your old family photographs. Depending upon how many photos you have to duplicate, how involved in this process you want to get, and how much money you are willing to spend, there are several options open to you. It would also be worth mentioning here that as photocopy machines get better and better, photocopying becomes a somewhat effective way to copy photographs.

> Jews who get a certain spiritual tonic from the reflection that they are somehow related to the creators of the Bible and to its ethical values forget that the relationship was passed on to them by the men who begot their fathers. Who were these men? Under what circumstances did they nurture the relationship for transmission? What tone and color had their lives? What purpose did they conceive themselves to be serving in their obstinate fidelity to the relationship? What hopes had they for themselves—and for their grandchildren?
>
> —Maurice Samuel, *The World of Sholom Aleichem*

Writing Letters

While it is almost always better to visit relatives when searching for family history, distance forces us to write letters at times. In addition, family historians use the mail to make inquiries to strangers who might be related or who might be of help. There are several "rules" or guidelines to follow when writing for family history information:

1) Try to avoid using a form letter, even if you are writing to many people for the same kind of information. You will get better results with personal letters.

2) Explain clearly at the beginning of your letter what you are doing and why. Many people are suspicious when it comes to talking about "family matters," especially since there are some companies which are trying to make money by offering to research your family tree. I have never had a problem with people suspecting my motives, but I think this is the result of my making it clear from the beginning.

3) Identify yourself in the letters. The more you say about yourself, the more other people will offer about themselves. Tell them about your family history, both to inspire them to do the same and to help them to trust you.

4) Promise that you'll write them again and that you will share your discoveries with them—and then keep your promise!

5) Do not ask too many questions in one letter. A letter filled with questions is not apt to get a response.

6) You might want to try a questionnaire, but keep it simple and short. It is more effective to ask a little with each letter than to try to "get everything" at once. Also, you do not want to "use" people. You want to establish friendships. The longer the relationship, the more rewarding it will be—both personally and informationally.

7) Always enclose a self-addressed stamped envelope. This is for the convenience of your respondent. While you should not expect everyone to answer every letter, a self-addressed stamped envelope will increase your rate of return. You cannot send such an envelope outside the United States, but you may want to send an addressed envelope and International Reply Coupons which can be purchased at your local post office. These coupons can be redeemed in other countries for stamps and this will serve the same purpose as sending stamps.

8) Finally, be warm, friendly, and polite in your letters. Do not insist that people send you information. Writing letters is an opportunity to be pleasant and to brighten someone's day (or more). Take that opportunity and use it!

Blessed is he that remembers what is forgotten!

—S. Y. AGNON

Phone Books

Contemporary phone books can be of help when searching for missing or new relatives. While it is almost impossible to use a telephone book looking for new relatives named Cohen or Levine, you might find it productive if your name is less common.

I have looked up the name Kurzweil in hundreds of phone books and have contacted many of the people whose names I have found. In a great number of cases, I have discovered relatives who did not know we were related—nor did I know about them until I made the contact. Often it was just a matter of asking a few questions to determine where on the family tree a newly discovered branch of the family belonged. Over the past several years I have discovered "lost" branches of my family in Israel, across the U.S., and in Poland.

Many large public libraries have good collections of telephone books. The New York Public Library Research Library, for example, has nearly every telephone book in the world! Many foreign telephone books have English editions which are also available.

When contacting a stranger, either by phone or through the mail, it is important that you identify yourself and explain what you are doing. You want to inspire trust. Tell him about yourself, something of what you have already researched, and promise to share it with him (and do it!).

I have sometimes found it difficult to call a stranger and to begin a conversation about family history, but it has almost always been rewarding.

Phone books which you should surely check if you have an uncommon last name are the Israeli phone books. There is an English language edition, and you might discover a branch of your family which settled there either before the Holocaust, or even afterward.

I never thought that I had relatives living in Israel until I looked up the name "Kurzweil" in the Israeli phone books. I wrote to several people, and when they wrote back, the information about their parents, grandparents, and towns in Europe from where they came matched with my family tree.

Several years ago I was eager to locate a cousin of my father who survived the Holocaust and was reported to have stayed in Poland. I did not know his address, nor did I know where he had been for the past thirty years. But I went to the Polish phone book of 1974 and found his name, address, and telephone number. I wrote to him, and a few weeks later I received a letter in return. It was, indeed, my cousin, whom nobody had been in touch with for years! We have since been writing to each other every few weeks, and I visited him and his wife and daughter in Warsaw. All because I looked up his name in the Polish phone book.

(See Chapter 3 for more on pre-Holocaust telephone books.)

Vital Records

Birth, death, marriage, and divorce records in the U.S. can be quite helpful, but it would be impossible to generalize as to what information each provides. This varies both from place to place as well as from year to year. Costs for these documents also vary, and you can never be sure of the current price either; I've seen prices fluctuate from one month to the next.

The best guides to these records can be found in a series of government pamphlets available from the U.S. Government Printing Office, Washington, D.C. 20402, or from their branch offices around the country (check locally). There are three pamphlets available on this subject:

Where to Write for Marriage Records
Where to Write for Divorce Records
Where to Write for Birth and Death Records

Each pamphlet costs 70¢ as of this writing, and each provides information on each state regarding the procedure required to obtain copies of these documents.

While the information on these documents is not standard and therefore will vary from place to place in the U.S. as well as from year to year in the same location, a few interesting examples of what I have found would be useful in illustrating the value of these American sources.

Often a person will say to me, "My great-grandmother came to the United States many years ago. She is no longer alive, nor is anyone else in her generation who can answer some questions. I cannot even find out the names of her parents." My immediate response is, "Have you obtained her death certificate?" More often than not, a death certificate asked (and still asks) the name of the parents of the deceased. While there might be no one alive today who knows the answer to that question, chances are someone *did* know at the time of her death.

One of my great-grandfathers came to America and died here. I wanted to know his parents' names so I sent for his death certificate. When it arrived, I learned his father's name and his mother's name. And most important, I learned the maiden name of his mother! When death certificates ask for the names of the parents of the deceased, they will usually include a request for the maiden name of the mother. So, when my great-grandfather's death certificate arrived, another branch of my family began to appear.

Interestingly, his mother's maiden name was the same as his wife's maiden name. So my first thought was that there must have been a mistake: How can his wife and his mother have the same last name? Unless, of course, they were related! I asked around in the family and was told that my great-grandparents were first cousins.

Marriage records are also of great value since these records will ask the names of the bride's parents and the groom's parents.

There is one additional thing to keep in mind when searching for these records. Often you will send to the appropriate agency for copies of these records and they will reply that they do not have them. A number of possibilities exist. It may be an error on the part of a clerk who made the search. Or it may be your error—perhaps your grandmother died somewhere other than where you think. Or possibly the record was lost. In any of these cases, do not give up. Try other alternatives. For example, if you cannot locate your grandmother's death certificate but are anxious to find her parents' names, try to locate the death certificate of one of her brothers or sisters. The same thing goes for marriage records: Try to find records of siblings. In other words, you must be a detective. You must think of every possibility and every alternative. It isn't always easy, but it's almost always worthwhile.

Be fruitful and multiply, and replenish the earth.

—Genesis 1:28

Census Records

The Federal Government has taken a census of the country's population every ten years since 1790. Census records can all be consulted for family history research, although some have restrictions on them. The only census which is not available is the 1890

Federal Census which was destroyed (except for small portions) in a fire.

The census records can be of enormous assistance to you when you are researching your family history. The information will be valuable on its own, and it will give you clues to seek additional facts. You will also be able to search the census records for people with your last name in an effort to locate new or unknown relatives. By reviewing the kinds of information to be found in the records, you can see how helpful they can be.

There are many differences among these census records from decade to decade. For example, the records of 1790 to 1840 list only the head of the household by name, whereas the later records list the names of each member of the household. You will have no choice, obviously, but to accept the difference among the records.

Each Federal Census from 1790 through 1900 is available on an unrestricted basis to researchers. While you can do your own research from the census records up to 1900, someone will have to do it for you for the records compiled since then.

Write to: U.S. Dept. of Commerce
            Bureau of the Census
            Pittsburg, Kansas 66762

and ask for form BC-600, if you want information from census records for 1910 to the present.

If your research takes you back before 1850 in the United States, you will be pleased to know that most of the censuses from 1790 to 1850 have been indexed and these indexes are in book form. The 1850 index in particular will be very useful for those German-Jewish families which arrived at the beginning of the major German-Jewish wave of immigration to America. Many of the National Archives branches have these indexes, as do major genealogical libraries.

The National Archives in Washington, D.C., has all of the Federal Census records from 1790 to 1900 on microfilm.

It is always best to do the research by yourself because you cannot be sure that anyone else has been thorough. Once I searched a Federal Census for a few hours until I found a part of my family in the records. I was sure they were listed (at least I believed they were) and it wasn't until I checked several alternate spellings of the name that I found it. Someone else probably would have given up after a few minutes—and rightfully so.

Census records before 1900 are filed geographically, so you must know the address of the individual or family in order to find the records. Often the use of a city directory (see page 94) is of help in this case. For the 1880 and 1900 census, there is a name index. This index is not alphabetical, however, but is filed by what is known as the Soundex System. In this system, the names are filed by "sound"—the phonetic sound to be exact. This is of great help since it avoids most problems of misspellings or alternate spellings.

Many local libraries have different parts of the Federal Census, and it would be worthwhile to check the nearest large public library to see what it might have. In addition, as we mentioned before, there are branches of the National Archives around the country. The following is a list of those branches:

Archives Branch
Federal Archives and Records Center

Boston:
380 Trapelo Road
Waltham, MA 02154
617-223-2657

New York:
Building 22-MOT Bayonne
Bayonne, NJ 07002
201-858-7252

Philadelphia:
5000 Wissahickon Avenue
Philadelphia, PA 19144
215-951-5591

Atlanta:
1557 St. Joseph Avenue
East Point, GA 30344
404-763-7477

Chicago:
7358 South Pulaski Road
Chicago, IL 60629
312-353-0161

Kansas City:
2306 East Bannister Road
Kansas City, MO 64131
816-926-7271

Fort Worth:
4900 Hemphill Street
Fort Worth, TX 76115
817-334-5515

Denver:
Building 48
Denver Federal Center
Denver, CO 80225
303-234-5271

San Francisco:
1000 Commodore Drive
San Bruno, CA 94066
415-876-9009

Los Angeles:
24000 Avila Road
Laguna Niguel, CA 92677
714-831-4242

Seattle:
6125 Sand Point Way NE
Seattle, WA 98115
206-442-4502

While each branch of the National Archives is known generally by the city listed on the left, as you can see, the branches are not always located in those cities. In addition, the areas which these branches serve include the states surrounding the branch. Your local public library should know which branch serves your area.

You should also send to the National Archives for their package of information on genealogical records. This material is free. A letter to the National Archives, Washington, D.C. 20408, asking for this information is all you need.

A final note must be mentioned regarding the accuracy of the census records, as well as all public records: You cannot be sure that anything is 100 percent accurate. There is always room for

World War I U.S. draft registration card of Morris Weisenfeld, born September 5, 1896 human error, and if you find two conflicting pieces of information, you must use your own judgment as to what is true.

The U.S. Department of Commerce, Bureau of the Census, has issued a booklet called "Age Search Information," which is an invaluable sourcebook for every family historian. Don't be misled by the title; this publication is far more than a guide to getting birth information.

In simple yet detailed form, it explains how to get census records, citizenship records, and military records, and gives information sources for local birth, marriage, and death records. The booklet also discusses resources at the Library of Congress, the Daughters of the American Revolution, the Mormon Church, state census records, and adoption records. There is also a section on "missing persons."

The publication provides the addresses of the state agencies which can give you birth and death records. It also gives the addresses of the National Archives branches throughout the country as well as dozens of other addresses to write to for genealogical information.

This booklet is a must for every family historian. The current price is $1.70, and it can be obtained from

> Superintendent of Documents
> U.S. Government Printing Office
> Washington, D.C. 20402

Send for this publication. It is well worth the investment.

Census Records (State)

In addition to the Federal Census, states have also taken censuses, often during years when the Federal Government did not. Check to see whether the states you are interested in have census records. You might inquire at your public library, state libraries, and genealogy libraries of local historical societies for this information.

To give one example, there was a 1905, 1915 and 1925 census for New York. 1915 and 1925 are available at the State Archives, Albany, New York 12230. All three are available with the respective county clerks throughout New York State.

> A clan and a family resemble a heap of stones: one stone taken out of it and the whole totters.
>
> —Genesis Rabbah

City Directories

A city directory looks very much like a phone book and serves much the same purpose—which is to identify people by name and address. City directories have been published in hundreds of cities and towns, large and small, since the 1800's. Some cities still publish these directories, while New York City stopped in the 1930's.

If a city of interest to you has ever published city directories, a collection of them is probably in the public library of that city.

Of what use is a directory? Suppose you know that your great-great-grandfather came to New York in the 1880's but you know little more about him. If you check the directories of New York City for that time period, you might find him listed. The listing might include his occupation (it usually does) and sometimes the directories even include a wife's name in parentheses next to the listed name. You will also learn his address. If you begin to check the directories by year for this period, you can determine what year he is first listed and what year he stops being listed. These are clues to the year he arrived in the city (and perhaps the country) as well as when he died (although he simply might have moved).

A city directory can also be useful in connection with census research. For most census records you must know the address of the person. Since phone books are relatively recent publications, a city directory is an excellent source of old addresses.

No father should give his son the name of a wicked man.

—RASHI

Synagogue Records

There is no systematic way of searching out synagogue records nor is there any guarantee that they exist for the particular location or time period that you want. Nevertheless, you should keep in mind that synagogues have generally kept records of different kinds, and it might be worth your while, if you know which U.S. synagogues your ancestors joined, to investigate the possibility that the synagogue still exists, or that the records do.

Synagogues have kept various different kinds of records, and again it varies from place to place. Often birth, marriage, and death records were kept, as well as membership records.

Inquire as to whether the synagogue still exists. If it does not, a local investigation might turn up a location of the synagogue's records.

According to Rabbi Malcolm Stern, genealogist for the American Jewish Archives, synagogues have been known to keep four types of records: 1) minute books of congregational meetings (which Rabbi

Stern says have often been lost); 2) account books which contained lists of membership (many of which have also been lost); 3) congregational histories and communal histories, which are often privately published and available from the synagogues themselves as well as from large Jewish libraries; 4) vital records, which include birth and circumcision records, Bar Mitzvah records, marriage records, and death records. Availability of all of these records varies from synagogue to synagogue and at this point there is no general accounting of these records.

Both the American Jewish Archives and the American Jewish Historical Society have collections of synagogue records. Their addresses can be found elsewhere in this book. It would be worthwhile to write to both of these organizations in an attempt to locate old U.S. synagogue records.

If an old synagogue to which your family belonged is still functioning, writing or visiting might prove worthwhile. Be aware, however, that the average synagogue is not staffed to search through records. They might be very hesitant to do a search for you—or even to let you search the records. There is no rule of thumb or formula for success here.

> Every man has three names: one his father and mother
> gave him, one others call him, and one he acquires himself.
>
> —Ecclesiastes R., 7:1-3

The National Archives

While we discuss the National Archives (Washington, D.C. 20408) in various other parts of this book, it would be useful to mention it here in a general context. The National Archives has millions of records in its collections. Among those of particular genealogical interest are:

> Census schedules 1790 to 1900
> Passenger arrival lists
> U.S. Military records:
>   Revolutionary War
>   War of 1812
>   Indian Wars and related wars
>   Mexican War
>   Civil War
>   Spanish-American War
>   Philippine Insurrection

> Burial records of soldiers
> Veterans' Benefits records
> Pension records
> Land records
> Passport applications

A complete description of these and other records can be found in the "Guide to Genealogical Records in the National Archives" available from the U.S. Government Printing Office, Washington, D.C. 20402, or from their local offices. You can also send to the National Archives itself for their "free pamphlets concerning genealogical records."

The records of the National Archives can prove invaluable, particularly if your family has been in the United States for several generations.

What If You Were Adopted?

The subject of an adopted child's search for his or her natural parents is a controversial one. Complex feelings exist on the part of all those concerned: the adopted child, the adoptive parents, the natural parents, and the people who keep the records.

A full discussion of the issue would not be possible or appropriate here. However, the subject of an adopted child's search for natural parents and the subject of genealogy have an obvious relationship. It is certainly an issue which must be continuously explored rather than avoided or feared. An observation of mine may be appropriate here: *Each and every* time that I have lectured on the subject of Jewish genealogy to children or teenagers the question is raised by someone in the audience regarding this issue. The question is usually a simple one: "How can someone who is adopted trace their family?" I have lectured to dozens of young groups and the question never fails to be raised, sometimes in front of the whole group and sometimes privately afterward by a young person who is struggling with this problem.

My response is always the same. I begin by noting that it is an important and deeply personal issue. I then add that the decision to search for one's natural parents is a serious one and that much thought must go into the decision in order to be considerate to everyone involved. I then mention that there are organizations which help in the process of searching for one's natural parents (as well as aid in the emotional issues which spring from this). But my concluding comments directed at the young questioner who most probably is an adopted child considering such a search is this: Jewish genealogy and family history offers a special and unique opportunity for someone who is adopted. If you were adopted I would strongly suggest that you research the family history of your adoptive parents. Just as they adopted you as their child, you can adopt their history as your own history. This is one powerful way for you to tie the link even more strongly between you and your parents—who are people who have loved you very much.

If you are an adopted child, there are organizations which can help you in your search for your natural parents—if you decide to make that search. They are:

ALMA	ALMA
P.O. Box 154	P.O. Box 112
Washington Bridge Station	Lomita, Cal. 90717
New York, N.Y. 10033	213-547-0147
212-581-1568	

ALMA (Adoptees' Liberty Movement Association) publishes a newsletter and a handbook called *Handbook for the Search*.

Also, it is suggested that you read *The Search for Anna Fisher* by Florence Fisher, which is the account of the author's search for her natural parents. Florence Fisher is the founder of ALMA.

An excellent book exploring the entire subject of adopted children searching for their natural parents is *Lost & Found; The Adoption Experience* by Betty Jean Lifton, New York, 1979. This book is worthwhile reading for all individuals involved in "the adoption experience." Also included in the book is a long list of "Adoptee Search Groups" around the country. This is the best and most moving book on this difficult subject that I have seen.

> To honor parents is more important even than to honor God.
>
> —SIMEON B. YOHAI
> Talmud J, Peah, 1.1

Canadian Research

The first step in beginning research on Canadian genealogy and family history is to obtain a booklet called *Tracing Your Ancestors in Canada*. It is available from Public Archives of Canada, 395 Wellington, Ottawa K1A ON3. This guide will give you an overview of Canadian sources and will describe what Canada has available to the researcher. In many cases the kinds of resources which

I have described for the U.S. are also available—in different format, years, and so on—in Canada.

For example, Canada has census records; birth, marriage, and death records; land records; military records; immigration records (including some passengers lists); and naturalization (citizenship) records.

Canada also has some important Jewish libraries, archives, and organizations which might prove useful in your searches. They include:

The Canadian Jewish
Congress Archives
1590 McGregor Avenue
Montreal, Quebec H3G 1C5

The Canadian Jewish
Congress Archives
150 Beverley Street
Toronto, Ontario M5T 1Y6

Jewish Historical Society of
Canada
150 Beverley Street
Toronto, Ontario M5T 1Y6

Toronto Jewish Historical
Society
21 Prince Charles Drive
Toronto, Ontario M6A 2H1

Ottawa Jewish Historical
Society
151 Chapel Street
Ottawa, Ontario KIN 7Y2

Jewish Historical Society of
British Columbia
950 West 41st Avenue
Vancouver, British Columbia
V5Z 2N7

Jewish Public Library of
Montreal
5151 Cote Ste.
Catherine Road
Montreal, Quebec H3W 1M6

In many cases there are sources in Canada equivalent to those in the U.S., particularly passenger-arrival records. There are three types of landing records maintained by the Canadian Government: records of arrival in Canada prior to 1900; records of arrival from 1900 to 1921; and records from 1921 to the present.

Arrival records prior to 1900. Records of ship arrivals at Quebec City from 1865 and Halifax from 1881 are kept by the Archives branch in Ottawa. You must know the name of the passenger, year and month of arrival, and the port into which the immigrant came. Send your inquiries to:

Archives Branch
Public Archives of Canada
395 Wellington Street
Ottawa, Ontario, K1A ON3

Arrivals from 1900 to 1921. Passenger lists (manifests) have been maintained for this period, but are on microfilm in chronological order. There is no index, which means that you must have fairly precise information concerning any individual in order to locate his or her records. Write to the address above for further information on how to obtain these records.

Arrivals from 1921. These records are the easiest of the three to obtain since they are filed alphabetically. If you have the correct spelling as it was upon arrival, the records can usually be located. Of course if you can provide additional information it will be that much easier for the Archives staff to be of help. Again, the Archives branch mentioned above should be contacted for more information.

While this is not an exhaustive list of Jewish sources in Canada, it is a good beginning. Do not think that these places will be able to do research for you, or that they will all know exactly where to send you for your research, but they have the most experience with genealogical inquiries and are a good place to start.

> Why did God create one man, Adam, rather than creating the whole human race together? It was to show that if anyone causes a single soul to perish, it is as though he caused a whole world to perish; and if anyone saves a single soul, it is as if he had saved a whole world.
>
> —Mishnah, Sanhedrin 4:5

Toledot: The Journal of Jewish Genealogy

In the winter of 1977, Steven W. Siegel, a free-lance Jewish researcher and archivist and secretary of the Jewish Historical Society of New York, and I got together to found *Toledot: The Journal of Jewish Genealogy*. In our view, a quarterly journal devoted to Jewish genealogy was badly needed. We were aware of the fact that before the Holocaust, in Germany, there was a Jewish genealogical periodical, but that Nazi activity forced it to close down. That prewar publication served the important function of informing its readers of new discoveries, techniques, and historical notes relating to Jewish family history. Steven Siegel and I wanted to do the same.

We found that we were continuously discovering sources for Jewish genealogical research. We also found that other people with similar interests were making their own new discoveries. Clearly a vehicle had to be formed which could publish, on a regular basis,

תולדות

TOLEDOT
the journal of jewish genealogy

VOLUME 2, NUMBER 1   SUMMER 1978

Front cover of *Toledot: The Journal of Jewish Genealogy*, currently published in New York

these new pieces of information. So, *Toledot* (the Hebrew word for genealogy) was born.

It is interesting to note that while there are hundreds of genealogy publications around the world, *Toledot* is the only Jewish one. *Toledot* reaches subscribers throughout the United States, in Israel, Europe, South America, Canada, and Australia.

What can you find in *Toledot?* Mostly "how-to" articles, each dealing with a different aspect of Jewish research. In-depth articles on German Jewish research, Polish Jewish research, and so on can be found in *Toledot*'s pages. *Toledot* also runs two regular features: a Jewish name column, written by Rabbi Benzion Kaganoff, and "The Jewish Family Finder." Kaganoff, a leading expert on the subject of Jewish names (and author of a book on the subject, discussed elsewhere in this volume), explains and theorizes about several Jewish names and their origins in each issue of *Toledot*. "The Jewish Family Finder" is basically a classified ad section where Jewish genealogists and family historians can announce to *Toledot*'s readership that they are looking for or willing to share information on particular surnames and locations. People have found valuable information through this column.

One very useful and popular series of articles in *Toledot* was the publication of the catalog of the Mormons' Jewish holdings (discussed elsewhere in this book).

Finally, *Toledot* informs its readers about obscure but possibly valuable resources of a very particular nature. For example, in one issue of *Toledot* there was a short article about a man who has spent his life researching the Jewish history of a small town in Hungary. If your family came from that town, it would be likely that he would have information for you. The chances of your family being from that town are remote, but the possibility exists. And you can find out about this and other related items in *Toledot*'s pages.

Subscriptions are $8.00 per year (four issues), $2.50 for single issues. Non-U.S. subscriptions slightly higher.

> Toledot: The Journal of Jewish Genealogy
> 155 East 93rd Street, Suite 3C
> New York, N.Y. 10028

Cardinal Rules When Dealing with Libraries, Archives, and Other Institutions

Throughout this book you will learn about libraries, archives, and other institutions which will be of interest when pursuing your Jewish family history. The following are basic principles to keep in mind when making contact with them.

1) Most historical institutions are understaffed and the employees are overworked and underpaid. Be friendly and polite when making your inquiry, and be appreciative when receiving your answer.

2) *Do not* expect the staff members of historical institutions to do research for you (unless they have a system whereby they charge by the hour for such a service). Librarians and archivists can and should help you to locate material, but just so that *you* can then do the research. They can be of general assistance in helping you to find material on your subject, but they cannot read the material with you or for you.

3) Much of the material of use to you in Jewish research is *not* in English. Staff members of Jewish historical institutions *cannot* translate for you. Translation is very time-consuming. Bring someone along who can translate for you.

4) The questions you are about to ask a librarian might be brand-new for you but have probably been asked a thousand times by a thousand others. Be patient with the librarian who is not patient with you. On the other hand, keep in mind that the staff of the library is there for you. Don't dominate their time, but use their skills. Most of all, appreciate their help.

5) When you write to an institution for information, always include a self-addressed stamped envelope. Not only is it the correct thing to do, but also, since most people do not do this, you will be appreciated by the receiver.

6) Most importantly, be prepared with an intelligent question. Of course, there is no such thing as a stupid question; it is stupid only if you do not ask. But librarians are always being confronted by people who have not done their own homework and think that the librarian should do it for them. For example, *do not* enter a Jewish library with an interest in researching your family history if you have yet to interview your family for basic information. The more information you can bring with you, the better the librarian will be able to assist you.

7) Specifically relating to family history and genealogy, avoid questions such as "I'm doing research on my family from Russia named Schwartz. Can you help me?" If all you know is that your family is from Russia and their name was Schwartz, you have not done your homework.

8) Finally, most Jewish institutions offer you their resources for free. But that does not mean that you are without a responsibility to that institution. Consider joining the organization if membership is offered. If not, a donation would be a nice idea.

Publishing Your Family History

There will probably come a time when you will want to publish your research findings for the benefit of the other members of your family who want a copy of what you have discovered. Hundreds of Jewish family histories have been privately printed and range from several typed pages that have been photocopied and stapled to hard-cover books of several hundred pages.

There are many things to consider when thinking about printing your family history. All considerations must include the price of production of course. If you have only a few pages of information, you can easily type them and get them offset rather cheaply. If you want to reproduce photographs, you can have them offset too. The more ambitious you are, the more it will cost. If you want to have a small book printed, the cost could be considerable. A conversation with a good printer can answer most of your questions.

I would suggest that you go to a large public library or any of the major Jewish libraries I have discussed in this book (especially YIVO and the Leo Baeck Institute). They will have many samples of Jewish families histories for you to examine, from inexpensive products to fancy volumes. Not only can you get an idea of what to aim for with your own project, but you can also see the various formats designed to record the information you have gathered. Don't decide against publishing a family history just because you cannot produce a fancy one. Even the most modest family history will become a cherished item for your family members.

> Rav Judah has said in the name of Rav: Ezra did not leave Babylon to go up to Eretz Yisrael until he had written his own genealogy.
>
> —Baba Bathra, 15a

Chapter 2

A Good Name Is Rather to Be Chosen Than Great Riches

Prov. 22:1

A link with our past, with Jewish history, and with our Tradition which each of us carries with us every moment is our names. Both our first and surnames represent, when analyzed, a piece of history. Whether it be our first names (which in European Jewish tradition are usually in memory of beloved persons who are deceased), or our surnames (which often contain fascinating clues to help us identify our ancestors), our names are not merely labels to distinguish us from others, but are rather special designations which place us in time and history.

Our surnames stretch back for generations. Like our heritage, our names have been passed down to us, generation to generation, until they arrived in the present. Our surnames, as we have said, provide us with clues about our early ancestors. At some point in time your surname was taken by (or given to) someone in your family's past, and it then continued through time to you. Of course, we must remember that while each of us has one surname, we are equally the descendants of many families with just as many surnames. Our custom has usually been to take the surname of our father, but we are just as much members of our mother's family. In addition, we are more than just the product of two families, since each of our parents is the product of two families. Therefore, it is important to keep in mind that when we discuss our surnames we are speaking of many more than one. In fact, as you discover the names of your ancestors and acknowledge the list of names which are *yours*, you will be able to understand more of your own personal history by examining the nature of your many surnames.

While our names are usually generations old, they are not ancient. Use of surnames by Jews is a relatively recent custom considering the length of Jewish history. In the Torah, there are no surnames, nor were there any used in Biblical times. It was sufficient to have one name which distinguished each member of a community from the others. In the later books of the Bible, we do find the first evidences of surnames, as in "Elijah the Tishbite" or "Uriah the Hittite." But while these names do add on place names to identify the individuals, they are not surnames as we know them today. If Uriah the Hittite moved to another location, his place name would probably change. In the same way, if Uriah the Hittite has a child, the place name would not be passed on. Rather, the child, if a male, would be called "——ben Uriah." This use of the term "ben" for "son of" or "bas" for "daughter of" is known as patronymics, and was the common way of identifying Jews for centuries before surnames as we know them today were used. But the use of additional names in Biblical times, such as place names and patronymics, were precursors of later sources of surnames. A current surname like Ginzburg is a place name, and a name such as Meyerson is a patronym.

Another kind of name used in the Bible foreshadows recent surnaming customs. Descriptive names are found in the Bible, such as Ha-kotz in Ezra 2:61. "Ha-kotz" means "the thorn," which is a descriptive term in the same way that a surname like Klein, meaning "small," is a descriptive surname of recent days. Names in the Talmud reflect the same kind of customs; while names of locations, patronymics, and also occupations are used, they are still not hereditary. Vocational names, which are not found in the Bible, foreshadow modern occupation names. Talmudic examples of this are Abba Jose the Potter and Daniel the Tailor. The more recent "Snyder" is the same occupational identification of a tailor.

Patronymics in the Talmud are quite popular. Simon ben Gamliel means Simon, son of Gamliel. There are even times when we find patronymics representing two generations, such as Raba bar bar Chana, which means that Raba was the grandson of Chana. (The term "bar" and the term "ben" both mean "son of.") We find nicknames appearing in the Talmud also. Zeira the Younger is an example of this. Also in the Talmud are examples of priestly designations, known to us in modern times by the surnames Cohen or Levy. In the Talmud we find individuals such as Ishmael the High Priest and Jose Ha-kohen. But again, these names would not necessarily be passed down to children.

For centuries, surnames were not used, as we know them, by Jews. Sephardic Jews adopted surnames from the Arabs who not only used a similar patronymic, that of "ibn" to designate "son of," but who also added the father's name without the use of "ibn." But Central and Northern European Jews, even throughout the Middle

Ages, generally did not use surnames. Jews were isolated from larger communities and simply did not develop the need to adopt family names. During the tenth and eleventh centuries we see the beginning of surname usage becoming popular because of the rise of cities and the rise of commerce, both of which stimulated the necessity of family names for practical reasons. But again it is largely the Sephardim who were affected by this. They developed a popular use of occupational names, nicknames, and place names. A famous Sephardic occupational name is Abulafia meaning "father of medicine," and another is Gabbai, which represents a synagogue official. Among place names, we are familiar with Cardozo from Spain and Montefiore from Italy.

The isolation of the Ashkenazim, as we have said, brought the use of surnames much later. It is interesting to note that in the fourteenth century there were only about 700 Jews in Frankfort on Main and in the sixteenth century, Prague had but 1,200 Jews. From this it is easy to see that the need for surnames just did not exist among the isolated Jewish communities of Northern Europe. When an official register of a city needed to record Jews for whatever reason, the designation "the Jew" was often used. Jews themselves continued to use place names, patronymics, occupation names, and other forms of family names, but these names lasted for just a generation or so rather than being kept as a permanent surname.

It was actually not until the late eighteenth century that surnames as we know them today were used commonly among Jews. This is why as we enter the period of Jewish history before this time it is exceedingly difficult to trace our own specific families back to these years. In all likelihood, if you are an Ashkenazi Jew, the surname which is yours today was not that of your ancestors in the 1600's or even a good part of the 1700's. This is because it was not until 1787 that Jews were first required to register last names, and this date reflects only one part of Europe, that of Austria. Switzerland, for example, did not require its Jews to register last names until 1863.

Of course, this does not mean that family names did not exist in these places before those dates. It does mean, however, that Jews were given the opportunities to change their names and register them permanently at these times. In some cases names were assigned to Jews, and at other times they had to be bought. In any case, surnames among Jews are a recent arrival, even though family names might have existed traditionally for much longer.

Jews in the Middle Ages, for example, did use names to identify their families and many families grew attached to those names and continued to use them. A fascinating development took place in Frankfort on Main during the Middle Ages. Jews were forced to live in a special section of the city called the Judengasse, and registration was done based on the house that each family occupied. Houses at this time were not numbered but rather were labeled by signs which hung outside. The signs were colorful and represented many kinds of images including animals, colors, and fruits. A famous surname which reflects a house sign of this time is Rothschild, which means "red shield." The name Loeb might reflect the use of the image of a lion on these house signs, as Gans would reflect the sign of a goose. These sign images were often carved on the tombstones of family members, adding to the permanence of the house signs as surnames. An interesting note pertaining to the use of house signs by Jews is that when the Jews in Frankfort's Judengasse were ordered in 1776 to use numbers on their houses rather than signs, there was such resistance that the whole Jewish community was fined.

We cannot say, however, that family names tended to be kept within families. Examples are known where names were changed by individuals themselves, and other examples where surnames appear to exist, but which change from parent to child.

The year 1787 is an important date in the history of the Jewish surname, for in that year an Austrian Empire order compelled the Jews to adopt surnames. This was the first time in history that Jews were forced to take surnames. Officers were appointed to register all Jews with these names, and if a Jew refused, the officers were to force a name upon them. It was at this time that many meaningless names were assigned to individuals, and this accounts, surely, for some names which we do not know the origins of at the present time.

On July 20, 1808, Napoleon issued a decree of a similar nature, insisting that Jews adopt fixed names. This was also done in Frankfort in 1807, and in Baden in 1809.

The same kind of legislation was enacted throughout Europe at different times. It happened in 1812 in Prussia, 1813 in Bavaria, 1834 in Saxony, and 1845 in Russia. In each case, Jews were required to register family names. There were several reasons for these enactments. The levying of taxes was made much simpler with permanent surnames, as was conscription of Jewish soldiers. A third reason was an effort to assimilate the Jews, at least in the cases

Beilage zum Amts-Blatt No. 1.

vom 7. Januar 1816.

General-Verzeichniß

der

am 24ſten März 1812 in der Provinz Pommern anſäßig geweſenen jüdiſchen Familien, welche zu Königl. Preußiſchen Staats-Bürgern angenommen ſind.

Nach den einzelnen Kreiſen und Städten geordnet.

Namen der Kreiſe und Städte.	Lau- fende Num- mer.	Vollſtändiger Name der Familienhäupter.	Beſtändiger Name, welchen die Familie angenommen hat.	Nummer, unter wel- cher die Familie in dem Staats- Bürger- Verzeich- niß aufge- führt ſteht
		I. Plattes Land.		
Kreis Belgard.	1	Lewin Marcus.	Marcuse.	1
	2	Aron Hirſch.	Arnholz.	2
Kreis Daber.	3	Jacob Lewin.	Blumenthal.	1
	4	Aron Lewin.	Agat Königsberger.	2
	5	Schmuel Lewin.	Haſelen.	3
Kreis Fürſtenthum.	6	David Joſeph.	David.	1
⸱ Greiffenberg.	7	Abraham Salomon.	Salinger.	1
⸱ Greiffenhagen.	8	Lewin Samuel.	Löwenherz.	1
	9	Abraham Moſes.	Maaß.	2
	10	Röſel Fränkel.	Fränkel.	3
	11	Iſrael Böhm.	Böhm.	4
⸱ Flemming.	12	Hirſch Michael.	Michaelis.	1
	13	Itzig Michael.	Michaelis.	2
	14	Leyſer Salomon.	Salomons.	3
				Namen

List of adopted family names, 1812, in Pomerania. (Courtesy Leo Baeck Institute, New York) where no specific list of names to be used was issued. When lists of restricted names existed, the exact opposite purpose was intended—to single out Jews among the larger community.

An additional reason for the requirement of surnames was its clever means of obtaining additional revenues for the government. This occurred when taxes were imposed for the registration of the names. It is also known that unfriendly local officials would either impose unattractive names upon Jews or threaten to do so unless a nicer name was "purchased." In response to Napoleon's decree, some of the names imposed upon Jews included Eselskopf (meaning "donkey's head"), Fresser (meaning "glutton"), and Lumpe (meaning "hoodlum"). In Austria in 1787, the unpopular names included Nussnacker (meaning "nutcracker"), and Puderbeutel (meaning "powder bag").

While those names were given with cruelty, nicer names often came at high prices. But there were also many opportunities to choose whatever name one wanted, and in Northeastern Germany, a series of names with "Rose" in them was common, such as Rosenzweig, Rosenthal, Rosenblum, and Rosenstein.

Amusing stories of how individuals and communities obtained their names have been preserved. It is known, for example, that in one community a rabbi opened a prayer book and went word by word assigning names to people from words in the book. In another case, an official asked a person for his name. He said "Yankele." The official asked him again, to which he replied "Poshet Yankele" which means "Simply Yankele." His name thus became Poshet. In a similar case, when a family was asked its name, and they replied "Anu lo neda," meaning "We don't know," they were called Neuda.

Often, I have imagined what it might be like to be forced to choose the surname which will be in your family permanently. It must surely have been a major decision, and this is reflected, perhaps, in the time periods given to the Jews to take a name. Several months of decision were allowed in some cases. But think of what it must have been like. Suddenly, you have got to choose from any name or word there is (except, of course, in the cases where a limited list was provided—in which case it is a different kind of incredible decision) and be satisfied. When the edicts were enacted, people must have thought that the choice would be a permanent one. I have pretended that I was put into this situation. I suggest that you do the same. What surname would you choose?

Our surnames today come from a large variety of sources, and it is often difficult, unfortunately, to know the meaning of the word, or for that matter the reason for the name being attached to the family. While it is likely that people with the family name Snyder had an ancestor who was a tailor, it is impossible to know what the reason behind a name like Schwartz might be. Meaning "black," the word might have been a description of someone's complexion, or it could have been chosen as the name of a color, or it could have been some other etymology that will never be found.

Nevertheless, there is much that we can learn from our names, and it would be useful to examine the different types of Jewish surnames, to help us to identify our own and make tentative conclusions as to the origins of our own names. Jewish surnames can be divided into several categories, and we will now discuss each of them.

Patronymics

As we have discussed, the patronymic is an early form of names, and while patronymics were originally not used as surnames as we now use them, they were eventually adapted to modern surname usage. It is known that when Jews were ordered to take surnames, many people simply used the patronymic form that they were currently using. This way, a man named Abraham ben Isaac would become Abraham Isaacs.

The patronym was the simplest way of forming a surname, and they can be found in every language. The Austrian and German patronym would be a name ending in "sohn," such as "Abramsohn," "Isaacsohn," or "Jacobsohn." The Slavic patronym is "vitch," as in Abromovitch. Other Slavic patronymics include the suffixes "-ov," "-off," "-eff," and "-kin," which all indicate "descendant of." Examples of these would include "Malkov" and "Rivkin." It is interesting to note here that these are not patronyms but rather matronyms—named after a female name. The two examples here would mean "descendant of Malka" and "descendant of Rivka." In Germany and Austro-Hungary, the mother's name was a frequent source of the establishment of a surname. Other examples of this are "Perles," "Gitles," and "Zeldes."

Another form of surname, though not a patronym, is a name based on the first name of a wife. This kind of name has been formed by adding the suffix "mann" on to a wife's first name, as in Estermann, being the husband of Esther, and Perlmann, being the husband of Perl.

There are suffixes for other languages as well which indicate a patronymic. Thus, the suffix "-wicz" is a Slavic ending, "-vici" is Romanian, and "-witz" is another German patronymic ending.

Place Names

Perhaps the largest group of Jewish surnames is the one based on locations. It is with place names that we are able to learn more specific information about our ancestors, assuming that they have surnames derived from places. If this is the case, it is fair to assume that an ancestor of yours once came from the location indicated by the name. If, for example, your surname happens to be Berliner, it would be logical to assume that someone in that line of ancestors came from Berlin.

Earlier than Ashkenazi Jews, the Sephardim often took place names as their surnames. We find Spanish surnames like "de Cordova" and "de Lima." From Portugal we have "Lisbona" and from Italy there is "Lucca" and "Padua," and from Holland we find a name like DeVries derived from the location of Friesland.

Every European country has inspired Jewish surnames, reflecting the extent to which Jews migrated around the Continent. Sometimes the name was as general as a country name. At other times it was as specific as the sign attached to a house. In fact, we find Jewish place-surnames as countries, regions, towns, streets, and houses. There is a mystery surrounding the derivation of surnames from places. It is not known why there are some towns with no surnames representing them. Even in the cases of towns with large Jewish populations, there are some which did not seem to inspire names.

There are several suffixes which have been added to places in order to turn them into surnames. The suffix "-er" is a common one, as in the example already given: "Berliner." The suffix "-man" is also used, as in Osterman, which means "a man who comes from the east," adding the notion of what direction a person comes from to our list of place sources for surnames.

We have already discussed house signs, but it is appropriate to mention them again in the context of place names. House signs would have represented on them various images which were later adopted as permanent surnames. We have already mentioned Rothschild ("red shield") as an example. Others would include: Schwarzchild ("black shield"), Blum ("flower"), Buxbaum ("box tree"), Lachs ("salmon"), and Baer ("bear"). One cannot be sure in all cases, however, whether the source of a name is actually from a house sign. Many Jewish surnames have been taken from names of flowers, fruits, plants, animals, and stones, but were chosen for their beauty rather than adopted because of a house sign. There is also an amusing story behind one common name related to house signs. A Frankfort family of priestly descent had the name of Kahn, which is commonly known as such a name. However, they took as their house sign the picture of a boat, since "Kahn" is German for boat. In later years, members of the same family used the sign of a ship and their name became "Schiff." The name went from "Kahn" to "Schiff" because of a house sign.

Vocational Names

Vocational names are another type of Jewish surname which offers a concrete clue to family history. In fact, it is vocational names which give historians an insight into the kinds of occupations either held or permitted to be held by Jews at a certain time. When we examine old tombstones and see occupational names corresponding to certain dates, we add to our knowledge of what kinds of jobs were done by Jews in certain eras.

Vocational names are less common among Sephardim than among Ashkenazim. We have already offered one example of a Sephardic vocational name—"Abulafia," meaning "father of medicine." Other Sephardic vocational names would include "Almosnino," meaning "orator" in Arabic, and "Mocatta" which is a "mason" also in Arabic.

Occupational names are taken not only from the exact title of the job but also from the materials used in the activity. A name such as "Leder" which means "leather" would stand for a tanner, just as a carpenter might have the name "Nagel" meaning "nail." Vocational names are also noted to range from the most common to the most highly respected types of occupations. We find names like "Dayan" meaning "judge," "Chazan" meaning "cantor," and "Spielman" meaning "player."

Descriptive Names

A large group of Jewish surnames comes under the heading of descriptive names. These, presumably, were descriptions of the original bearer of the name. These types of names can be separated into two different groups: physical descriptions and personality characteristics.

In the category of physical characteristics, we have names such as "Klein" meaning "small," "Kurtz" meaning "short," and "Geller" meaning "yellow," which we assume to be a hair color. In the same way, "Graubart," which means "gray beard," represents another general subheading of this group.

As for personality characteristics, we find names like "Selig" which means "happy," "Biederman" which means "worthy man," "Baruch" meaning "blessed" and "Gottlieb" which means "God loving."

Another kind of descriptive name is the nickname, many of which have become surnames. We find names like Purim and Lustig (happy) among this category.

My own name, Kurzweil, can be seen perhaps as a descriptive name, although this name is one which might fall under any of several different types. The word "Kurzweil" literally means "short time," though as a compound word the meaning changes to "pastime." An additional definition of the word—as a German word— is an "entertainer" or someone who entertains by telling stories. An even earlier meaning of the word is that of a "jester" in the more official sense of court entertainer. Therefore, while all the definitions have similar meanings, it is interesting (for me) to note that the name could be a simple word, a personal characteristic, or an occupation. I find it all the more fascinating when I discovered that there is one personal attribute which people have repeated over and over in order to describe people in my family, and in particular my ancestors, and that is that Kurzweils are jokesters.

Names from Abbreviations

One of the most unusual sources for Jewish surnames is that of abbreviations. A popular surname—Katz—is not generally known to be an abbreviation but is just that. While the source of "Katz" is commonly thought to be a form of the animal "cat," it is actually a short form of the phrase "Kohen Zedek" or "priest of righteousness." In the same way, the surname "Schatz" is an abbreviated form of "Sheliah Tzibbur" which means "minister of the congregation." Likewise the name "Segal" (also Segel, Seigel, etc.) is said to come from "segan leviyyah" meaning "assistant to the Levites."

Another form of abbreviation which resulted in surnames was that of the letters formed from a man's name and/or his father's name. So, for example, the name Schach is derived from Sabbatai Cohen. The name Bry comes from Ben Rabbi Israel, Brock is from Ben Rabbi Akiba, and Basch is the abbreviated form of Ben Shimeon.

There is another custom within the Jewish Tradition concerning the abbreviation of names. During the Middle Ages, it was somewhat common to abbreviate names by initials. While these names were not surnames, they did not become the general way of identifying the individual. The three most popular examples of this are "Rashi" who was actually Rabbi Solomon ben Isaac, "Rambam" who was Rabbi Moses ben Maimon, and "Besht" which is an abbreviation of Baal Shem Tov.

A final type of surname for this category (though not truly an abbreviation or actually a surname) is the custom of referring to an individual by his *magnum opus,* his finest literary work. Perhaps the most famous of these is Israel Meir Ha-Kohen who is known as "Hafez Hayyim" after his work by that name. Two other examples of this are "Roke'ah" who is R. Eliazer b. Judah, and "Tur" who is R. Jacob b. Asher. Again, these were not surnames, but were abbreviated forms, in a sense, of lengthier names.

Matronymics

In the same way that a patronym is a name derived from a male source (usually a father), a matronym comes from a female source, usually the mother. Many Jewish surnames come from this source and include names such as Perle, Rose, Hinde, Freude, and Gutkind (from Gute).

In general, the origins of surnames can be determined by considering the several different sources which we have discussed. However, there can be little certainty about this. Despite the fact that a surname can potentially be an excellent clue for insight into family history, a warning must be issued that this is speculation. In the same way that there are many sources for surnames, there are a great variety of circumstances which might have resulted in the establishment or adoption of a family name. While the name "Snyder" means "tailor," we cannot be certain that there was a tailor in our past who adopted that name to reflect his profession. The name might have been imposed upon him, or he may have chosen it for other reasons.

Another issue regarding surnames within Jewish Tradition is the custom of taking the surname of one's father. While this is common today, there have been times in our past when this was not the case universally among Jews. Often a child would adopt the maiden name of his or her mother and not the father. The reason for this was often as follows: When a Jewish child was born, often the parents were not married through civil law but only through Jewish law. Therefore, it was not uncommon for the civil law to refuse to recognize the legitimacy of the birth. This resulted in the child being required, by civil law, to take the name of the mother. This is something to keep in mind when doing family history research. It is not wise to assume that a surname automatically leads to the father of a child.

It should be repeated, however, that the study of surnames is a fascinating part of Jewish history and the history of your family. We are each the descendants of a countless number of families, and each of those families has its own surname. Each of those families has its own history as well, and each of those histories directly affect who you are.

Examples of Jewish surnames originally nicknames or personality characteristics:

EHRLICH	honest
KLUGER	wise
FROHLICH	happy
LUSTIG	happy
FRUHLING	spring
SOMMER	summer
SONNTAG	Sunday
DIENSTAG	Tuesday
GITTELSON	son of good little one
FRIEDMANN	free man
SHALOM	peace
SHOLEM	peace
SOLOMON	peace
GOTTSCHALK	God's servant
GOTTLIEB	God loving
LIPGOTT	God loving

Examples of Jewish surnames from occupations:

BECKER	baker
FLEISCHER	butcher
BREUER	brewer
WEBER	weaver
FARBER	painter
GOLDSCHMIDT	goldsmith
KRAMER	merchant
WECHSLER	money changer
ACKERMANN	farmer
BRENNER	distiller
GERBER	tanner
LEDER	tanner (leather)

NADEL	needle (leather)
SCHER	shears
NAGEL	nail (carpenter)
RABAD	"Resh av beth din" (rabbi)
BABAD	"ben av beth din" (son of rabbi)
RABINOVITCH	son of rabbi
SCHECTER	slaughterer
SCHOCHET	ritual slaughterer
SINGER	cantor
CANTOR	cantor
KAUFFMAN	merchant
DRUCKER	printer
BOOKBINDER	bookbinder
ZIMMERMAN	carpenter
BAUMAN	builder
BAUER	builder
FELDMAN	shepherd
BERGER	shepherd
SCHLOSSER	locksmith
KOSTER	door-keeper
SCHUSTER	shoemaker
SCHNEIDER	tailor
SNYDER	tailor
WALDMAN	woodman
SANDLER	cobbler
METZGER	butcher
SCHNITZNER	carver
ROKEACH	spice merchant
KUNZLER	artist

Examples of Jewish surnames from animal names:

WOLF	Wolf (also Wulf, Wolk, Seiffer, Lopez)
LOWE	lion
HIRSCH	stag (also Hartwig, Harris, Herschel, Herzl, Cerf)
BAR	bear (also Beerman, Berman, Berish)
OCHS	ox
FUCHS	fox
ADLER	eagle
GEIER	vulture

FINK	finch
HAHN	cock

Examples of Jewish surnames from physical characteristics:

ALT	old
BRAUN	brown
GELBER or GELLER	yellow
KLEIN	small
KURTZ	short
JUNG	young
GROSS	large
NEU	new
REISE	giant
ROTH	red
SCHNELL	fast
SCHWARTZ	black
SCHON	beautiful
STEINHART	hard as stone
STARK	strong

Personal Names

Ever since the first humans, Adam and Eve, people have had personal names. A great amount of significance has always been given to names, beginning in the Bible when we witness, among others, Abram becoming Abraham, Sarai becoming Sarah and Jacob becoming Israel. The change of one's name, in this Biblical setting, symbolizes a major change in one's personality and one's being.

Throughout history we find similar examples of customs and beliefs which reflect the seriousness with which we have looked upon names. Popular in the Middle Ages and still practiced among many in modern times is the custom of changing the name of a person who is seriously ill in the hope that the Angel of Death would be confused and be unable to locate the person. One of the most popular names given at this time was Chaim, meaning "life," in order to add still another significance to names. The power of this custom is reflected in my own family. My father was renamed Chaim because he was very ill as a young child. When he grew up his parents told him of this, and he in turn has told me. The story which my father told me of his "renaming" as a child became a favorite of mine. It was a deeply powerful story for me, inspiring my imagination to envision the Angel of Death, the renaming ceremony, and a young child (who grows up to be my father) getting well after a prolonged illness. Stories, as well as names, can have a profound effect on a person. This custom, which is known as "meshanneh shem," can be found in the Talmud.

The same type of belief is found in a custom which was, in good probability, begun by Judah the Pious. He forbade his immediate descendants from bearing his name or the name of his father during their lifetime in the belief that since a man's soul was bound up with his name, the soul would be deprived of its rest if someone else bore it. While this is not a universally accepted custom, it is generally true that children are not named after living relatives. Among the reasons for this custom is that the Angel of Death might be unnecessarily confused and might take the wrong person. Finally, the custom of naming children after relatives who are deceased is based on the notion that to do this would be an honor to the deceased. It is also an attempt to "inject" the child with the qualities of the deceased.

It has been customary to name children after deceased relatives or other individuals who are greatly respected. It is common, for example, to name a child after a man's teacher. In European Jewish communities it also became common to name the eldest son after the paternal or maternal grandfather. Because of this, it is curious to examine the repetition of certain few names within many generations. For example, in one family we find the following: Meshullam b. Moses b. Ithiel b. Moses b. Kalonymus b. Meshullam b. Kalonymus b. Moses b. Kalonymus b. Jekuthiel b. Moses b. Meshullam b. Ithiel b. Meshullam. The interesting aspect of this genealogy is that among the fourteen people who span three centuries, we find only five names.

Ever since I can remember, the notion that I was named after someone has intrigued me and captured my imagination. I learned at a young age whom I was named for (my great-grandfather Abusch) and I have been drawn to him in a somewhat mystical way. In fact, while I have very little interest or attraction to mysticism, this is one area where I cannot seem to resist it. Through stories which I have solicited about my great-grandfather, I have developed a personal relationship—I daresay—to him which I find difficult to describe.

As we have seen in our discussion of surnames, there was a time when individuals had only one name. Then the surname was introduced and it became universal. Today, many Jews have three names: a first, a surname, and an additional first name. Many Jews have secular and Hebrew first names. At various points in history, depending upon the location, Jews began to use secular first names. This inspired the custom of giving Jewish children separate Hebrew first names to use during religious ceremonies and for religious purposes. Naming ceremonies have developed for just this purpose.

In modern times, two occurrences of note relating to names have been witnessed among Jews. The first is the changing of names, usually without the consent of the individual, during the days of great immigration at United States ports. There are many stories of name changes which occurred when an immigration official "renamed" a Jewish immigrant by mistake, or on purpose. Of course, it often happened that immigrants would change their names without "assistance." The motive for this voluntary change of names might relate to the second phenomenon to be mentioned and that is the adopting of new names by individuals who move to Israel. It is customary for a new Israeli to abandon his or her original name and replace it with a new one. Both of these customs may very well reflect a belief in the power of names. When a name changes, a person changes.

WHAT'S IN YOUR NAME

For Whom Were You Named?

In my family, I am named after my great-grandfather, my father is named after his great-grandfather and my grandfather is named after his grandfather. My mother was named after her great-aunt. My brother was named after another great-grandfather, and that great-grandfather was named after his own father's rebbe.

Whom were you named after? What do you know about the person? Why did your parents name you after that person rather than someone else?

Speaking of being named after people, often an older relative will not remember who his or her great-grandparents were until you ask, "Who were you named after?" There's a good chance they were named after the great-grandparent whom they couldn't remember.

You can also try to figure out the names of people early in your family tree by noticing the names which keep repeating. While

List of adoption of family names, 1809, in Baden. (Courtesy Leo Baeck Institute, New York) you cannot come to any definite conclusions with this method, a repeating name might jolt someone's memory about an early ancestor with the same name.

One's name has an influence on one's life.

ELEAZER B. PEDAT, Talmud: Berakot, 7b

What If Your Name Was Changed at Ellis Island?

We have all heard stories of how Jewish names were shortened, misspelled and changed at Ellis Island or other ports by immigration officials. Jewish names were also tampered with at other times and under other circumstances after arrival in America. If there is no one to ask or no one who remembers what the original name was, how can you find out the original name?

It is, of course, important to discover what your name was in the Old Country because without this knowledge, it will be impossible for you to bridge the ocean and find out about relatives and ancestors who never came to America.

There is a way to research your original name—assuming that it was changed from the one your family used in Europe—and this is by locating your immigrant ancestors' steamship passenger list (see page 169). Follow the directions for the various ways of obtaining the name of the ship and its date of arrival. If you send for a copy of the passenger list for your immigrant ancestor, it will contain his or her original name since these lists were usually made *before* the ship sailed—that is, before arrival in America when the name was changed.

Of course, when you get the passenger list, you will not find the name that you know. Therefore, you will have to be a detective and try to determine who on the list was your ancestor. There are many ways of doing this because the lists will offer various clues to work with including the person's place of birth, occupation, age, and so on. Something ought to match—and you will then discover what your name was originally!

Names changes, both voluntary and involuntary, present obvious problems for genealogists. If a person has his or her name changed, it is almost impossible at times to locate the individual. A woman who marries and takes her husband's last name suddenly disappears from the records in her original name. An immigrant who either changes or shortens his own name or who has his name changed by an immigration official also cuts himself off from the family history. In Israel this situation is common. Huge numbers of Israelis have dropped their European names and replaced them with modern Israeli or Biblical names. Sometimes the change is as simple as translating a European word into a Hebrew word. For example, an Israeli with the European name of "Singer" has changed his name to "Zamir" which is the Hebrew word for singer.

I am against name changes because it cuts off a person from his or her history. While I can understand the symbolic meaning of a Black American adopting an African name or an Israeli adopting a modern Hebrew name, it once again cuts the person off from his past. It might be linking that person with the distant past, but the recent past—for better or worse—is still a part of our experience. Recently, an Israeli who has maintained his European surname said to me, "I keep my old last name as my own personal memorial to the Holocaust victims in my family."

There is one recent name-change which I like, however. The well-known author Irving Wallace has a son named David Wallechinsky. Together, the two of them have co-authored *The People's Almanac* and *The People's Almanac #2*. Why do father and son have different yet similar last names? As the "About the Authors" page in *The People's Almanac #2* says, "David Wallechinsky was born in Hollywood, California, in 1948. In 1972 he adopted the original family name of his grandfather, whose name had been changed to 'Wallace' by an immigration agent at Ellis Island."

Some name-changes are terrific!

> Names were changed as readily as clothes. From Yacov (Hebrew) or Yankel (Yiddish) to Jacob and finally to Jack. From Hyman to Howard, Leybel to Lester or Leon, Berel to Barnett or Barry, Chai-Sura to Sarah, Breina to Beatrice, Simcha to Seymour, Chatzkel to Haskell, Meyer to Max, Moishe to Mossir, Aaron to Allan.
>
> —MILTON MELTZER, *Taking Root*

Sexism in Genealogy

Sexism has crept (or marched) into almost every aspect of our lives and genealogy is no exception. Genealogy and Jewish Tradition both make it difficult for the family historian when it comes to family-tree research regarding women.

Early Federal Census records, for example, list the head of the household (male) by name, and then simply put the number of others in the family and house.

Generally, children take the last name of their father which results in most family trees being able to stretch farther back on male lines than on female lines. Even in documents where a woman's name is given, her maiden name usually is not, and this brings that particular line to a halt.

Within Jewish Tradition, we see that tombstones usually refer to an individual and his or her father but not his or her mother. Ketubot (marriage documents) and other items also fall into this category.

Not only in records, but also in attitude is genealogical sexism evidenced. I must admit this in my own case. As noted, I did research for nearly seven years on my father's family before getting to my mother and her family. This is mostly because I had an interest in my last name (my father's), and this is simply the result of our naming customs—which, again, are male-oriented.

I mention this as a warning and also to encourage you not to neglect the researching or recording of female names, maiden names, and the maternal branches of your family tree.

> Properly, I ought to begin this account by telling when I was born. But—I am ashamed to admit it—I do not know. You see, I was only a Jewish girl, and in my day and time, in the place where I was born, female births were not recorded.
>
> —Rebecca Himber Berg, from her memoir, "Childhood in Lithuania"

Names Can Help You with Dates
Because it has been a Jewish tradition for many generations to name a child after a deceased member of the family, or a deceased member of a community who is well respected—such as a rebbe or teacher—names can help you determine dates.

Let us illustrate this by using an example.

Look at the family tree below and notice the dates of birth indicated for the children named Abraham. As you can see, there is no date listed for the children's grandfather who is also named Abraham.

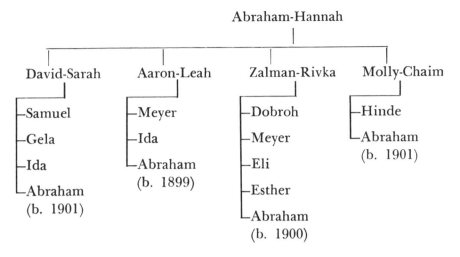

It is clear from this three-generation family tree that the four families all named a child Abraham, undoubtedly after the grandfather. They all named a child Abraham about the same time, though the earliest date was 1899. If this example represents a typical family in Europe, all four families probably named their next child after the death of Abraham. Since a child cannot, by tradition, be named after a living person, it is safe to assume that the grandfather died before 1899, and probably in that year or the year before.

While you cannot know this for sure, nor can you know the exact date, it is reasonable to write "ca. 1899" on your family tree. The abbreviation "ca." means "circa" or "approximately."

Using this method, it is often possible to figure out older dates by the dates—and names—that you already have.

> What is a good pedigree? A good name.
>
> —AL-HARIZI, *Tahkemoni*, ca. 1220

Last Names from the Maternal Side

Do not assume that children always took the last name of their father, or that when a couple got married they took the husband's last name.

Often the woman's surname was used. Frequently, people were married in Europe by religious ritual but not with a civil license. Because of this, the children from the marriage were not recognized as legitimate by the civil authorities (while they were legitimate as far as Jewish Law and the families were concerned!). Subsequently, the children took the mother's surname.

There existed at various times and places anti-Jewish legislation limiting Jewish marriages. Because of this, Jews often got married secretly. Again, the children were considered illegitimate by civil law, and the mother's name was adopted.

A good name is rather to be chosen than great riches.

—PROV. 22:1

Hebrew, Yiddish, and English Names

Most Jews have two names: a secular name and a religious name. The secular name is in the language of the country where the person resides, and the religious name is Hebrew.

Many immigrants had three names: a Hebrew name, an English name, and a Yiddish name. This is because they had two names in Europe (the Yiddish was their secular name), and they adopted an additional secular name on arrival in America. My grandfather, for example, was Julius (English), Yudl (Yiddish), and Yehudah Yaakov (Hebrew-religious).

When charting your family tree, you will come across different names for the same people—sometimes even more than three when nicknames are also used. It has been my practice to record all the names used rather than to "standardize" them. I have seen Jewish genealogies where all Abes, Abbies, and Abrahams became Abraham. It's more important to record a person's name as it was used from day to day than to suddenly become formal when building a family tree. Keep track of all the names used, and when deciding which name to use on a family tree, use the one which was most common, or the one that the person himself or herself liked—if you know.

> One thing is certain, I have no real feeling about my first name. I can only guess why this is. It seems to me that it may be because my parents gave it to me without any particular feeling, simply because they "liked it" (and why did they like it? because at that time it was "different"; only later were there other Franzes in the Jewish community of Cassel). It's as though my parents had seen it in a window shop, walked inside, and bought it. It has nothing traditional about it, no memory, no history, not even an anecdote, scarcely a whim—it was simply a passing fancy. A family

name, a saint's name, a hero's name, a poetic name, a symbolic name, all these are good: they have grown naturally, not been bought ready-made. One should be named after somebody or something. Else a name is really only empty breath.

—FRANZ ROSENZWEIG

What Does Your Name Mean?

The finest popular source for the meaning of Jewish surnames is *A Dictionary of Jewish Names and Their History* by Benzion Kaganoff (Schocken Books, New York, 1977). Rabbi Kaganoff has pursued his hobby of Jewish names for more than twenty-five years. This book is the result of his years of research and study. The first half of the volume is a history of the development of Jewish names, first and last. The second half of the book is a Jewish surname dictionary. The *probable* meanings of nearly 1,000 Jewish last names appear. "Probable" because as Kaganoff himself admits, there is much speculation which must be done when trying to determine the origin of a surname.

What if your names are not included in Kaganoff's dictionary? Rabbi Kaganoff contributes a regular column to *Toledot: The Journal of Jewish Genealogy* (see page 100). In this column, he answers inquiries from readers who write in queries about Jewish surnames.

The literature on the study of Jewish names is vast. In 1977, a bibliography of that literature appeared, making it somewhat easier for the researcher who wishes to explore the history of his or her surnames in depth. *Jewish and Hebrew Onomastics; A Bibliography* by Robert Singerman (Garland Publishing, Inc., New York and London, 1977) is a classified bibliography (by subject) of nearly 1,200 sources for research on the subject. "Onomastics," in case you are wondering, is the study of names.

There are men whose names are beautiful but their acts ugly.

—Genesis Rabbah

Chapter 3

Six Million Jewish People Is One Jewish Person—Six Million Times

Six million Jews were murdered in the Holocaust.

That phrase, "six million," slips out of our mouths so quickly, so easily, too often even thoughtlessly. Six million. We speak the number as if . . . as if we know what six million human beings means. As if we can understand such proportions of death through murder.

Six million. The number is unfathomable.

Six million Jews were murdered in the Holocaust.

That word, "murdered," is spoken without difficulty, as if we can grasp those murders, as if they are calculable. We say "murdered" but we do not mean simply murdered. Not like the killings we see so often on our televisions where life is taken every few moments without pause.

And "Holocaust." Its nine letters are supposed to add up to the six million murdered, as if . . . as if a word, any word, can grasp, can include, can measure the loss, the tragedy, the meaning of what happened. We speak the word "Holocaust" often, but some things should remain nameless, since no name or word will do. No label, no phrase, no sentence, can measure the unmeasurable.

When something is named or defined, it is imprisoned by the very limitations of the combination of letters tacked on to it. As if it can now be filed away, dealt with, understood, grasped.

Six million Jews were murdered in the Holocaust.

Yes. But, no—it was more than that. So much more that to say just this is to perhaps betray the lives of the victims.

There are no graves for the victims. No markers stand as their memorials. Yes, throughout the world there are monuments, museums, posters, plaques, statues, and sculptures commemorating their lives and paying tribute to them. But who were they? Who were the "six million murdered in the Holocaust"?

Some names ought to be given, some ought not.

Perhaps the deaths in total of six million Jews should remain nameless.

But the people should not remain nameless.

Have we made a mistake by naming the Event but not naming the murdered?

We have labeled the murders, added them up, written about them as if they were a phenomenon, but do most of us know the names of those in our families who were stolen from us and killed?

Education about the facts of the Jews during World War II is inferior enough. Schools often spend too little time on it; when it is discussed, the terms are broad and therefore, vague. We learn about the Holocaust as a subject, as a phenomenon, as an historical event with causes and results.

What shall we tell our children? How shall we explain to those who do not remember the event, or, as time goes by, are farther and farther removed from it? In what way shall we keep the memory alive?

Elie Wiesel, a survivor of the Death Camps, taught a course at City College in New York on the Holocaust. One day, a student asked, "What shall we tell our children?"

"And what if they don't believe us?" a girl in the class added.

"They won't," a third student answered. "I'm convinced that in a few years, a few generations, it will all be forgotten."

"I am not sure I can agree," Wiesel said. "I have heard a theory, a fascinating, intriguing theory. Irving Greenberg told me this. He said that when one considers the Exodus of the Hebrews from Egypt, to those Hebrews, their exodus did not have much of an impact. But consider the impact it has had since. Consider the impact of the Exodus on Jews today. This observation might be applied to the Holocaust. Who can know? It may be the same."

"But, since we weren't there, what should we say to the next generation?" a young man asked. "You have said that we will never understand what happened. If so, how can we tell people about it?"

"Yes," Wiesel said. "You will never know. But you will know that there was something. You will know one incident. One tear. That will be yours to tell."

Wiesel went on. "In my books, I don't like to repeat stories. Once I did. One story I told in two books."

He then told the legend, a Chassidic tale. It was a tale that contained many of the Chassidic Masters. It began with the founder of Chassidism, the Baal Shem Tov, the Master of the Good Name. It seems that when there was a disaster about to strike, the Baal Shem

went into a certain spot in the woods, lit a candle and said a prayer—
and the disaster was prevented. Then, a disciple of his was faced
with a disaster. He knew where the special spot in the woods was
located, he knew how to light the candle, but he did not know the
prayer. But the disaster was averted. Then another disciple was
faced with calamity. He knew where the spot in the woods was
located, but he did not know how to light the candle, and he did
not know the prayer. But the disaster was prevented. Then a final
disciple was faced with a disaster. He did not know how to light the
candle, he did not know how to say the prayer, and he did not know
where the spot in the woods was located. *All he knew was how to tell
the story*. And then, too, was the disaster avoided.

The Chassidic tale was instructive to the class, but Elie Wiesel
wanted to be even more explicit in response to the question. So,
when a student said, "What is the story we should tell?"

Wiesel responded: "In a few years, a very few years, there will not
be one survivor left. Not a single survivor will be alive. Their numbers are decreasing at a very fast rate. Soon, there will be no one
who was there.

"What can you tell your children? Tell them that you knew the
last survivors. As the survivors were alive when it happened, you
were alive to hear their story. Tell them that: You knew the last
survivors.

"They will listen. And they will ask the same question: What
shall we tell our children? They will tell them: We knew people
who knew the last survivors. We heard the story from people who
heard the last survivors. The very last.

"And the question will again be asked. And the story will be
told. Again and again. It will be told."

Wiesel looked with complete seriousness at his students.

"This is what we hope for," he said. "That it will be remembered. It is up to you."

The easiest way for the Holocaust to become nothing more than
one more chapter in Jewish history is to be satisfied with an imper-
sonal approach to the understanding of it. If we allow the murders
of our people to be "written up" in the history books to be put on
a shelf for future reference, we will be helping to forget. It is
incumbent upon us to remember. As Jews, we are a people of
memory, a people whose history should be part of each of us. We
cannot let the Holocaust become just another subject for books and
articles and for nameless monuments in cemeteries.

We have to make a personal connection with the Holocaust. Each of us must understand the Holocaust in the most personal of terms. Who was murdered? Where were they? What are their names? How old were they? Who were in their families? Where did they die? How did they die? What is their relationship to me?

It is not enough to know that "the Jews" were killed, or that "six million were murdered," or even that "my people were slaughtered." We must try to find out who they were, these people of ours. We must know their names and their fates.

There are no gravestones for them. Our knowledge of them might be their finest memorial.

How do we discover who the victims were? How do we determine what their names were, when they were last heard from, or where they died? How do we find out what their relationship was to us?

The first step is to ask. Begin to make inquiries in your family as to who remained in Europe rather than immigrate to the United States, Israel, or some other country. You will probably discover quite quickly, sad as it is to say, that close members of your family were taken to Death Camps or murdered in their towns.

Often the best sources for this kind of information are survivors of the Holocaust. Inquire as to who in your family was there and survived, and arrange to talk to these relatives, or write to them if distance is too great. Often we are hesitant about talking to people who lived through the experience. We think that we will stir up old memories as if survivors of the Holocaust have, themselves, forgotten about it. This is obviously not the case. Often survivors are silent for other reasons. As Elie Wiesel has said, "They are either silent because they are afraid you will not understand, or they are silent because they are afraid you will understand."

Survivors of the Holocaust are also sometimes silent because they have not been asked. They feel that they do not want to volunteer the information but are waiting to be asked. Always remember the difficulty of speaking about the subject, but keep in mind its importance as well.

When you arrange to speak to a survivor in your family, ask if you can bring a tape recorder. Needless to say, a tape recording of the memories of a Holocaust survivor is important for future generations. If you become the one who helps to keep the memory of the Holocaust alive, you will be performing a fine deed.

You will discover that people in your family who have survived the Holocaust will be knowledgeable about the people in your family who did not survive. The question of "Why did I survive while they did not?" will surely have passed through many minds. Remember to tape or write down the names of the Holocaust victims in your family, and to determine what their relationship to you is. It is best to do this in the form of a family tree. Not only will this permit you to see the relationships among relatives better, but the family tree will also become the memorial to these people.

Not only survivors, but also other family members as well will remember people in your family who were killed. Often after the War, families in the United States made inquiries to try to locate family members. It was at this time that people began to discover who did not survive. Try to locate the people in your family who were involved with these inquiries. They will be your best resources for discovering the answer to your questions. You will watch the branches of your family tree grow when you are doing this research. But never forget that if not for your inquiries and your research, the names which you are gathering will be lost in another generation. You are making an effort to keep the memory of these deaths and of the Holocaust alive. It is one thing to know about "the six million" and quite another to have the names of the people in your family who were there and who were murdered.

The Search for Victims and Survivors

In 1943, the Committee on Displaced Populations of the Allied Post-War Requirement Bureau, located in London, observed the obvious: As a result of the war and particularly because of persecution, there was extensive displacement of populations. They decided, therefore, to establish the National Tracing Bureau in different countries with the aim of locating people who were missing or who had been deported. In 1944, the Supreme Headquarters of the Allied Expeditionary Forces, known as SHAEF, gave orders to register all displaced persons on index cards, to aid in the location process. By 1945, SHAEF established a tracing bureau which was given the task of collecting name lists of displaced persons as well as persons incarcerated in concentration camps. This effort was aided by the United Nations Relief and Rehabilitation Administration (UNRRA) and was located in Versailles. Together, however, UNRRA and SHAEF relocated to Frankfort on Main.

In July of 1945, SHAEF was dissolved and the Combined Displaced Persons Executive, known as CDPX, established a collecting center for documents as well as a tracing bureau. This Central Tracing Bureau had as its goals to trace missing persons—military and

L i s t e
-.-.-.-.-.-.-.-

der am 22. August 1942 nach Theresienstadt abgewanderten Juden aus Baden

Lfd. Nr.	Familienname:	Vorname:	Geburtsort & Tag:	Wohnort & Wohnung:
1.	...dler geb. ...likann	Mina S.	Hagenbach/Pf. 9.11.70.	Mannheim B-7-3
2.	...ugust geb. Strauss	Nanette S.	Mannheim 19.2.51.	Mannheim Charlottenstr.7
3.	Bur geb. Erlanger	Anna S.	Stuttgart 27.9.70.	Mannheim B-7-3
4.	Baer	Jenny S.	Bruchsal 15.6.63.	Karlsruhe Westendstr.69
5.	Bamberger	Emilie S.	Heidelberg 12.10.52.	Mannheim B-7-3
6.	Barth geb. Schönfarber	Jeanette S.	Mainbernheim 16.11.72.	Mannheim B-7-3
7.	Behrens geb. Cohn	Julchen S.	Berlin 25.12.49.	Heidelberg Blumenstr.4
8.	Besag	Adolf I.	Bühl 7.2.73.	Freiburg/Brsg. Erbprinzenstr.8
9.	Besag geb. Maier	Pauline S.	Malsch/K'ruhe 20.3.75.	"
10.	Biedermann geb. Hilb	Rosa S.	Oberdorf/Wtbg. 7.9.68.	Mannheim B-7-3
11.	Billig geb. Brechler	Rosa S.	Stanislau/Pol. 28.1.68.	Karlsruhe Wilhelmstr.25
12.	Bischofsheimer	Fanny S.	Feuchtwangen 9.1.70.	Mannheim B-7-3
13.	Bloch	Laura S.	Freiburg/Brsg. 26.10.75.	Freiburg/Brsg. Starkenstr.39
14.	Bloch geb. Lion	Regina S.	Ettenheim 20.11.73.	Freiburg/Brsg. Ludwigstr.32
15.	Bloch	Sofie S.	Rheinbischofsheim 16.4.57.	Mannheim B-7-3
16.	Bodenheimer	Frieda S.	Wiesloch 17.8.70.	Wiesloch Blumenstr.6
17.	Bodenheimer	Regina S.	Wiesloch 25.1.72.	"

Nazi deportation list of Jews during Holocaust, from Baden. (Courtesy of Leo Baeck Institute, New York)

civilian—of countries which were members of the United Nations, as well as to collect and preserve all documents concerning non-Germans and displaced persons in Germany. It was also given the task of assisting in the reuniting of families that had been separated by the War.

In 1946, the Central Tracing Bureau moved from Frankfort on Main to Arolsen. It was renamed the International Tracing Service, as it is still called today.

At present, and since 1955, the International Tracing Service has been directed and administered by the International Committee of the Red Cross.

In its beginning, this organization was involved mainly with displaced persons. However, when the International Tracing Service (ITS) came into possession of concentration camp documents, the function of the organization changed. Suddenly, ITS became involved with furnishing proofs of death that occurred in the Death Camps. It is mainly this function of ITS that concerns us here.

The historical background of the International Tracing Service has been provided here to offer an understanding of why the major source of information on concentration camp victims is located in Germany. ITS continues to receive hundreds of thousands of inquiries from all over the world and provide a research service which is free to all interested parties.

Basically, the International Tracing Service has the most acceptable information of concentration camp victims and displaced persons in the world. While it is true that Yad Vashem Archives in Jerusalem has a complete duplicate collection provided by ITS, Yad Vashem is not set up to do the kind of research for people that ITS is financed to do. In fact, Yad Vashem directs many inquiries to ITS. To be clear, ITS will, under the right circumstances which we will explain, provide information for you free of charge.

The International Tracing Service has, as perhaps the most important feature in its archives, a Master Index. This index is a file, by name of individual, of all names appearing on all the documents in the archives. The reference cards include the name, personal data available, and the description of the document in which the name is mentioned. At present, this Master Index contains 39,700,000 cards. It is interesting to note that the index is not filed alphabetically but rather phonetic-alphabetical in order to account for different spellings of the same surnames. Another rather remarkable resource used by ITS in this regard is a two-volume set of books listing first names and their many variations. This is obviously useful for location of individuals. The list of first names contains 48,096 forms of names.

The Master Index is, however, just the axle about which the collections within the archives revolve. A closer look at the contents of the archives will show how useful ITS can be.

In the International Tracing Service Archives the following are contained:

> Indexes and name lists of concentration camps.
>
> Indexes and name lists of Gestapo and Sipo Offices.
>
> Name lists of persons.
>
> Deportation lists of Jews.
>
> Index cards and name lists of towns and communities, district magistrate offices, labor offices, health insurance firms, etc., concerning foreigners who were registered during the War in Germany, mainly in the area that is now West Germany.
>
> Index cards and name lists concerning children who had been separated from their parents or close relatives during the War or immediately after the War.

While the holdings of ITS archives are vast, one should not think that the material is complete. For example, while the concentration camp material in the archives is the largest, it is not a collection of all concentration camp material that existed. ITS rates the completeness of its concentration camp collection as follows:

Buchenwald	almost complete
Dachau	almost complete
Flossenburg	incomplete but quite numerous
Mauthausen	trivial gaps
Mittelbau	trivial gaps
Natzweiler	not complete but quite numerous
Stutthof	not complete but quite numerous
Niederhagen-Wewelsburg	not complete but quite numerous
Ravensbruck	incomplete
Auschwitz	very incomplete
Gross-Rosen	very incomplete
Sachsenhausen	very incomplete
Neuengamme	very incomplete

| Lublin | very incomplete |
| Krakow-Plaszow | very incomplete |

According to ITS, there are 3,735,000 individual documents in the collection just described.

Another collection of ITS is the Post-War Documents which generally concern displaced persons who were registered from 1945 to 1951. Included in these documents are lists of the inhabitants of the DP camps.

The Historical Section of ITS archives is also of great value. Here are contained documents of a more general nature including concentration camps, Jewish towns, Nuremberg trial records, and information of the persecution of Jews in different countries. If you are interested in certain Jewish communities in Europe during the Holocaust, you will find these archives at ITS to be excellent.

The International Tracing Service is currently in the process of establishing a subject index to its concentration camp material for use by researchers. They are also publishing a volume on concentration camps detailing the inner workings of each of the camps.

One might think that the "tracing" function of the International Tracing Service has outlived its usefulness, but ITS reports that during the last five years the average number of inquiries per year has been 8,000. After more than thirty years, people are still looking for lost relatives—and are sometimes finding them. It is sad to note, of course, that often ITS offers verification regarding the concentration camp deaths of individuals.

Finally, the International Tracing Service has a staff of personnel who can answer inquiries in the following languages: Czech, Dutch, Estonian, Finnish, Greek, Hungarian, Italian, Lithuanian, Polish, Russian, Serbocroation, Slovakian, Spanish, English, French, and German. Inquiries in Hebrew and Azerbaijan can also be answered with the aid of other organizations, reports ITS.

I once naively thought that my family had escaped the Holocaust. It was my belief that since I was born in the United States and since my parents were in the United States, and since even my grandparents were not in Europe during the War, our family "got out in time."

It was not until I found an old family photograph and asked my great-uncle to identify people in the picture that I realized how wrong I was. The photograph contained twenty-one people and included my great-grandfather, who also came to America, as well

Abteilung für innere Verwaltung
Matrik und Beerdigungswesen.

Theresienstadt, am 7.Feber 1943.

G E B U R T E N :

Am 1.Feber 1943 wurde in E VI ein Knabe geboren.
Vater: BERTHOLD ISRAEL HOCHBRUCK
Mutter: SELMA SARA HOCHBRUCK, Trs.Nr. 779/III/2

Am 1.Feber 1943 wurde in E VI ein Mädchen geboren.
Vater: ALFRED FINKLER Trs.Nr.203/AAw
Mutter: THERESE FINKLER,geb.Machlup, Trs.Nr. 204/AAw

Am 2.Feber 1943 wurde in E VI ein Knabe geboren.
Vater : LEO PICK, Trs.Nr. 234/Ck
Mutter: THEA PICK,geb.Baumann, Trs.Nr. 324/Aaq

S t e r b e f ä l l e

vom 5.Feber 1943.

Lfd.Nr.:		Trs.Nr.:	Geb.-Jahr:	Ubikation:
1	Abraham Marie Sara,g.Wagner	8343/I/71	1870	L 504
2	Altmann Gidel Sara,geb.Eisenheimer	21/II/26	1865	L 213
3	Bechhöfer Gustav Israel	863/II/18	1868	L 425
4	Benger Johanna Sara,geb.Hurwitz	338/IX/1	1873	Q 501
5	Bergenthal Regina Sara	43/II/26	1869	Q 301
6	Bergheim Hedwig Sara,geb.Brauer	10289/I/83	1870	Q 608
7	Birnbaum Gisela Sara	820/IV/7	1875	A II
8	Bloch Sascha	701/Ck	1926	B V
9	Böck Bertha,geb.Löwy	539/Co	1879	L 306
10	Brühl Oskar Israel	60/V/2	1873	Ea III
11	Caspary-Lilienthal Röschen Sara	10617/I/86	1864	L 504
12	Danziger Else Sara,g.Kramer	7429/I/65	1873	E VI
13	Dienstag Moses	10626/I/86	1857	L 504
14	Drill Max Israel	8/IV/13	1906	B IV
15	Ebenstein Anna Sara,geb.Lehves	10005/I/80	1863	E VI
16	Eisler Rosalie,geb.Suran	986/Cn	1865	L 124
17	Fanzl Emil	966/AAw	1870	B V
18	Feldmann Irma Sara,geb.Weiss	336/IV/8	1884	Ea III
19	Fischer Jetti Sara,g.Gottlieb	7357/I/65	1873	Q 506
20	Fischer Leopold	115/Bz	1864	L 504
21	Fleischmann Amalie Sara,g.Thormann	89/II/25	1865	A II
22	Frank Hanna Sara	584/II/26	1866	L 206
23	Frank Regina Sara,geb.Stein	7431/I/65	1863	Q 303b
24	Frankl Lilly	794/Ca	1921	E VI
25	Freud Antonia Sara,geb.Fürst	625/IV/4	1868	A II
26	Fried Chaje Sara,geb.Adler	104/XVI/1	1863	Q 704
27	Fried Klara Sara,geb.Wolf	281/XVII/1	1875	L 213
28	Friedrichs Lina Sara,geb.Kaufmann	9149/I/71	1856	H V
29	Glückauf Salomon	386/Cm	1864	Q 317
30	Feldmann Josef	682/Ae	1866	E VI
31	Goldschmidt Julchen Sara	120/XI/1	1869	L 312
32	Gotthelf Laura Sara,geb.Matzdorf	7081/I/65	1860	L 504
33	Grombacher Süssmann Israel	1008/XVII/1	1876	Q 615
34	Grünebaum Minna Sara,g.Baumblatt	227/XII/1	1873	L 223
35	Handel Fanni Sara	1130/IV/11	1865	L 306
36	Halporn Friederike Sara,g.Weiss	889/IV/10	1883	Q 403

Birth and death list, Theresienstadt Concentration Camp. (Courtesy of Leo Baeck Institute, New York)

Kurzweil Family in Dobromil, Poland, ca. 1925. Of the twenty-one people in this photograph, fourteen were murdered in the Holocaust.

as my father, aunt, uncle, great-uncle, and grandmother. That added up to six people of the twenty-one whom I could recognize from the photograph. Who were the others?

I didn't think much about the other people in the photograph when I first found it. After all, my grandmother and her three children were in it, and I knew all of them. Perhaps I was also preoccupied with the fact that my grandfather was not in the picture. He was already in America at the time, earning enough money to send for the rest of the family.

Yes, "the rest of the family." Since my grandmother and her three children were finally sent for five years after my grandfather came to America, I always thought, as I said, that we "missed it."

Today, I know the truth: In addition to the six people whom I recognized in the photograph, only one other person survived the Holocaust. The other fourteen people were murdered. Out of twenty-one family members, two thirds were killed.

When I asked my great-uncle Sam who the other people in the picture were he said, "This is my brother Elya, his wife Dobroh, and their two children. This is my brother Hersh, his wife Anna, and their five children. And this is my sister Reisl, her husband

Shimon, and their two children. Only Mechel, the oldest son of Hersh and Anna, survived. You know him. The others were all killed."

As I looked at the photograph, I thought again of my grandfather in America, working to earn the money which would bring his wife and three children, one of whom was my father, to this country. Had my grandfather stayed, had he continued his life with his brothers and sisters in the town in which they were born and raised, his family, like the others, would have probably been killed.

In all, at least 103 people in the Kurzweil family alone were murdered in the Holocaust. That's just one branch of my family.

And I thought we escaped it.

HOLOCAUST RESEARCH

The International Tracing Service

As has been described, the International Tracing Service is the best source for locating information about Holocaust victims. While Yad Vashem has a duplicate collection of the International Tracing Service's holdings, it is ITS which will be more helpful. This is because ITS has, as its function, the role of doing research for individuals for free, while Yad Vashem does not do research for persons. If you write to Yad Vashem, they will suggest you contact ITS.

If you know the name of a relative and you want to find out his or her fate during the Holocaust, write to ITS and give them as much information about the person as you can. They require more than just a name since their files contain so many duplicate names. ITS usually asks for a person's name and birthdate, but if you do not know that (even an approximate date will help) then try to supply any other information which will narrow the field for the researcher.

What ITS *will not* do is send you information on everyone in their files with a certain surname. Remember: it is a tracing service of individuals.

The ITS has all the available records kept by the Nazis at the concentration camps but, as noted, its collection is not complete. It also has a great number of other types of records. This means that its files include not only Holocaust victims who were killed, but also others who survived.

It usually takes a few months for ITS to fill your request, but it is their policy to send you a note telling you that they have received your inquiry. However, even this note takes several weeks to arrive. Nevertheless, when you do receive their final reply, it might include some extremely meaningful information.

As we have mentioned, ITS also has information concerning the fate of towns during the Holocaust. Along with your inquiry pertaining to individuals, you might want to ask about certain localities.

When you write to ITS, simply state that you are interested in knowing whatever they have in their files on your family members and then list those individuals along with additional information as explained earlier. Again, ITS, which is under the auspices of the International Red Cross, does not charge for its research—nor should it.

Write to: International Tracing Service
         D-3548 Arolsen
         Federal Republic of Germany

> The one million Jewish children murdered in the Nazi holocaust died not because of their faith, nor in spite of their faith, nor for reasons unrelated to faith. They were murdered because of the faith of their great-grandparents. Had these great-grandparents abandoned their Jewish faith, and failed to bring up Jewish children, then their fourth-generation descendants might have been among the Nazi executioners, but not among their Jewish victims. Like Abraham of old, European Jews sometime in the mid-nineteenth century offered a human sacrifice, by the mere minimal commitment to the Jewish faith of bringing up Jewish children. But unlike Abraham they did not know what they were doing, and there was no reprieve. This is the brute fact which makes all comparisons odious or irrelevant. This is the scandal of the particularity of Auschwitz which, once faced by the Jewish believer, threatens total despair.
>
> —EMIL L. FACKENHEIM

Mauthausen Death Books

The National Archives in Washington, D.C., has two rolls of microfilm which contain seven volumes known as the *Mauthausen Death Books*. These books recorded the deaths of about 100,000 victims at that Nazi Death Camp. The volumes are chronological—by death (!)—and include such personal data as name, date of birth, date of death, and other comments.

These volumes were introduced by the U.S. prosecution staff before the International Military Tribunal, commonly known as the Nuremberg Trials.

There is no index to these Death Books, so it is quite difficult to find specific names. However, if you have reason to believe that family members were killed in Mauthausen, and you care to do the research, these rolls of microfilm are available. You can also view these rolls of microfilm if you want to witness a frightening example of Nazi sickness.

These and other National Archives holdings are available to you on interlibrary loan. The code number for the Death Books is (T 990). Ask your local library for details concerning the interlibrary loan of these materials.

Yad Vashem

Yad Vashem is a national institution in Israel dedicated to perpetuating the memory of the victims of the Holocaust. Their stated goal is "to gather in material regarding all those Jewish people who laid down their lives, who fought and rebelled against the Nazi enemy and their collaborators, and to perpetuate their memory and that of the communities, organizations, and institutions which were destroyed because they were Jewish. . . ."

In addition to administering a museum devoted to the Holocaust, Yad Vashem is a research institution which collects material and publishes books and periodicals in Hebrew and English. Yad Vashem also aids in bringing Nazi war criminals to trial through the information which it provides to legal authorities throughout the world.

While Yad Vashem will not endeavor to do research for individuals with general requests, one department of Yad Vashem is of great interest to those who wish to locate information about Holocaust victims. This is the Pages of Testimony Department. Yad Vashem has thousands of pages of testimony, written by individuals, regarding Holocaust victims. The testimony is arranged by name, and if you can supply the names of persons who you believe were murdered by the Nazis, or if you do not know the fate of individuals who were in Europe during the Holocaust, the Pages of Testimony Department might have information on these persons.

A useful aspect of the pages of testimony is the fact that not only is the name of the Holocaust victim on file, but so is the name of the individual who made the testimony—(i.e., the person who filled out the form). If you find the name of a victim who was in your

YAD VASHEM
Martyrs' and Heroes'
Remembrance
Authority
P.O.B. 84 Jerusalem, Israel

דף־עד
עדות־בלאט
A Page of Testimony

יד ושם

אינסטיטוט צום אנדענק
פון אומקום און גבורה

THE MARTYRS' AND
HEROES' REMEMBRANCE
LAW, 5713—1953
determines in article No. 2
that —
The task of YAD VASHEM
is to gather into the homeland
material regarding all those
members of the Jewish people
who laid down their lives, who
fought and rebelled against the
Nazi enemy and his collaborators, and to perpetuate their
memory and that of the
communities, organisations, and
institutions which were destroyed because they were Jewish.

ב י ל ד
Photo

דאס געזעץ צום אנדענק פון אומקום און גבורה — יד־ושם, תשי״ג 1953

שטעלט פעסט אין פאראגראף נומ׳ 2:

די אויפגאבע פון יד־ושם איז איינצואמלען אין היימלאנד דעם אנדענק פון אלע יידן, וואס
זענען געפאלן, האבן זיך מוסר נפש געווען, געקעמפט און זיך אנטקעגנגעשטעלט דעם נאצישן
שונא און זיינע ארויסהעלפער, און זיי אלעמען, די קהילות, די ארגאניזאציעס און אינסטיטוציעס,
וועלכע זענען חרוב געווארן צוליב זייער אנגעהעריקייט צום יידישן פאלק — שטעלן א דענקמאל.

(געזעץ־בוך נומ׳ 132, י״ז אלול תשי״ג, 28.8.1953)

Family name *	1. פאמיליע־נאמען *
First Name (maiden name)	2. פארנאמען
	(פאמיליע־נאמען פאר דער חתונה)

Place of birth (town, country)	ארט פון געבורט 4. (שטאט, לאנד)	Date of birth	3. געבורטס־דאטע
Name of mother	נאמען פון מוטער 6.	Name of father	5. נאמען פון פאטער

Name of spouse (if a wife, add maiden name)	7. נאמען פון מאן אדער פון פרוי און איר מיידלשע־פאמיליע
Place of residence before the war	8. שטאביליער וואוינארט
Places of residence during the war	9. וואוינערטער בעת דער מלחמה
Circumstances of death (place, date, etc.)	10. ארט, צייט און אומשטעגנדן פון טויט

I, the undersigned .... איך, דער אונטערגעשריבענער

residing at (full address) .... וואס וואוינט (פולער אדרעס)

relationship to deceased .... קרובישאפט

hereby declare that this testimony is correct to the best of my knowledge.
דערקלער דערמיט, אז די עדות וואס איך האב דא איבערגעגעבן,
מיט אלע פרטים, איז א ריכטיקע לויט מיין בעסטען וויסן.

Place and date .... ארט און דאטע   Signature .... אונטערשריפט

״...ונתתי להם בביתי ובחומתי יד ושם...אשר לא יכרת״ ישעיהו נ״ו, ה

״...even unto them will I give in mine house and within my walls a place and a name...that shall not be cut off.״ Isaiah, LVI.5

---

* ביטע אנשרייבן יעדן נאמען פון אומגעקומענעם אויף א באזונדער בלאט.
* *Please inscribe the name of each victim of the Holocaust on a separate form.*

Blank "Page of Testimony" in English, Yiddish, and Hebrew, from Yad Vashem in Jerusalem. Yad Vashem asks individuals to testify on these forms regarding victims known to them.

family, you can also find the name, possibly, of a living person who knew the victim. Relatives who lost contact with each other have found one another through the written recording of a Holocaust victim!

To make a request for pages of testimony, write to:

> Yad Vashem
> Pages of Testimony Dept.
> P.O.B. 3477
> Jerusalem, Israel

Note: The Pages of Testimony Department works both ways—giving information and receiving information. If you already have names and other facts about people who were murdered during the Holocaust, you will want to ask Yad Vashem for blank pages in order to send them *your* testimony.

Everything new must have its roots in what was before.

—SIGMUND FREUD

Memorial Books as Sources for Learning about Holocaust Victims

If you can find a Memorial Book devoted to a town from which your family has come (see page 192), you might find a listing of Holocaust victims from that town. Often Memorial Books publish lists of individuals murdered during the Holocaust, in order to keep their memory alive. Even if you think your family left its ancestral home before the Holocaust, these listings might provide names of family members who stayed. While you cannot assume that people with the same surname as yours appearing on these lists are related, there is a good chance that they are—especially if it was a small town. If you find names in Memorial Books which are familiar, you should ask your relatives, particularly your older relatives, if they remember them.

Landsmannschaften (see page 207) can also be a good source for learning about the fate of your family and your ancestral towns during the Holocaust. Often the members of landsmannschaften are survivors and have much to share regarding this part of your family experience.

Locating Survivors

I write this section of this book with great hesitation. While it is nearly thirty-five years after the Holocaust, I have met many

	Name	Age	Place and Time of Death
218.	Edelman, Yente	59	Skala Sep. 1942
219.	Edelman, Moses	30	Borszczow 1942
220.	Edelman, Aron	64	Skala Forest 1943
221.	Edelman, Golda	60	Borszczow 1943
222.	Edelman, Liba	35	Skala Sep. 1942
223.	Edelman, Rywka	59	Borszczow 1943
224.	Edelman, Moshe	35	Turylcze 1943
225.	Edelman, Eli	30	Turylcze 1943
226.	Edelman, Tonia	25	Turylcze 1943
227.	Edelstein, Hersch	68	Borszczow 1943
228.	Edelstein, Liba	64	Borszczow 1943
229.	Edelstein, Dora	30	Borszczow 1943
230.	Edelstein, Sara	75	Skala Sep. 1942
231.	Edelstein, Chaya	40	Skala For. Sep. 1943
232.	Edelstein, Alter	15	Skala 1943
233.	Ehrenberg, Mendel	71	Skala Sep. 1942
234.	Ehrenberg, Ita	71	Skala Sep. 1942
235.	Ehrenberg, Dvora	45	Skala Sep. 1942
236.	Ehrlich, Meier	58	Cygany Unkn.
237.	Ehrlich, Gitel	56	Cygany Unkn.
238.	Ehrlich, Brana	19	Cygany Unkn.
239.	Ehrlich, Motio	17	Cygany Unkn.
240.	Ehrlich, Sima	16	Cygany Unkn.
241.	Eisenfeld, Mendel	67	Cygany Unkn.
242.	Eisenfeld, Ratze	63	Cygany Unkn.
243.	Eisenfeld, Zeide	70	Skala 1942
244.	Eisenfeld, Szyfra	68	Skala 1942
245.	Elkes, Nachum	43	Gluboczek c.c. 1942
246.	Elkes, Sosia	43	Skala Sep. 1942
247.	Elkes, Pepa	17	Skala Sep. 1942
248.	Elkes, Wolf	15	Janowska c.c. 1942
249.	Engelbach, Sima	76	Skala Sep. 1942
250.	Engelbach, Eli	42	Borki c.c. 1942
251.	Engelbach, Frima	35	Skala Sep. 1942
252.	Engelbach, Leizer	7	Skala Sep. 1942
253.	Engelbach, Chaim	72	Skala 1942
254.	Engelbach, Mariem	69	Skala Sep. 1942

From the list of more than 1,400 Jews murdered by the Nazis. The "List of Martyrs" was published in the Skala Memorial Book. Lists of murdered Jews are usually included in Memorial Books.

people who still have hopes that one day they will find their relatives who have been missing since the War. Every once in a while a news item will stimulate more of this hope. "A brother and sister, separated by the Holocaust, find each other decades later." While these stories are true, they are few and far between. Nonetheless, if the hope is there, a distant dream might one day be fulfilled.

Yet, I write this section with hesitation because I do not want to raise false hopes. I do not want to give the impression that one can easily find lost relatives. I do not want to add to the thought that "they might be alive" only to bring on greater disappointment when they are not found.

So, I ask the reader to understand the situation: Hope in finding a lost relative is very slight. Yet, if the possibility exists and if you have the strength to pursue the question, you may want to attempt the research. Finally, before I describe this next source, you should understand that the odds are greatest, sadly, that your missing relative is not alive and was murdered.

After the Holocaust, a major activity of Jews around the world was searching for missing relatives. The question in everyone's mind was, "Who was killed and who survived?" Immediately after the War, Jews were asked to return to their hometowns. This was, perhaps, the best way to find out the fate of one's family and friends. If everyone returned "home," even for a short time, the survivors could learn the fate of their loved ones. In addition, if any of the family's personal effects were still there, this would be an opportunity to claim them.

There are an enormous number of post-War horror stories relating to this very subject. How often a surviving Jew returned to his or her village only to be murdered—after the War!—by anti-Semites in the town. In my family, there are eye-witness accounts by many people of just this situation. A cousin of mine returned to our shtetl only searching for his missing relatives and was killed by the local people.

For the Jews who returned to their homes, their experience was mixed with joy and sadness. In many cases a survivor's wildest dreams were fulfilled: Others in his family survived. But in most cases, perhaps every case, the death of many loved ones was discovered.

But not everyone returned home. Some refused ever to go back to the town where they were originally from—not even for a day. Others were physically unable to travel great distances to return

REGISTER
of
JEWISH
SURVIVORS

II

LIST OF JEWS IN POLAND

(58.000 NAMES)

JERUSALEM 1945
PUBLISHED BY THE JEWISH AGENCY FOR PALESTINE
SEARCH BUREAU FOR MISSING RELATIVES

Kurc   — 157 —   Kwaśniewska

Kurc Grynberg Nina, Łódź
Kurz Regina, Tarnów
Kurtz Regina, Będzin
Kurc Regina, Radom
Kurz Rena, Peterswaldau
Kurc Rywka, Łódź
Kurc Szajndla, Warszawa
Kurc Szlama, Łódź
Kurz Urszula, Tarnów
Kurzbard Dawid, Warszawa
Kurzbard Dawid, Lublin
Kurzbard Jola, Częstochowa
Kurzbard Judka, Warszawa
Kurzbard Mania, Częstochowa
Kurzbard Piskun, Łódź
Kurchart Salomon, Łódź
Kurchlat Szlama, Łódź
Kurchaum Fradla, Łódź
Kurchaum Frajdla, Łódź
Kurzer Abraham, Lwów
Kunzer Leib, Nowy Sącz
Kurzer Regina, Lwów
Kurzer Tema, Lwów
Kurcfeld Mordko, Łódź
Kurcfeld Moszko, Łódź
Kurcfeld Regina, Sosnowiec
Kurcfeld Ruchla, Peterswaldau
Kurcfeld Sara, Łódź
Kurzman Moses, Gorlice
Kurzrok Jan, Kraków
Kurcrok Józef, Lublin
Kursztag Jakub, Warszawa
Kurzweil Samuel, Przemyśl
Kurzwöld Regina, Kraków
Kurtza Ryfka, Zambrów
Kurcz Rywka, Łódź
Kurdelas Its, Skierniwice
Kurdelas Szmul, Skierniwice
Kurek Abram, Łódź
Kurek Aron Alie, Łódź
Kurek Kajla, Łódź
Kurgan Mina, Łódź
Kuriańska Roza, Łódź
Kuriańska Tylda, Katowice
Kuriański Ignacy, Łódź
Kurland Anna, Częstochowa
Kurland Chaim, Częstochowa
Kurland Estunia, Sosnowiec
Kurland Estera, Rychbach
Kurland Gustawa, Częstochowa
Kurland Idel, Częstochowa
Kurland Mala, Sosnowiec
Kurland Maria, Sosnowiec
Kurland Noe, Częstochowa
Kurland Noech, Częstochowa
Kurland Rachmil, Częstochowa
Kurland Sura Frajdla, Częstochowa
Kurlandzki Adam, Warszawa
Kurlender Jakub Szaja, Częstochowa
Kurmann Bella, Oświęcim
Kurnatowska Maria, Warszawa
Kurnik Dola, Warszawa
Kurnik Róża, Warszawa

Kurnik Sara, Łódź
Kurnik Sura, Warszawa
Kuronczyk Róża, Częstochowa
Kuropatwa Józef, Łódź
Kursztein Leon, Chełm
Kurt Izrael, Oświęcim
Kurta Izio, Warszawa
Kurta Zofia, Warszawa
Kurutkowski Stanisław, Kraków
Kurweit Gustaw, Lwów
Kurycka Basia, Bydgoszcz
Kurycka Benia, Bydgoszcz
Kurycka Fruma, Warszawa
Kurycka Genia, Bydgoszcz
Kuryski Abram, Łódź
Kus Abram, Łódź
Kuss Mania, Częstochowa
Kusbaum Mania, Łódź
Kuskel Izrael, Lwów
Kuko Dawid, Łódź
Kuś Abram, Kraków
Kuśmierak Adam, Warszawa
Kuśmierak Irena, Lublin
Kuśmierak Ignaś, Lublin
Kuśmierak Krystyna, Warszawa
Kuśmierak Teofila, Warszawa
Kuśmierc Majer, Lublin
Kuśmirak Abram, Łódź
Kuśmirak Hendla, Łódź
Kuśmirak Herez, Łódź
Kuśmirak Małka, Łódź
Kuśnier Gerez, Lublin
Kuśniewski Chaim, Sosnowiec
Kuszel Zelma, Łódź
Kuszer Olszewska, Warszawa
Kuszer Binem, Piotrków
Kuszer Symcha, Warszawa
Kuszerman-Koperwas Chaja Sura, Radom
Kuszerman Frymeta, Radom
Kuszerman Szlama, Radom
Kuszmarin Iljasz, Kalisz
Kuszner Bronisława, Warszawa
Kuszner Marian, Warszawa
Kuszner Feiwl, Trzciane
Kuszner Karola, Częstochowa
Kuszner Roza, Trzciane
Kusznir Alexander, Warszawa
Kusznir Chaja, Częstochowa
Kusznir Lowa, Częstochowa
Kuszyńska Hanka, Łódź
Kuszyński Henryk, Łódź
Kuszyński Lajb, Częstochowa
Kuszyński Lajb, Częstochowa
Kurzyłaki Lajb, Łódź
Kuszyński Ludwik, Łódź
Kutajner Gota, Warszawa
Kutas Mina, Katowice
Kutas Wolf, Łódź
Kute Herszek, Drzewica
Kutkowski Zelik, Warszawa
Kutner Chaja, Lublin
Kutner Dienkle, Bydgoszcz
Kutner Estera, Warszawa

Kutner Ewa, Łódź
Kutner Lajb, Łódź
Kutner Moazek, Łódź
Kutner Roza, Bydgoszcz
Kutner Sala, Łódź
Kutner Sara, Bydgoszcz
Kutner Sara, Łódź
Kutner Szlama, Łódź
Kutner Szprynca, Warszawa
Kutnowski Szlama, Warszawa
Kutowski Szlama, Łódź
Kuwartowski Miotek, Łódź
Kuwent Symcha, Zychlin
Kuzda Jadwiga, Bergen-Belsen
Kuzecki Abram, Częstochowa
Kuzecki Alter Chaim, Częstochowa
Kuzner Krautman Emma-Helena, Kraków
Kuzne Abram, Będzin
Kuznier Izrael, Chełm
Kuzniecow Gela, Łódź
Koźnicz Maria, Warszawa
Kuźnic Ryszard, Warszawa
Kwal Marceli, Warszawa
Kwala Jak, Łódź
Kwalber Jakub, Matthausen
Kwalwasser Henia, Sosnowiec
Kwalwasser Sonia, Kraków
Kwaśniewski Józef, Kraków
Kwaśniewski Maksymilian, Kraków
Kwaśniewski Marian, Warszawa
Kwaśnik Noach, Łódź
Kwejman Henryk, Łódź
Kwekzylber Mojżesz, Warszawa
Kwiatek Chaim, Łódź
Kwiatek Józef, Łódź
Kwiatkowski Stanisław, Kraków
Kiecień Julian, Warszawa
Kwinta Dawid, Częstochowa
Kwinta Izrael, Sosnowiec
Kwinta Leja, Częstochowa
Kwinta Mirka, Częstochowa
Kwinta Zalma, Częstochowa
Kwintner Izrael, Lublin
Kintner Izrael Mordchaj, Łódź
Kzmer Abram, Katowice
Kwart Bronisław, Warszawa
Kwart Dina, Białystok
Kwart Dyna, Warszawa
Kwart Lola, Warszawa
Kwart Rubin, Łódź
Kwart Srul, Lublin
Kwart Szulim, Łódź
Kwartler Roza, Kraków
Kwas Eugenia, Warszawa
Kwastel Motek, Sosnowiec
Kwaśniewska Bronisława, Łódź
Kwaśniewska Chana, Chmielnik
Kwaśniewska Helena, Kraków
Kwaśniewska Judzia, Łódź
Kwaśniewska Janina, Warszawa
Kwaśniewska Sala, Rychbach

Cover and sample page from one of many lists of Jewish survivors published after the Holocaust.

home. Still others were too ill to make the journey. Other circumstances also prevented many Jews from going "home." In addition, usually a person had family in several different towns. A survivor could not be in all places at once. Yet the survivor was desperately anxious to learn news about his family.

Because of this situation, various agencies attempted to aid in the search for missing relatives. The Jewish Agency for Palestine in 1945 established the Search Bureau for Missing Relatives. The World Jewish Congress established the Division for Displaced Persons. Other organizations, such as the Czechoslovak Jewish Committee, the Relief Committee of Jews from Czechoslovakia, the American Federation for Lithuanian Jews, Inc., and many others, also joined in to help Jews find survivors.

The major effort of these organizations was to gather and publish information about survivors in the form of alphabetical lists of names. The Jewish Agency for Palestine's Search Bureau for Missing Relatives published a 300-page book in 1945 called *Register of Jewish Survivors*. It was a list of 58,000 Jews in Poland in June of that year.

But this was just one of many such published lists. Here is a list of titles of some of the published lists:

SURVIVING JEWS IN WARSAW AS OF JUNE 5th 1945

SURVIVING JEWS IN LUBLIN

LIST OF PERSONS LIBERATED AT TEREZIN IN EARLY
    MAY 1945

LIST OF CHILDREN AT TEREZIN

DISPLACED JEWS RESIDENT IN THE CZECHOSLOVAK RE-
    PUBLIC 1948

LIST OF JEWS RESIDING IN RIGA

JEWISH REFUGEES IN ITALY

JEWS LIBERATED FROM GERMAN CONCENTRATION
    CAMPS ARRIVED IN SWEDEN 1945-6

SURVIVING JEWS IN JUGOSLAVIA AS OF JUNE, 1945

A LIST OF LITHUANIAN JEWS WHO SURVIVED THE NAZI
    TYRANNY AND ARE NOW IN LITHUANIA, FRANCE,
    ITALY, SWEDEN, PALESTINE, 1946

JEWS REGISTERED IN CZESTOCHOWA

AN EXTENSIVE LIST OF SURVIVORS OF NAZI TYRANNY PUBLISHED SO THAT THE LOST MAY BE FOUND AND THE DEAD BROUGHT BACK TO LIFE.

These are just some of the lists which were published. The titles of many of the lists are, in themselves, quite moving.

Where are these lists located? At the present time I am aware of only one place where a large collection of these books is gathered and that is at YIVO Institute for Jewish Research, 1048 5th Avenue, New York, N.Y. 10028 (see page 191). Be aware that the YIVO staff *cannot* do research for you. They *cannot* look in these books in search of names. However important this search might be to you, the YIVO does not have the staff to do searches.

How can these lists serve you? While the International Tracing Service has all available data on Holocaust victims and survivors, I have already explained that ITS is a *tracing* service. In others words, if you give it a name of a person (and additional identification) it will check to see if it has information on the person. However, what if I am looking, for example, for information about people with the name Kurzweil? The International Tracing Service cannot and will not supply me with information on every Kurzweil in its files. As they have told me through correspondence, their files have information about more than 200 Kurzweils! They cannot send me all of that information, but they can check their files if I ask them about certain specific names. Again, they are a tracing service of individuals.

This is where the lists come in. If I check the survivors lists for the surnames which I am interested in, I might find people with the same surnames. As you can see from the illustrations of the pages from these lists, the names of the towns are also listed. These towns are the ones where the people were at the time the list was compiled. Since most Jews registered in their hometowns, this is often the town where they lived before the Holocaust. If the town matches one in your family history, you *may* be on the right track in locating a relative. Once you find a listing of interest, you can photocopy the page and ask family members if they recall this person. Then you can send it to the International Tracing Service. They will check their files for the name. Finally, you can check phone books (see page 88) and you might match the name on the list with a listing in the Israeli phone books, for example, or other phone directories as well.

Once again, these lists are a way to possibly locate missing people. While the lists were published more than three decades ago, they might be an aid in discovering some valuable information. On the other hand, I must repeat that the chances are still slight, and your hopes must not be raised too high.

Missing Relatives in Israel

If you are looking for a missing relative in Israel, the following organization would be of help:

> The Jewish Agency
> Missing Relative Department
> P.O. Box 92
> Jerusalem, Israel

Deportations from France during the Holocaust

A remarkable book was published in 1978 that should be of great interest to anyone researching Holocaust victims in France. Titled *Le mémorial de la déportation des Juifs de France* and written and compiled by Serge Klarsfeld, this book lists all of the Jews deported from France during World War II. The book contains the names, birthdates and birthplaces of nearly 80,000 Jews who were deported.

This large volume costs thirty dollars and is available from the Beate Klarsfeld Foundation, 515 Madison Avenue, New York, New York 10022.

Death Books

At YIVO Institute for Jewish Research in New York, along with their collection of lists of survivors, are a few examples of lists of murdered Jews. There are no gravestones for the millions murdered. These lists, in effect, become their memorials.

Examples of such books are two volumes published by the Jewish Labor Committee in 1947. The titles of the two books are: *Memorial Dates of the Martyred Jews of Dachau—Jews Born in Lithuania, Latvia, Estonia and White Russia,* and *Memorial Dates of the Martyred Jews of Dachau—Jews Born in Poland.*

Both books were compiled by Jesef Lindenberger and Jacob Silberstein, themselves Dachau survivors.

These kinds of lists, while being possible sources for research, also serve as a further inspiration. We must try our best to learn about those members of our families who perished during the Holocaust. We ought to know their names and to write them down on our family trees. We ought to print these family trees and distribute them to our family members so that everyone knows who perished and how we are connected to them. Their memories must live.

> Whoever teaches his son teaches not only his son but also his son's son—and so on to the end of generations.

> —Talmud: Kiddushin, 30a

Holocaust Calendar of Polish Jewry

According to Jewish Tradition, the anniversary of the death of a family member is to be observed. On that day, each year, a candle is lit in memory of the individual who has departed.

The Holocaust, which stole six million Jews from our families, caused most of our families to observe these death anniversaries. The problem, of course, is that in most cases we do not know the exact date of death. Whole towns were often destroyed at once with nobody to recall the date. Many Jews were marched or taken to concentration camps. The precise date an individual Jew died is nearly impossible to determine.

Desiring to fulfill the religious obligation to observe the anniversary of the death, many Jews who have family members who were killed during the Holocaust will use the date that the town was attacked or evacuated as the day to remember.

In 1974, Rabbi Israel Schepansky published an 88-page book called *Holocaust Calendar of Polish Jewry*. The *Holocaust Calendar* is essentially a town-by-town list of communities in Poland. The book provides the name of the town, the population, the dates and ways of "liquidation," as the author puts it, and in many cases other information about the town. Rabbi Schepansky is a well-respected scholar, the editor of the Jewish magazine *Or Hamizrach*, and on the editorial board of the *Talmudic Encyclopedia*.

The *Holocaust Calendar* is available for $3.50 from Rabbi Israel Schepansky, 2220 Avenue L, Brooklyn, N.Y. 11210. Be aware that the book is in Hebrew. Nonetheless, you can surely find someone who can translate for you, if it is Polish Jewry that is your interest.

Unfortunately, there is no single reference source for the dates of other Jewish communities in Eastern Europe. Some dedicated scholar ought to do the same thing for Hungary, Czechoslovakia, etc., that Rabbi Schepansky has done for Poland.

On the other hand, as you do research on the histories of your European communities, you will find these dates and other information about your towns during the Holocaust. The day that the Nazis destroyed your town is an important date for you to remember and to keep as a part of your family history.

> Mid-nineteenth century European Jews did not know the effects of their actions upon their remote descendants when they remained faithful to Judaism and raised Jewish children. What if they had known? Could they have remained faithful? Should they? And what of us who know, when we consider the possibility of a second Auschwitz three generations hence. (Which would we rather have our great-grandchildren be —victims, or bystanders and executioners?) Yet for us to cease to be Jews (and to cease to bring up Jewish children) would be to abandon our millennial post as witnesses to the God of History.
>
> —EMIL L. FACKENHEIM

The author's two cousins, Jozef and Ani Schlaf, who still live in Warsaw and were discovered as a result of family history research. Photo taken in 1978.

Pre-Holocaust European Phone Books

The New York Public Library Research Division attempts each year to obtain current phone books from all over the world. They also save their old phone books.

One day I wondered how far back the oldest Polish phone book went in the library's collection. The New York Public Library Annex on 43rd Street keeps these books. At the annex I found two volumes of the 1936 Polish telephone directories.

Since most of my family who came to America arrived in the early part of the 1900's, and since even those who came later arrived before the Holocaust, one might wonder why these phone books would be of use to me. In addition, you might ask, "What Jews had telephones in Poland in 1936?!"

In answer to the second question, the fact of the matter is that many Jews in Poland in 1936 had phones. The myth is that every Eastern European Jew was as poor as Tevye the Dairyman. As for my family being in the U.S. before 1936, the truth is that many cousins did not come to America—and were murdered in the Holocaust.

Upon examining the 1936 Polish phone books, I discovered that the books were arranged by town. Some towns had only two phones. Others had more. In one of the towns in my family history there was a listing of about twenty phones. Two of the names, to my great surprise, were slightly familiar to me. I photocopied the page and brought it to a man in the family who was from the same town and in fact had the same last name as the people listed. When I asked him if he knew who the two people listed were, he said, "Of course. One is my uncle and the other is my father."

They were both killed during the Holocaust, but in 1936 both had telephones. My cousin was then able to tell me about some of the other people who were listed as having phones in the same town. It was an excellent way to discover new people as well as to stimulate a memory to recall stories about people who had not been seen for thirty-five or more years.

The following is a listing of which pre-Holocaust telephone books can be found in the New York Public Library Annex:

Austria: Vienna, 1928-30, 1932-34, 1936-38
Niederösterreich
Burgenland
Oberösterreich

Salzburg
Steiermark
Karnten
Tirol
Vorarlberg

Czechoslovakia: Prague, 1932-38, 1940
Bohemia, 1934/35, 1935/36, 1936/37, 1938/39
Moravia and Silesia, 1932, 1933, 1936
Slovakia and Russian Lower Carpathia, 1934, 1935

Germany: Berlin, 1913, 1926-38
Düsseldorf, 1931-36
Frankfurt, 1928-37
Hamburg, 1927, 1930-35
Leipzig, 1932-34
München, 1932-37
Stuttgart, 1936
(It is interesting to note that many people who do research to claim war reparations as well as to hunt Nazis use these rare pre-Holocaust German phone directories.)

Hungary: Budapest, 1913, 1928-34, 1936-38, 1940

Poland: Warsaw, 1931-35, 1936/37
All districts except Warsaw, 1936

Yugoslavia: Belgrade, 1934

This is an incomplete list of cities and countries, of course.

The New York Public Library also has post-Holocaust phone books which may aid in tracking down missing relatives.

All our ancestors are in us. Who can feel himself alone?

—RICHARD BEER-HOFMANN, *Schlafied für
Miriam,* 1898

Chapter 4

Someone in Your Family Left Home

Generally, we look at Jewish history in terms of broad categories of time. The arrival of Jewish immigrants to the United States, for example, has been broken down into stages spanning many years for each stage. Most of us are familiar with the well-known era of American Jewish history during the years just before and after the beginning of the twentieth century, when vast numbers of Jews arrived in the Port of New York. Steamships carrying Jews from Europe arrived daily, pouring Jews into the United States.

We see that period of history, when the Lower East Side of New York filled up with immigrants, when other cities in the United States saw a rapid growth of their Jewish population because of this immigration, when the United States emerged as a center of world Jewry, as a phenomenon. The phenomenon of Jewish immigration has been written about, studied, and celebrated literally since it began. Books appear constantly on the subjects of the Lower East Side, Jewish immigration, and related topics. As an era, as a category of history, as an event, the years we are speaking about are seen in mostly broad perspectives.

While it is quite useful to see history in terms of the eras, stages, and time periods which are usually used, it is equally, if not more, useful to go from the general to the specific to see where, in fact, we fit into those broad descriptions of history. We know that steamships arrived in the ports of the United States daily during the active periods of immigration, but which boats brought us—meaning our ancestors—to those ports? What were the names of the ships which took our family to America? What did they look like? What route did they travel? When did they arrive? How long did it take to make the journey? Who traveled with whom? How old were your ancestors when they arrived? Where did they go when they got off the ship? Where did they live?

Again, we can understand the general history of different eras, or we can move in closer and examine details. We can see the crowd or we can examine the individuals.

As you read this, chances are you are sitting in or near your home. How long have you been living where you currently reside? How long has your family lived in the area where you are now? Whatever the answers are to those questions, if you are like most Jews in the United States, you have not been here for too many generations. Just as the United States is a nation of immigrants, so too are you and your family part of that collection of people whose ancestors arrived here sometime in the recent past. Most of us live our lives as Americans, rarely remembering that the United States is a relatively new experience for our families.

Do you know when your family arrived in America? Perhaps you yourself are an immigrant, in which case you are well aware of the arrival of your family to the United States. Or perhaps your parents were immigrants, in which case you might also have a good idea of the story behind your arrival in this country. Let us take a look at the Jewish immigrant experience in the United States and see where we fit into the large picture. Our examination of this era of Jewish history will be like a gradually moving close-up in a motion picture. We will begin with a wide-angle shot of the phenomenon of immigration. Slowly we will focus in on a more and more narrow portion of the picture until we arrive at a single detail in the original scene: you.

Jewish immigration to the United States can be seen in five different stages, and different branches of your family will fit into each of these time periods. Remember that unless you yourself are an immigrant, the arrival of your family to America will vary. Branches of your mother's family might have arrived in the United States in 1908, while your father's family—or parts of it—might have been in this country since before the Civil War.

American Jewish history can be divided into many different stages. For our purposes we will look at it from the following time periods:

    1654 to 1825
    1825 to 1880
    1880 to 1929
    1929 to 1945
    1945 to the present

Let us examine, in brief, each of these periods.

1654 TO 1825:

The year 1654 is a famous one in Jewish history for in that year the first Jewish settlement was established in North America. It consisted of twenty-three individuals and was located in Dutch New Amsterdam. There has been much research done concerning this group and the years that followed through the Colonial period in America. The number of Jews during that period was small, and assimilation was great. Jewish settlements appeared throughout the early Colonial period, however, and we find them quite early in Virginia, in Rhode Island, and in Maryland. By 1733 each of the thirteen colonies had Jewish populations. During this wave of settlers, most of the Jews were of Spanish descent, but after 1700, we find that German Jews were arriving in the colonies in small numbers. By 1750, the German Jews had outnumbered the Sephardic Jews. Nevertheless, the Jewish population of the United States by 1790 was a mere 1,500.

When the American Revolution broke out, most Jews were Whigs, that is, supporters of the Revolution. Having little or no tie to England, they were much more interested in independence. A great deal of historical material exists on this early period of Jewish history in North America, including the Jewish role in the Revolution. While the history is often fascinating, we are still aware of the fact that assimilation was the most common experience among the Jews in this period, and the reason that the Jewish population remained fairly stable was because of the balance between the Jews who faded out of the Jewish community and the trickle of Jewish immigration that continued throughout this time. By 1800, there were 2,000 Jews in the U.S. and by 1826 there were approximately 6,000. Most of these Jews, by this time, were native born and completely acculturated. Intermarriage was common.

1825 to 1880:

The second period of American Jewish history is one of enormous growth. In fact, the period can be seen as the American Jewish community going from a small group of little significance to a major world Jewish community. A quick look at population figures tells the story:

1826	6,000
1840	15,000
1860	150,000
1880	280,000

The increase in population was mainly the result of foreign immigration. Most of the immigrants were Germanic Jews, coming from Bohemia and Bavaria. Large numbers also came from Hungary. An interesting aspect of this migration was that many of the Jews who arrived in America did not remain on the East Coast. In fact, one of the great contributions of the Jews in America at this time was the continued opening up and development of the West. The older Jewish communities such as Charleston, South Carolina; Newport, Rhode Island; and Norfolk, Virginia, saw a decline during this westward movement across the country by Jews. Other cities began to develop Jewish communities. These included Cincinnati, Louisville, New Orleans, Chicago, St. Louis, Cleveland, Newark, Albany, Syracuse, Buffalo, Detroit, Milwaukee, and Minneapolis. Many Jews who arrived at the time of the Gold Rush traveled to California and were among the first to settle in San Francisco. By 1854, there were Jewish communities in dozens of cities across the entire country. As a result of the European revolutions of 1848 to 1849, the early 1850's evidenced the greatest wave of immigration of this entire period.

This was also the great era of the Jewish peddler and traveling salesman. Because of the lack of retail outlets to be found in a still developing nation, the Jewish peddler contributed to the growth of the American economy by traveling to cities throughout the country. In fact, many of the major giant department stores of today such as Macy's, Gimbel's, and Abraham and Straus had their beginnings in this period as tiny retail outlets, sometimes in the form of a horse-drawn wagon.

The middle of the nineteenth century in American Jewish history was dominated by the German Jew. With the arrival of so many German Jews came the establishment of German theater, newspapers, cultural societies, and other groups. These were often devoid of much Jewish content, however. But at the same time, the development of Reform Jewry as a major force in Jewish thinking took place. Major figures in the history of the Reform Movement emerged at this time, and synagogues as well as schools representing Reform Jewish ideology appeared.

Since many Jewish communities were well intact by the 1860's, Jewish participation in the Civil War was significant. Jews lived both in the North and the South and tended generally to support the war effort of the region in which they resided. After the Civil War, industrial expansion in the U.S. was great, but Jews were generally excluded from most of the industries which developed at this time such as oil, railroads, shipping, and banking. The area of business which was then wide open was retailing, and in large part this is the reason for the Jew in the U.S. being associated with retail markets.

1881 to 1929:

In 1880, the Jewish population of the United States was 280,000. By 1925, it had increased to 4,500,000. Those figures, by themselves, begin to tell the story of the few decades that are a major event in Jewish history. Between 1880 and 1925, some 2,378,000 Jews arrived in the United States.

The reasons for this huge migration of Jews from Eastern Europe, where most of them came from, are simple and at the same time complex. The simple reason is that life in Eastern Europe was becoming more and more unbearable. Pogroms were widespread during certain years, Jews were expelled from different regions, and anti-Semitic violence was a constant threat. But underlying those more immediate reasons were other factors: The Jewish populations in Eastern Europe grew at a pace which often made it impossible for a community to survive economically. In addition, the movement from Eastern Europe was continually building momentum. As more people arrived in the United States, the notion of America as a land of the free made its way back to the villages of their ancestry. Eastern Europe was literally buzzing with the idea of America and this helped considerably in the migration of such masses to the United States. The immigrants to America were mostly from Russia, Poland, Romania, and Austro-Hungary during this period. It is during these years that most of our ancestors came to the United States.

Within the years of this era, the pace of immigration increased with each decade. Between 1881 and 1892 approximately 19,000 Jews arrived, on the average, each year. Between 1892 and 1903 the annual average was 37,000. Between 1903 and 1914, the yearly average was 76,000. By 1918, the United States contained the largest Jewish community in the world.

Most of the immigrants arrived in New York. Many went to Philadelphia, Boston, Detroit, Cleveland, Chicago and other places, but the Lower East Side of New York City became the center of the world for the largest group of newly arrived Jews. With the start of the First World War, immigration came to a temporary halt. After the War, a series of bills passed in the United States Congress also served to slow up immigration considerably.

This period in American Jewish history is perhaps the richest and most well known. It was a milestone in the history of the Jews, transplanting families from one side of the world to the other. Individuals and families left their ancestral homes of generations to establish new roots in America. The quantity of material written

Emigrants to the United States in the Warsaw office of the Hebrew Immigrant Aid Society (HIAS), 1921. (Courtesy of YIVO Institute for Jewish Research)

during and about this period is vast, and entire libraries could be filled with the story of this era.

1929 TO 1945:

The time period from the beginning of the Depression to the end of World War II can be seen as another era in American Jewish history. However, it is here where we can see that to divide history into specific eras has its problems. So much can happen within just a few years that to lump several years together does not serve much of a purpose. While this is particularly true of this era, the same can be said of the other time periods already discussed. History is a complex unraveling of time, and hardly a generalization can be made without there being an exception quickly found.

We do see that there was very little immigration during these years, particularly in comparison with the years of the period before this one. The key date during this era is 1933, the year that Nazism arrived in Germany. With the vicious anti-Semitism increasing in Germany as well as in Poland and Romania, the number of Jews driven to leave and come to the United States increased. Those seeking immigrant status in the U.S. came up against difficulties in this period which were unknown just a few years before. Because of the economic situation in the United States coupled with anti-immigrant sentiment on the part of U.S. consuls empowered to grant visas, immigration was not as great as it could have been. During the years 1933 through 1937, total immigration did not exceed 33,000. The rate increased between 1938 and 1941, however, and the total for this period was 124,000. The increase was the result of the extreme worsening of the situation for Jews in Germany as well as in the lands recently taken over by Germany. But by the end of 1943, Jewish immigration to the United States had virtually stopped.

1945 TO THE PRESENT:

During the years 1947 to 1951, a little more than 119,000 Jews immigrated to the United States. The large majority of them were Holocaust survivors, more than 63,000 of them entering the country by the Displaced Persons Act of 1949. Between 1960 and 1968, about 73,000 Jewish immigrants arrived, made up of Israelis, Cubans, and Near Easterners. In recent years, Jewish immigration to the United States has come from the Soviet Union and Israel for the most part.

Canada

While the Jewish history of Canada parallels that of the United States in many ways, it would be useful to take a glimpse of Jewish migration to Canada.

The year 1759 begins the Jewish history of Canada. It was then that a permanent settlement arose in the country. At this time, the Jews were concentrated in the city of Montreal. The community was quite small, however, and by 1831, the population of Jews in Canada was only 107. In 1851, the Jewish population had increased to 248, and in 1861 there were 572 Jews in the country. By 1871, the population was 1,115 split fairly evenly between Quebec and Ontario. Finally, in examining the total Jewish population of Canada just before the period of mass migration in 1881, we find that there were 2,393 Jews.

The sources of these immigrants were the same as that of the United States immigrations. Most Jews came from Western and Central Europe with a minority coming from Eastern Europe in the middle of the nineteenth century. As in the case of the United States, it is really after 1881 that the bulk of the Canadian Jewish population arrived. The present-day Jewish population of Canada consists mainly of families descending from the post-1881 migrations. By 1891, the Jewish population of Canada was up to 6,414, and by 1920, the figure was more than 125,000.

Since the United States introduced a quota system for immigration after the First World War, Canada saw an increase in immigration but with the arrival of the Depression, restrictions tightened in Canada as well, limiting immigration severely. Again, as in the case of the United States, the rise of Nazism in 1933 in Germany led to another increased effort at immigration by Jews. Pressure in Canada by its Jewish leadership attempted to keep the doors open for oppressed European Jews. But restrictions and anti-immigrant and anti-Semitic sentiment kept the figure low.

Between 1930 and 1940, 11,000 Jewish immigrants arrived in Canada. After World War II an additional wave of Jewish immigration occurred, the number totaling 40,000 between 1945 and 1960.

The major Jewish centers in Canada have been and still are Quebec and Ontario, with Montreal, Quebec, Toronto, Hamilton, and Ottawa being the leading Jewish cities.

Israel

Not all European immigrants went to the United States. In fact, there were years during which migration to the United States was at a standstill and other countries were sought out by those looking for a better life. Israel, or Palestine, is not merely an alternative to America; a "return to Zion" has been a part of Jewish Tradition for centuries, and whether or not individuals who migrated to Israel saw it as a Biblical "return to Zion," it remains a major destination of many Jews.

Throughout history, there have been several reasons expressed for migration to Israel. The first is the ancient notion of a "return" as we have just mentioned. A second reason has been the desire to study Torah where the Sanhedrin and the great academies were located. There has also been a belief that a person who is buried in Israel will reap "other world" benefit from this.

Another motive for migration to Israel, or aliyah as it is called, has been the belief that only in Israel can mitzvoth be fulfilled. There has also been the belief that Israel will cure illness as well as barrenness. A belief that an increased population in the Land of Israel will hasten the Messiah has been another motivation for aliyah. Finally, we find that large numbers of people went to Israel— even since the thirteenth century—to escape persecution in Europe.

In modern times, migration to Israel has been motivated by combinations of the above-mentioned reasons in addition to national and ideological factors which have inspired great numbers of Jews to "make aliyah."

During the period after 1881, which as we know was the height of Jewish exit from Europe, there was considerable migration to Palestine. The stages of migration to Palestine and Israel are known by the phrases "First Aliyah," "Second Aliyah," and so on. The dates of the First Aliyah are considered 1882 through 1903. By 1903, approximately 10,000 Jews had settled in the region. The Second Aliyah was the period from 1904 through 1914, the beginning of World War I. The First and Second aliyot combined saw about 70,000 Jews migrate to the country, though it must be noted that many of them left because of the hardship of life there. There is no question but that the United States was the major attraction of Jews relocating during this period. Of all the Jews who were intercontinental migrants between 1881 and 1914, only 3 percent arrived in Eretz Israel.

As immigration to the United States slowed down considerably after the First World War, aliyah picked up. Between 1919 and 1926 nearly 100,000 Jews made aliyah. When the 1930's arrived, Palestine became enormously important as a destination for Jewish migrants. Anti-Semitism was worse than ever because of the rise of Nazism, and the United States had slowed down acceptance of immigrants drastically. Therefore, Palestine became exceedingly important. Between 1932 and 1939, which is known as the Fifth Aliyah, almost half of the intercontinental migrants went to Palestine. In that same period, the United States and Canada received but a fifth of the intercontinental migrants. The period of World War II is of course the most tragic. Most Jews were unable to leave Europe, though between 1940 and 1945, nearly 45,000 Jews reached Palestine—where the British turned many back. The British also denied entrance to Palestine to many Jews in the years following the Holocaust, between 1945 and May, 1948. Fewer than 70,000 Jews were able to enter Palestine. In May, 1948, Palestine became the independent nation of Israel, and from that time until the present, Israel has become the most popular destination of Jewish intercontinental migrants. The United States, Canada, and France (in the 1960's) were also the destination of many migrants of this period. But again, Israel was clearly the leader. Between May, 1948, through 1951, almost 700,000 Jews went to Israel. It was only in the mid-1960's that migration to Israel began to slow down considerably.

The brief descriptions of Jewish migrations and population growth in the United States, Canada, and Israel are the backbone of the Jewish history of the time periods covered. Basic to the understanding of a particular history and a particular people are the answers to the questions: Where were they from? how did they get there? what did they do?

As we have said, if you examine the general periods of recent Jewish history, you should be able to place your own personal family histories in these eras. So, for example, if your great-great-grandfather was a German Jew who arrived in this country in 1852, you can easily see that this particular branch of your own family background was a part of a special era in Jewish history. Of course, in order to know this, you must know the history of your own family. It is not enough to think that your ancestors were immigrants and that they came to America one day. Your own personal history is wrapped up in the choices made by your ancestors. To lump them together in a category called "the past" is a disservice to them, their risks, their strengths, and their lives. Again, the question remains: Where do you fit into Jewish history?

One of the results of tracing your family history and creating a family tree is that at one point, for each of the branches in your direct ancestry, you will discover your immigrant ancestor. Eventually, when you follow each branch back, your mother and your father, your four grandparents, your eight great-grandparents, your sixteen great-great-grandparents, and so on, one individual in each line will be an immigrant. For some of us, it may be found very soon; our own parents might be the immigrants. Or it may be just two generations back to our grandparents who were the immigrants in our families. In any case, none of us are without immigrant ancestors, obviously. That is, unless you are an immigrant.

While each person in your family history is special for his or her own contributions to your life, your immigrant ancestors surely have a unique distinction among the others. While we know that it was often hardship, anti-Semitism and fear which pushed immigrants to America, that final decision—to make the journey—must have often taken immense courage. All you have to do to know what the experience may have been like is to imagine for yourself leaving your home, family, friends, familiar environment, and everything that you have known for a lifetime, never to see it again. The result of that kind of imagining is dramatic. To envision your grandfather at age fifteen leaving his parents, his brothers and sisters, and an entire life to journey by himself to America never to return is a powerful experience and an education. It strains the mind to realize the number of divided families, the number of children who said farewell to parents, the number of sisters who said goodbye to brothers, or the husbands who left behind wives and children to save enough to send for them.

Another frightening image is to think about what the fate of your family might have been (in most cases) had your ancestor not made the decision to take the risk, the journey, and leave his home. As you build your family tree, you will often notice that your direct ancestors—grandparents, great-grandparents, and so on—had brothers and sisters whose decisions were quite different from each other. You will also come to understand that it was the decisions made by your direct ancestors which, in large part, are responsible for your very existence. If yours is like most Jewish families, you will undoubtedly find siblings of some of your direct ancestors who made different kinds of decisions—and their descendants were never born. This is understandable, of course. When you think of the radically different kinds of decisions that brothers and sisters make all the time, it is easy to comprehend why some lines of your family still exist and why some did not survive. But what you ought to understand above all else is how the choices made by your ancestors are so profoundly linked to your own life. If any one of your sixteen great-great-grandparents had chosen a different life from what he or she did, you might not be where you are today. You might not exist at all. Imagining this is not a senseless game, but is, rather, a serious invitation to attempt to understand the lives of your ancestors and the paths they traveled.

It is possible to enter Jewish history in a dramatic way through the history of your family as we have said and will say many times in this book. One of the most important points in the history of your family as well as in the history of the Jewish People is in the recent migrations. In the last 150 years nearly every Jewish family has made a radical move geographically. The Jewish population pockets of today are extremely different from 150 years ago, or even 100 years ago for that matter. In Eastern Europe, where the center of world Jewry existed for a few hundred years, the Jewish community today is almost non-existent. The United States, whose Jewish population was so small just 100 years ago, is one of the two centers of world Jewry today.

It will probably not be difficult for you to determine, for each of your family lines, who your immigrant ancestors are. Jewish migrations to this country were recent enough to make this task easy in most cases. If your family stems at all from a German-Jewish

Page from *Judisches Adressbuch (Jewish addressbook) fur Gross-Berlin, 1929–30.* (Courtesy of Leo Baeck Institute Library, New York)

family which migrated in the 1850's, the chore mght be more difficult than others, but will still be generally easy since records exist
often where memories of family members fail. Along with your
search for the names of your immigrant ancestors, you will want to
concern yourself with other questions as well. When did each immigrant ancestor arrive in this country? What towns and countries did
they come from? Let us treat each of those questions separately.

When did your immigrant ancestors arrive in this country? The
answers to this question relate directly to the summaries of the
different eras of Jewish history and migration which we have discussed. When you know the year that an ancestor of yours arrived
on America's shores, you can then link up to general Jewish history
and understand your part in it. For example, let us assume that
your grandfather arrived in the United States in 1907. From that
simple piece of knowledge, you will know, from your understanding of American Jewish history, of what era and what phenomenon
your grandfather was probably a part. A Jew who arrived in the
United States in 1907 was a part of the major wave of Jewish immigration to this country, a mass migration unequaled in Jewish history. Suddenly, when you read a description of the arrival of Jewish
immigrants to a port in the United States in this era, the history is
not anonymous. It is your history.

The date of arrival of a direct ancestor of yours is a special event
in your own personal history regardless of how long ago it took
place. It does not take much of an imagination to understand the
profound impact that the decision to leave and the arrival in
America had, not only on your ancestor but on you as well. There
are many dates which we all have been taught as significant in
history. The date of arrival of an immigrant ancestor should be
among such dates for each of us. Unlike the famous dates of history
shared by all, these dates are personal and meaningful to us as individuals. We each have a personal history as well as a common
history. It is important to know both.

What towns and countries did they come from? This is another
question of importance when pursuing our family histories. How
many of us know the names of the towns left behind by our
immigrant ancestors? How many of us know what the conditions
were like in those towns which forced or provoked our ancestors
to leave? General history tells us about the anti-Semitism, the
economic hardships, and other conditions which plagued Jewish
communities throughout Europe. But what, specifically, was it like
in the places where our families lived for generations in the Old

Country? This is a question which we discuss at greater length in Chapter 5.

Once the decision was made to journey to America, money had to be saved and a steamship ticket had to be purchased. While steamships made their way back and forth across the Atlantic throughout the years, it is hardly enough to know that the type of vehicle used to transport Jewish immigrants was, in fact, a steamship. Rather, how much more alive Jewish history and your own personal history becomes when you know the name of the ship traveled on by your ancestors, and what the ship looked like, both from the outside as well as the conditions lived in for the days of the long journey.

When the ship arrived, it landed in a port. Most often, that port was New York, though Boston, Philadelphia and other seaports were also used. Do you know where your immigrant ancestors arrived? Do you know, in addition, where your ancestors went after they arrived in America? Did they stay in the city of their port of arrival? Or did they travel to some inland city which was the location of a relative who had arrived in America earlier? Or perhaps they went to some unexplored location? Maybe they were sent by an organization set up to aid and relocate immigrants to some rural community or to a job opportunity? The encounter that your immigrant ancestor had with his new country must have been what we now call "culture shock." The United States was very different from the Old Country. The people were different, the language odd, the customs strange. Where did they go? How did they deal with the shock of an alien culture? What organization might they have joined, or helped found, which made life in the United States more manageable?

There are many questions that can be asked and hopefully answered regarding the experiences of your immigrant ancestors. Suppose you discover that an ancestor settled in Richmond, Virginia, but that you have lived all of your life in New York. You will want to learn more about the Jewish community of Richmond at the time that your ancestor was there. Here is one more example of Jewish history coming alive through your family history: Though the history of the Jewish community of Richmond might have once been the farthest thing from your mind, it is now important for you to learn about it—in order for you to understand yourself. When was the Richmond Jewish community founded? Was there a Jewish section of the city? What synagogues existed when my ancestor lived there? Is there a Jewish cemetery there which might have

family members buried? What occupations did Jews have at that
time in Richmond? What made people go to Richmond to live
and what made them leave? Are there any old photographs of the
Richmond Jewish community for that time period so that I can
get an idea of what life was like then and there? Is there a photo
of the street on which my ancestor lived? What other information
can I discover about the city to add to my understanding of my
ancestor's life?

The question of where your ancestors lived is not one of concern
exclusively regarding your immigrant forebears. This is particularly
true for families who have been in America for several generations.
If many generations of some branches of your family have been in
this country for years, you will have the same kinds of questions
for each of them. Where did they live? What were their occupations?
When did they arrive in the places they lived? When did they
marry? What did their homes, their streets, and their neighborhoods
look like? Which synagogues did they belong to? For each generation
before you, back until your immigrant ancestors, you will want to
approach the same questions with interest and research. You will
want to enter their lives as much as possible, knowing the streets in
which they walked, the occupations which earned their living, and
the choices which molded their lives—and yours.

Immigrants often joined and formed organizations known as
landsmannschaften. A landsmannschaft, as noted earlier, is an immigrant benevolent organization formed by the ex-residents of a
particular city, town, shtetl, or region. For example, if you were
an immigrant from Pinsk, you might belong to the Pinsk Society.

Before 1880, landsmannschaften were generally synagogues, each
formed by individuals and families from the same European locality
for the purpose of having a place to pray among one's "people."
However, the rise in Jewish immigration after 1881 brought more
secular organizations of this kind into being. These later benevolent
societies often had synagogues as well, but their purposes were
expanded to include other functions. Often, the landsmannschaften,
as their first order of business, would raise money to buy a burial
plot for the use of families of the membership. Membership would
also offer other advantages, such as sick benefits, interest-free loans,
aid to families during a mourning period, and overseas aid to
members of the town who were still in Europe. The landsmannschaften were also often instrumental in arranging for individuals
and families to come to America. (It should be noted that landsmannschaften have existed and continue in some places to exist in

Latin America, the U.S., Western Europe, and Israel.)

Many cities throughout the U.S. had landsmannschaften. Since New York City and Chicago represent two of the largest Jewish communities in the United States, it is understandable that they had hundreds of landsmannschaften in their midst. In 1914, there were at least 534 landsmannschaften in New York, for example. As time went on, the ancestral home of immigrants faded from their minds. This and the deaths of members over the decades has brought the existence of landsmannschaften almost to a close. While there are still many such organizations functioning, the numbers are minute in comparison with the days when landsmannschaften were major societies. The decline of these groups was well underway by the beginning of the Second World War, although there was a slight revival of activity after the Holocaust when many groups published Memorial Books in honor of the towns which were destroyed (see Chapter 3).

The total experience of your immigrant ancestors, including their homes in the Old Country, their decision to travel to America, their journey aboard a steamship, their arrival in the United States or wherever else they landed, and their lives in their new home, all should have meaning for you. Most importantly, there are many ways in which you can learn about and document those journeys and those lives, to begin to see the experiences of your family as Jewish history, and to see yourself as a part of it as well. Enter Jewish history through the lives of your ancestors and make your own personal connections with your past and your people.

TRACING YOUR JOURNEY

How to Find the Ship Which Brought Your Ancestors to America

The steamships on which your ancestors traveled to America and the dates of their arrival are important in the context of your family history. In the same way that the *Mayflower* was the celebrated ship which took early settlers to the American continent, so too should the steamships in your family history be noted as turning points in your own history.

It is not always easy to find the names of ships, or their arrival date, but with a little detective work, you should be able to do it.

1) The first step, of course, is to ask your relatives if they remember. In cases where your family has been in this country for generations, you cannot expect anyone to know, but in families with more recent arrivals, it is possible that they know. I tried to track down the steamship of my grandmother Helen for a long time with no luck. My grandmother is one of those people (whom you will surely encounter) who does not care to talk much about family history. But one day I decided to ask her if she knew the name of the ship on which she came to America. It did not take her a second to answer, *"The Fatherland."* This was the same woman who refused to tell me her place of birth for months! All of my research time could have been saved if I had begun by asking the immigrant herself. Since then I have asked many immigrants if they knew the name of the ship which took them to America. Most people remember—as if it was yesterday.

2) If your immigrant ancestor is alive and does not remember, ask if he or she came alone or with others. If you get names of others and they are alive, ask them. You have to become a detective, trying to locate leads wherever you can find them.

3) If you have partial information on the ship and its arrival, you might be able to narrow the field by using the *Morton Allen Directory of European Passenger Steamship Arrivals.* This volume, which is a standard book in large public and research libraries, and especially genealogy collections, includes the following information: a year-by-year listing of arrival by steamship companies, dates of arrival, ports of arrival, and the exact names of the steamships. The information is for all vessels arriving in New York between 1890 and 1930, and in Baltimore, Boston, and Philadelphia between 1904 and 1926.

How can you use this directory? Let us assume that you have been told the exact date of arrival (someone might remember the day but not the ship) and the port. The *Morton Allen Directory* has an easy-to-find listing of the ships which arrived in the above-mentioned ports for each day. This will surely narrow the field to just a few. Or you may know the ship and the approximate date, but not an exact date. Again, you can narrow the possibility down considerably by using the directory. In either case, this might be helpful if you are forced to use step number 6 below.

4) One of the pieces of information often given on Petitions for Naturalization or Declarations of Intention is the name of the steamship and date of arrival for the individual who applies for citizenship. See "Naturalization Records." (Page 176.)

5) If you can locate the passenger list of the steamship on which your ancestors arrived in America, you can obviously identify the name of the ship. See "How to Find the Steamship Passenger Lists with Your Ancestors on Them." (Page 171.)

6) A final means of locating this information is the most difficult and time consuming but is certainly a good last resort. Steamship passenger lists are on microfilm at the National Archives and various genealogy libraries. If you know the approximate time of arrival and the port of arrival, you can search through the microfilm looking for the names of your ancestors. See "Your Ancestor's Steamship Passenger Lists."

How to Find the Steamship Passenger Lists with Your Ancestors on Them

One of the most intriguing documents relating to the history of your family is the actual passenger lists of the steamships on which your ancestors traveled. The National Archives has more than 11,000 reels of microfilm containing copies of most passenger lists since 1820.

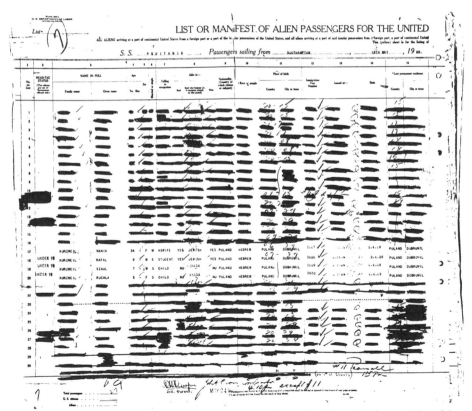

Passenger list of steamship *Aquitania*, arrived in New York on May 24, 1929. The National Archives blackened all names but those in author's family because of confidentiality of information not older than fifty years.

If you know the name of the ship and the date of arrival for an ancestor, the National Archives will check its collection and make copies of the lists for you (and they will bill you; the current fee is $3.00 per list). Or, if you are in Washington, D.C., you can do the research yourself, provided that the ship arrived more than fifty years ago. Lists of ships which arrived since then are confidential. They can be searched, however, by the staff of the National Archives, and they will provide you with the information pertaining to your family alone.

In some cases, the passenger lists have been indexed by name, thereby relieving you of the problem of locating the name and date of the ship by yourself.

To obtain copies of passenger lists, you must fill out GSA Form 7111. Send to:

> National Archives and Records Service
> General Services Administration
> Washington, D.C. 20408

While the information provided on the passenger lists varies from ship to ship and year to year, some of the lists contain quite a bit of information including name, age, occupation, closest living relative at last residence, place of residence, place of birth, and destination in the U.S. These and other facts will be of interest and might serve as the missing clues for additional information.

For example, many passenger lists give place of birth. You might only know the last place where an ancestor lived. This will give you an additional town where your family lived.

The Mormon Church (see page 215) has a microfilm collection of a rather unusual set of passenger lists which are worth noting. Lists were kept in Hamburg of all passengers who left from that port and went to the United States (and elsewhere). The lists provide each passenger's name, occupation, place of birth and residence, age, sex, name of vessel, captain's name, destination, and departure date. The lists were kept from 1850 to 1934 and are indexed by year and first letter of the surname. In other words, if an ancestor of yours went through the port of Hamburg on the way to America, he or she should appear on these lists. If you know the date, you can look in the index under the first letter of the last name and hopefully find it. If you do not know the year, checking various dates would be necessary of course. This resource is more valuable than it might seem at first since many Jews in addition to those from Germany came through Hamburg.

Passenger list of *Mauretania,* arriving in New York on September 23, 1927.

Sometimes the decision to change names was not the immigrant's own. Immigration officials at the ports of entry refused to be bothered with exact transcriptions of a new arrival's difficult name. Down on the forms went totally new or easy names—Smith, Jones, Johnson, Robinson, Taylor, Brown, Black, White, Green. And then there were Jews who named themselves after old streets on the Lower East Side—Clinton, Rivington, Delancy, Rutgers, Stanton, Ludlow. Or when children went to school, teachers who found a name unpronounceable put down on the records something close enough but easier to say. After a time the parents would accept the new name the children brought home.

—MILTON MELTZER, *Taking Root*

How to Obtain Photographs of Your Ancestors' Steamships

While the ships which took our ancestors to America were often overcrowded, uncomfortable, and in poor condition, they were still a profoundly important part of our history. Therefore, an interesting and unusual addition to your family history would be photographs of the steamships themselves.

The Mariners Museum in Newport News, Virginia 23606, has a huge collection of steamship photographs, and their collection is indexed by the name of the ship. You can either write to the museum and allow its staff to choose the photographs for you, or you can consult a large library in your area to see if it has the *Catalog of Marine Photographs* published by the Mariners Museum.

The Mariners Museum will sell you reproductions of its photographs. Send for their price list and details.

Another equally excellent source for these photographs as well as for additional information about steamships and their history is the Steamship Historical Society, 414 Pelton Avenue, Staten Island, N.Y. 10310.

If you want information about the society, write to the above address. However, if you want to obtain photographs of steamships from its huge collection, write to the University of Baltimore Library, 1420 Maryland Avenue, Baltimore, Md. 21201.

The Steamship Historical Photo Bank is located at the University of Baltimore. The collection contains more than 30,000 photos.

Jewish Historical Societies

Many Jewish historical societies can be found around the United States and would be worth contacting for information concerning the regions of which they are a part. Most of these societies hold regular meetings and some publish historical material on a regular basis. If you live in the vicinity of any of these societies you may want to join. Historical societies are always looking for new members.

CALIFORNIA
Western Jewish History Center
2911 Russell Street
Berkeley, California 94705

Southern California Jewish
  Historical Society
6505 Wilshire Boulevard
Los Angeles, California 90048

COLORADO
Rocky Mountain Jewish
  Historical Society
Center for Judaic Studies
University of Denver
Denver, Colorado 80208

CONNECTICUT
Jewish Historical Society of
  New Haven
169 Davenport Avenue
New Haven, Connecticut 06519

Jewish Historical Society of
  Greater Hartford
335 Bloomfield Avenue
West Hartford, Connecticut
  06117

DELAWARE
Jewish Historical Society of
  Delaware
101 Garden of Eden Road
Wilmington, Delaware 19803

FLORIDA
Jewish Historical Society of
  South Florida
c/o American Zionist
  Federation
605 Lincoln Road
Suite 600
Miami Beach, Florida 33139

ILLINOIS
Chicago Jewish Historical
  Society
618 So. Michigan Avenue
Chicago, Illinois 60605

INDIANA
Indiana Jewish Historical
  Society
215 E. Berry Street
Fort Wayne, Indiana 46802

MARYLAND
Jewish Historical Society of
  Annapolis
24 Romar Street
Annapolis, Maryland 21403

Jewish Historical Society of
  Maryland
5800 Park Heights Avenue
Baltimore, Maryland 21215

MASSACHUSETTS
North Shore Jewish Historical
  Society
4 Community Road
Marblehead, Massachusetts
  01945

MICHIGAN
Jewish Historical Society of
  Michigan
21720 Parklawn Avenue
Oak Park, Michigan 48237

NEW JERSEY
Jewish Historical Society of the
  Raritan Valley
1050 George Street, Box 1-L
New Brunswick, New Jersey
  08901

Jewish Historical Society of
  Trenton
999 Lower Ferry Road
Box 7249
Trenton, New Jersey 08628

NEW YORK
Jewish Historical Society of
  New York
8 West 70th Street
New York, New York 10023

NORTH DAKOTA
Jewish Historical Project
c/o Ms. Toba Geller
417 Oakland
Fargo, North Dakota 58103

OHIO
Cleveland Jewish Archives
Western Reserve Historical
  Society
10825 East Boulevard
Cleveland, Ohio 44106

Columbus Jewish History
  Project
Ohio Historical Society
1-71 and 17th Avenue
Columbus, Ohio 43211

OREGON
Jewish Historical Society of
  Oregon
6651 S.W. Capitol Highway
Portland, Oregon 97219

PENNSYLVANIA
Philadelphia Jewish Archives
  Center
625 Walnut Street
Philadelphia, Pennsylvania
  19106

RHODE ISLAND
Rhode Island Jewish Historical
  Association
130 Sessions Street
Providence, Rhode Island 02906

(The South)
Southern Jewish Historical
  Society
Valdosta State College
Box 179
Valdosta, Georgia 31601

WASHINGTON
Jewish Archives Project
University of Washington
  Libraries
Manuscripts Collection
Seattle, Washington 98195

WASHINGTON, D.C.
Jewish Historical Society of
  Greater Washington
701 Third Street N.W.
Washington, D.C. 20001

WISCONSIN
Wisconsin Jewish Archives
State Historical Society of
  Wisconsin
816 State Street
Madison, Wisconsin 53706

CANADA
Jewish Historical Society
Archives and Museum of
  Western Canada
Suite 403
322 Donald Street
Winnipeg, Manitoba R3B 2K3

Jewish Historical Society of
  Western Canada
365 Hargrove Street
Suite 402
Winnipeg, Manitoba R3B 2K3

Toronto Jewish Historical
  Society
21 Prince Charles Drive
Toronto, Ontario M6A 2H1

Ottawa Jewish Historical
  Society
151 Chapel Street
Ottawa, Ontario K1N 7Y2

Jewish Historical Society of
  British Columbia
950 West 41st Avenue
Vancouver, British Columbia
  V5Z 2N7

UNITED STATES
American Jewish Historical
  Society
2 Thornton Road
Waltham, Massachusetts 02154

We cannot rid ourselves of the past without destroying our present and ruining our future.

—HARRY WOLFSON, "Escaping Judaism"

Naturalization Records: An Important Genealogical Source

Finding naturalization records is not like looking for a needle in a haystack. It can be worse. First you have to find the haystack. (It's not easy to find the "haystacks" of naturalization records since they are scattered all over the place, look different, and are often hidden under haystacks of other kinds of documents.) Once you find the haystack, looking for the needle (the papers that *you* want) requires you to have certain amounts of knowledge, skill—or luck. But the final problem is this: however difficult it might be to find a needle in a haystack, the saving grace is your assumption that the needle is in there somewhere. But in searching for naturalization records of an ancestor, you can never know if you will find what you are looking for. In fact, you can never be sure that the documents even exist.

With that pessimistic introduction, we have to attempt to tackle the problem of naturalization records because they often are profoundly important sources of information—genealogically. One personal illustration will suffice: after sending for my great-grandfather's naturalization records, I received a reply from the Immigration and Naturalization Service which gave me my great-grandfather's birthdate, place of birth (in Europe), place of last residence (in Europe), his first wife's name (she died in Europe and never came to America), the date of his arrival (this allowed me to get a copy of the passenger list of the ship), and the names and birthdates of all his children—some of whom were killed in the Holocaust and whom I would never have been able to learn much about!

How did I get the document which provided me with so much information? I simply sent a letter to the Immigration and Naturalization Service, telling them what I wanted. They sent back a form. I filled it out. And in a few weeks I received the information. All for $5.

If it's that easy, then what was the "needle in a haystack" business all about?

The answer is that it can be easy, and it can be terribly difficult, depending upon when your immigrant ancestor arrived in America and petitioned to become a citizen.

But let's start at the beginning. We are looking for naturalization records, better known as citizenship papers. On your family tree, only your immigrant ancestors might have naturalization records on file. Ancestors of yours who never came to America would not have become citizens, obviously, and those ancestors (or family members) who were born in the United States were automatically citizens—and therefore never had to fill out papers. But for your immigrant relatives, citizenship papers might very well be on file somewhere in the United States. As a genealogist you should be interested in finding those records.

There are three different types of naturalization records. The first is the Declaration of Intention which was filled out by an immigrant who wanted to become a citizen. This Declaration of Intention was commonly known as one's "first papers." Then there is the Final Petition which was completed just prior to becoming

Form 2200
U. S. DEPARTMENT OF LABOR
NATURALIZATION SERVICE

DUPLICATE
(to be given to the declarant of intention)

No. 114411

UNITED STATES OF AMERICA

DECLARATION OF INTENTION

☞ **Invalid for all purposes seven years after the date hereof**

State of New York,
Southern District of New York, } ss.:

In the District Court of the United States.

I, **Samuel Leib Gottlieb**, aged **32** years,
occupation **Salesman**, do declare on oath that my personal
description is: Color **white**, complexion **dark**, height **5** feet **6** inches,
weight **140** pounds, color of hair **brown**, color of eyes **brown**,
other visible distinctive marks **none**,
I was born in **Borgo Prund, Hungary,**
on the **8th** day of **June**, anno Domini 1 **890**; I now reside
at **217 East 66th St.,**, New York City, N. Y.
I emigrated to the United States of America from **Bremen,**
on the vessel **Cronprinzessin Cecilia,**; my last
foreign residence was **Hungary,**; I am **married**: the name
of my wife is **Helen**; she was born at **Hungary**
and now resides at **with me.**
It is my bona fide intention to renounce forever all allegiance and fidelity to any foreign
prince, potentate, state, or sovereignty, and particularly to
Hungary of whom I am now a subject:
I arrived at the port of **N. Y.**, in the
State of **N. Y.**, on or about the **16th** day
of **Jan.**, anno Domini 1 **907**: I am not an anarchist; I am not a
polygamist nor a believer in the practice of polygamy; and it is my intention in good faith
to become a citizen of the United States of America and to permanently reside therein:
SO HELP ME GOD.

X *Samuel Leib Gottlieb*
(original signature of declarant.)

Subscribed and sworn to before me in the office of the Clerk of said Court

[SEAL.]

at New York City, N. Y., this **1** day of **Feb.**,
anno Domini 19 **23**.

Deputy Clerk of the District Court of the United States.

"Declaration of Intention" of Samuel L. Gottlieb to become a U.S. citizen in 1923. (Courtesy of Samuel L. Gottlieb)

a citizen. And finally there is the Certificate of Naturalization which is the document given to the new citizen which declares that citizenship has been granted.

Among old family papers you can often find the Certificate of

Naturalization, but this is the least valuable document in terms of information about the individual. The Declaration of Intention and the Final Petition are the most valuable because they often asked several personal questions of genealogical interest, such as occupation, date and place of birth, name of ship and date of arrival, and details on spouse and children.

There are a few more things to know before we discuss the locations of naturalization records. While we may assume that immigrants became citizens (unless we know for sure that someone did not), it is possible that an immigrant ancestor of yours never applied for citizenship. Indeed, you may have a grandparent still alive who was an immigrant and who is not a citizen.

Also be aware of the fact that children under sixteen automatically became citizens when their parents were naturalized, and furthermore that until 1922 a wife automatically became a citizen either by marrying a citizen or by the naturalization of her husband.

The key date in the story of naturalization records is September 26, 1906. It was on that date that citizenship procedures became a Federal function. If you are looking for the naturalization records of someone who was naturalized on or after September 26, 1906, you will usually have an easy time of searching. How do you know if your ancestor was naturalized on or after this date? You don't. But by asking a few questions within your family you will probably have a good sense of when the immigration occurred and therefore when the naturalization could possibly have taken place.

If you have reason to believe that the naturalization of interest to you took place after this date, you are advised to write to: U.S. Immigration and Naturalization Service, Washington, D.C. 20536.

Ask them for a few copies of Form G-641 (Application for Verification of Information from Immigration and Naturalization Service Records). Don't write them a long letter describing your great-grandmother and her trip to America or any other information of a personal nature. No matter what you write, however long, short, or interesting, if it has to do with naturalization records, they will send you Form G-641. So, you might as well ask for it right from the start. And again, ask for a few; it will save you time when you want more.

Fill out the form as best you can. Do not be alarmed when you find that you cannot fill out but 3 percent of the form. The Immigration and Naturalization Service has the nice policy of working with whatever information you can give them. If *all* you have is your ancestor's name, then fill that in and leave everything else blank. But the more you can fill out, the better chance you have of locating the document—or the right document. (Once, when all I knew was the person's name, I received the papers of someone with the same name, but an entirely different individual.)

After you fill out the form and send your check (current fee is $5.00) you will wait a few weeks (sometimes more) and will hopefully receive the information you are looking for. One thing I have yet to figure out is the Immigration and Naturalization Service policy on sending information. Sometimes I receive photocopies of the desired documents and sometimes I receive a letter which contains a transcription of the information on the original documents.

What if you are sure that a person was naturalized but the Immigration and Naturalization Service tells you they have nothing? Then, either the person was naturalized before September 26, 1906, or a clerk made a mistake (which wouldn't be the first time). As far as a clerical error is concerned, all you can do is try again (unless you want to—and are able to—examine the documents yourself, which we will discuss in a little while). But if the person was naturalized before our key date, then the fun begins.

Before September 26, 1906, naturalizations were a local function and naturalization proceedings took place in just about any court, Federal, state, or local. While naturalizations took place in courts around the country after our key date, it was only then that the courts were required to send the information to the Federal Government for processing and filing.

Besides the lack of centralization of these documents before 1906, the procedures also varied. Therefore, different questions were asked of the potential citizen and different records were kept. So, while the type of information on post-1906 naturalization records is basically standard, the pre-1906 information varies from next to nothing but the person's name and former country on up.

Let us say that you are looking for the naturalization records of someone who arrived in the United States well before September 26, 1906. I say "well before" because if the immigrant arrived shortly before that cutoff date, there is still a good chance that the naturalization took place after the 1906 date. It is here where excellent detective work is essential. What you must try to determine is where the immigrant whose papers you are looking for entered the United States (which port) and where he or she resided right after arrival.

Once you have determined this (to any degree of accuracy), you must try to determine to which court the immigrant might have gone to file "first papers." Of course, there is no guarantee that the immigrant filed for citizenship immediately upon arrival. He might have waited ten years (at which time he could have been living in another city) or he could have never gotten around to becoming a citizen.

But we have to assume that the immigrant became a citizen, and we must also begin somewhere in our search. The best bet is to start at the location where the person entered the country and first resided. Finding the right court is not easy. It takes patience, time, and lots of letter writing—unless you can travel to the city in mind, in which case you might either get the search done quickly or you might reach a dead end. If this all sounds very negative, it is meant to.

The process of searching for pre-1906 naturalization records can be difficult, especially if you have little information to go on. Of course, if someone entered the U.S. in Boston and then spent all his life there, the search would not be too difficult. You would have the field narrowed, and it would just be a limited amount of leg work. But the more vague your information is, the more difficulty you will have.

An excellent book which tackles this very problem head-on is well worth the purchase or use if you are searching for naturalization records. This book is *Locating Your Immigrant Ancestors, A Guide to Naturalization Records,* by James C. Neagles and Lila Lee Neagles, published in 1975. (Available for $7.00 from The Everton Publishers, Inc., P.O. Box 368, Logan, Utah 84321.) The bulk of this volume is a state-by-state, county-by-county, listing of courts and what records they have, for what years. In addition, if the records are indexed the book will indicate this. (The subject of indexing is quite important since locating the court of a certain naturalization is not the same as locating the document that you want; if the documents are not indexed in some way, then you are not only looking for a needle in a haystack but rather in a barn!)

While we are on the subject of indexes, we might as well discuss a body of indexes of naturalization records which can save years of work, depending upon the location you are dealing with. During the Great Depression, the Works Progress Administration (WPA) put people to work doing various interesting and unusual tasks. One of them was the photocopying and indexing of pre-1906 naturalization records for certain locations. If the naturalization which you are looking for took place in the states of Maine, Massachusetts, New Hampshire, or Rhode Island, or in New York City, you're in luck. The National Archives in Washington has the Soundex indexes and photocopies for these New England states.

Since New York City was not only the entering point for most Jews to the United States but also the home of the greatest number of Jews, it would be justified to go into more detail here regarding naturalization resources for New York City.

The Federal Archives and Records Center located in Bayonne, New Jersey (Building 22 at the Military Ocean Terminal) has an excellent collection of naturalization records for New York City.

The holdings in Bayonne are a large, but not complete, collection of New York City naturalizations. For example, the county clerk of each county in New York has the records of those naturalizations which occurred in the State Supreme Court of that particular county. Other records are scattered elsewhere as well. In fact, this situation of the non-centralization of these records is a good example of what the researcher has to often face when trying to locate naturalization records.

A trip to the Records Center in Bayonne would be worthwhile for all people doing searches of these documents for the New York City area. If you are unable to travel to Bayonne, you can write them at:

> National Archives and Records Service
> Federal Archives and Records Center
> Archives Branch
> Building 22—MOT Bayonne
> Bayonne, NJ 07002
> Phone: (201) 858-7245.

There is one important reason why a trip to the Records Center (or any archives) is worthwhile. A clerk will try to answer a specific question. However, in my opinion, you and you alone can do an adequate search. You can look for a dozen alternate spellings of a name while a clerk will usually only check the spelling provided. In addition, every researcher knows that you always learn more than just what you are looking for—*if* you do it yourself!

Finding naturalization records is not easy but is certainly worthwhile. Be aware, of course, that the earlier the naturalization took place, the less information there is likely to be. However, you can never know what you might find until you try.

> With our despised immigrant clothing we shed our impossible Hebrew names. A committee of our friends, several years ahead of us in American experience, put their heads

together and concocted American names for us all. Those of our real names that had no pleasing American equivalents they ruthlessly discarded, content if they retained the initials. My mother, possessing a name that was not easily translatable, was punished with the undignified nickname of Annie. Fetchke, Joseph, and Deborah issues as Frieda, Joseph, and Dora, respectively. As for poor me, I was simply cheated. The name they gave me was hardly new. My Hebrew name being Maryashe in full, Mashke for short, Russianized into Marya, my friends said that it would hold good in English as Mary; which was very disappointing, as I longed to possess a strange-sounding American name like the others.

—MARY ANTIN, *The Promised Land*

American Jewish Historical Society

The American Jewish Historical Society (AJHS) functions as a library, an archive, an organization, and a publisher. Its publication, *American Jewish History*, formerly *American Jewish Historical Quarterly*, is an excellent journal devoted mainly to American Jewish history. Often in this journal you will find specialized articles on the history of a particular location or family.

As a library and archive, the AJHS can be most helpful in your family history research when it comes to synagogue records, family histories which have been published, genealogies, Jewish organization records, and town histories (towns in the U.S.). The library staff is quite helpful. I have made many inquiries through the mail over the years and I always receive a prompt and thorough reply. However, it would be best to visit the society if you can, particularly if a reply through the mail indicates material of interest; you cannot expect the librarians to do too much research for you.

It would be appropriate to mention the AJHS as a good depository of Jewish records—if you have records of your own. Too often, people discard records of synagogues, charitable organizations, landsmannschaften, and the like, throwing away gems of history. If you know of any Jewish records or other items of Jewish historical interest, contact the American Jewish Historical Society or the American Jewish Archives (see page 184).

American Jewish Historical Society
2 Thornton Road
Waltham, Mass. 02154

The future of Judaism belongs to that school which can best understand the past.

—LEOPOLD LOEW, Hungarian rabbi

American Jewish Archives

This archive, founded in 1947, is devoted to collecting historical documents relating to American Jewry. Of special interest to the family history researcher is their collection of family trees and family histories, both numbering in the hundreds. The AJA also has a large collection of synagogue records (mostly Reform, though others as well, because of their affiliation with the Reform Movement) which would be quite valuable if your family belonged to one of the synagogues whose records are deposited there.

The AJA answers inquiries through the mail and often will photocopy relevant material. You cannot expect them to do much research for you, but they are willing to make initial searches to determine whether they have something of interest.

For doing research regarding a town or city in the U.S. they also have much material of worth.

If you have published a family history, town history, or even have simply drawn a family tree, it would be nice to send a copy to the AJA. Not only will this make your work available to others, but they may also print a reference to it in an issue of their publication *American Jewish Archives* alerting their readership to it. Your work will then become a part of their holdings; you can never tell when a person might check the AJA for a certain surname and it will be yours. Depositing your research at the AJA is also serving the cause of American Jewish history. The address is:

American Jewish Archives
3101 Clifton Avenue
Cincinnati, Ohio 45220

Research into the past, as an aim in itself, without the present, is not worth a bean.

—BIALIK

Sending for Family History Documents Is Legitimate

As you send for all of the different kinds of documents available which will help you to research your family history, you might wonder whether the U.S. Government and local government agencies

Marriage record, 1858, from Congregation Bnai Jeshurun, New York City. (Courtesy of American Jewish Archives, Cincinnati) see your requests for information as important enough for them to help you. *Never worry.* Not only are you entitled to see the kinds of records which are described in this book, but you will also be paying for almost everything. Government documents cost generally between $2 and $10—and considering the simple process required for most document searches, it becomes a rather lucrative business for government agencies.

So, never feel that your family history is not "important" and that you will get a response only if you are on "official" business. Family history and genealogy is a legitimate and accepted endeavor.

> Everything that typified the old country, in family names as well as first names, had to go. The Russian -skis and -vitches were dropped. Levinsky became Levin, Michaelowitch, Michaels. Russian and Polish names were Anglicized: Bochlowitz to Buckley, Stepinsky to Stevens, Shidlowsky to Sheldon, Horowitz to Herrick, Willinshky to Wilson. Davidowitz became Davidson, Jacobson became Jackson. The Germanic names too were readily translated into English: Weiss-White, Preiss-Price, Reiss-Rice, Rothenberg-Redmont.
>
> —MILTON MELTZER, *Taking Root*

Rabbi Malcolm Stern

When I first began my own Jewish genealogy research I wrote a letter to Rabbi Malcolm Stern, the genealogist of the American Jewish Archives. Although Rabbi Stern's expertise is early American Jewish history, I wrote to him because he was the only person I could find "in print" on the subject of Jewish genealogy. Rabbi Stern had published a monumental book, *Americans of Jewish Descent*, which is essentially a collection and compilation of genealogies of Jewish families who were in North America before the year 1840. The book traces these "early" American Jewish families from their arrival in America to the present.

While my family arrived in this country long after 1840 (Rabbi Stern's cutoff date), I wrote him, asking for clues and hints as to how to do my family research. Rabbi Stern wrote me several long letters in reply to my letters. While he was not aware of much by way of Eastern European research or recent Jewish migration, he was able to share some information and much encouragement. I was honored to receive such long letters from him, and it was not until years later, when Rabbi Stern and I became friends, that I saw his letter file: He had written, over the years, hundreds of similar letters to others who also had asked for advice. Rabbi Malcolm Stern is not only "the dean of American Jewish genealogists" as he is often called, but is also one of the kindest and most generous men I have ever met.

An updated version of Rabbi Stern's book has been published. Titled *First American Jewish Families*, the book consists of 600 genealogies from 1654 to 1977. The index contains more than 40,000 names. The book is available from:

> KTAV Publishing House
> 75 Varick Street
> New York, N.Y. 10013

If your Jewish family arrived in the U.S. before 1840, it is probably in this book. If it is not, Rabbi Stern would like to know about it and he can be reached c/o:

> American Jewish Archives
> 3101 Clifton Ave.
> Cincinnati, Ohio 45220

He has a great future, for he understands the past.

—HEINRICH HEINE

Chapter 5

Walking the Streets
of Your Shtetl

It is startling to realize the extent to which we are affected by the lives of our ancestors.

It is equally startling to realize the extent to which we are distant from the lifestyles of those same ancestors.

The more we examine the past from which we have come, the more we make these discoveries. We find many aspects of our family histories which have survived throughout generations, and we also find many aspects of the lives of past generations which are strange to us, as if we were examining an alien culture.

Of course, the lives of our ancestors *are*, to a significant degree, alien. Life in a European shtetl was far different from, say, urban life in the United States. Our language is different, our educations are different, the pace of our lives is different, and the structure of our communities is different. When we take a journey back through time and arrive at the places where our ancestors lived, we must be introduced to the streets, the houses, and the faces as if we were strangers.

If you are like most Jews in America, it is merely a few generations ago, at most, when your parents, grandparents, or great-grandparents, walked the streets of European cities, towns, and villages. Of course, there are those Jewish families who have been in America for more than a century, and there are others who do not come from Europe, but generally, the Jewish community in the United States can find its roots in the Eastern European shtetlach which peppered the map a mere generation ago.

The Jewish towns and villages which were the homes of our ancestors for generations no longer exist in Eastern Europe. Most of the Jews in those places were murdered; many of the towns were destroyed. To imagine this is almost impossible. Millions of Jews living in thousands of towns, and suddenly, in a few years, it is all gone.

Yet we yearn to know those places, to see the streets on which our ancestors, as children, played; to see the shops in which our ancestors, as adults, earned their living. We want to see the fields, on which they tilled the soil, to enter the shuls in which they prayed to God and celebrated their Jewish lives. We want to know those places. We want to understand what it was like to live in those communities. We want to know what our ancestors wore, what issues concerned them, and how they lived their lives. We want to enter the school rooms and see the chairs on which we might ourselves have sat, had our families not left, or been chased out, or been destroyed. We want to know where our families lived and through them where *we* lived.

We cannot return to those places. We can take journeys to those towns and see different worlds from the ones which our ancestors left. We can walk the streets today, and wonder what the roads look like beneath the pavement that has since been laid. Often we can visit a town of our ancestors and see the synagogue which still stands, or visit the Jewish cemetery which may still be intact. But we can never return, through space, to those places of our ancestors.

Weinstein family from Pinsk, Russia, ca. 1895. (Courtesy of Bella Lande)

Yet we can journey to them—in Time. We can travel there in our imaginations, helped along by that which has survived: facts, photographs, and tales all adding to the stories of our families, all helping us to understand from where we came.

Each Jewish community in the world, whether it be in Eastern or Western Europe, Asia, the Americas, or elsewhere, has its own history, and the telling of each community history would be impractical or impossible here. Our ancestors each came from different spots on the globe, and the time in which they lived in these places will change the perspective taken to understand their lives. For example, if an ancestor lived in Germany, the history of that particular family would differ greatly depending upon what period of history we are speaking. A Jewish family in Germany in 1812 had a very different experience from a Jewish family in Germany in 1934. Another example is the shtetl where my father was born. When asked, "Where were you born?" he would answer, "Dobromil, Poland." When I ask his uncle where he was born, he would say, "Dobromil, Austria." If I were to visit Dobromil today, I would go to Russia. The same thing is true for many locations in Europe. The history of that continent is filled with border changes, sometimes so frequent that each generation finds itself in the same town, but in different countries.

But we still want to visit those places, in Time, trying to recreate what it was like for our forebears. We want to know whatever we can about the lives of our ancestors, so that the more we know of the places where they spent their lives, the more we will know about them.

What has remained of those towns, cities, shtetlach, and villages which were once the homes of our ancestors? What can we discover about them?

We can find photographs of these places, helping us to imagine the streets that our ancestors walked and the buildings in which they lived and worked. We can find histories that have been written about the tiniest locations where Jewish communities existed. We can learn about the religious life of the communities, discovering which rabbis taught in which communities and what these rabbis wrote and taught. This would allow us to understand some of the religious influences upon our ancestors. We can learn quite a bit about the most remote places, mostly because of the historical instinct of so many people who have come from these towns. In a vast number of cases we find examples of individuals who knew the worth of recording the present which, for us, has turned into precious history. Our Jewish libraries are filled with a wealth of information about the Jewish communities which are no longer here. It is up to us to discover those communities, to enter them in our minds, to relive those experiences, and to connect with our past.

DISCOVERING THE OLD COUNTRY

YIVO Institute for Jewish Research

The YIVO Institute for Jewish Research, located at 1048 Fifth Avenue, New York, N.Y. 10028, is a pot of gold at the end of the rainbow for the student of Eastern European Jewry. The YIVO library and archives collections are filled with material on seemingly every aspect of the history of Eastern European Jewry. Equal to their superb collection is their helpful staff, who are aware of the fact that many of us cannot read the material in all the languages represented there and do everything they can to help the researcher. But, do not expect them to translate for you! This would be unreasonable to request.

YIVO (whose initials stand for Yidisher Visnshaftlekher Institut) was founded in Vilna in 1925. Its history is a story in itself, particularly in light of the fact that the Germans seized YIVO's collection in 1940. Much of it was recovered. Today, the institution can be found on the corner of 86th Street and Fifth Avenue in Manhattan, right down the street from the Jewish Museum. YIVO must be visited by anyone interested in the Jews of Eastern Europe.

While YIVO cannot be of much help when you are doing research on individual family members, there is no finer place to find background material on locations in Eastern Europe. Reference to various parts of YIVO's collection are mentioned throughout this book. Of particular note, however, are the several photography collections there. There is a collection of more than 10,000 photographs, for example, indexed by town, for Poland and Russia. In other words, there is a good possibility that you can find photographs of the smallest towns at YIVO. There are several other photograph collections at YIVO as well, all indexed by location, so that it is easy to locate pictures of specific locations throughout Europe.

It would take weeks to discover all of the resources at YIVO, and this would be time well spent. I myself discovered the first reference to my great-great-great-grandfather, the Stropkover Rebbe, at YIVO.

In 1977, Schocken Books published a beautiful book drawn from YIVO's Polish photograph collection. Titled *Image Before My Eyes; a Photographic History of Jewish Life in Poland, 1864-1939*, the book is the result of the skillful and scholarly efforts of

Lucjan Dobroszycki and Barbara Kirshenblatt-Gimblett. An historian and folklorist at YIVO respectively, the two authors have produced a book which should be in the home library of anyone with the slightest interest in Jewish history in general and Polish-Jewish history in particular. One of the most remarkable results of the book's publication has been the large number of people who have recognized people in the old photographs in the book.

> Yesterday did not vanish, but lives.
> —ELISHEBA, Hebrew poet

Memorial Books

One of the best sources for learning about Jewish communities are Memorial Books, mentioned before. These volumes, also known as Yiskor Books, are books of several hundred pages, which tell the story of the Jewish community of one town (or a town and surrounding villages). The Memorial Books have been published and continue to be published by landsmannschaften. Members of landsmannschaften, because of their affection for their old community as well as their admirable historical sense, have published these books as a tribute to their old homes and the people who were murdered during the Holocaust.

Several hundred Memorial Books corresponding to the same number of villages, shtetlach, and cities have been published. Often the tiniest village will have a large book devoted to its history, reflecting the devotion of the survivors. The bulk of the Memorial Books have been published since the Holocaust, though many books of a similar nature were published before the current era. Often a book would be written and published to describe a tragic event in the life of the community, and to memorialize the victims of that event. Many books can be found in response to pogroms, for example.

The post-World War II Memorial Books usually take the same or similar format. There are historical articles about the location, photographs, maps, illustrations, and names of Holocaust victims. Often advertisements can also be found in the books; in these cases, space was sold to survivors in order to raise publication money. These advertisements are good sources in themselves for information about individuals. The ads often contain photographs.

The Memorial Books have usually been written by many people. The landsmannschaften gather articles on different aspects of life in the location, and these are collected for the book. While the

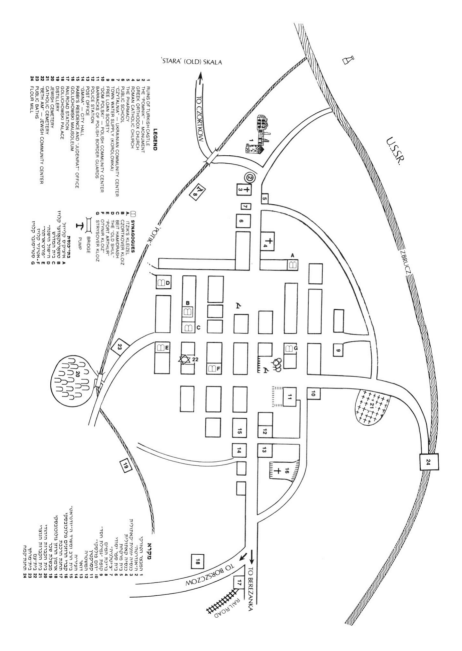

Map of the shtetl Skala in Poland. Most Memorial Books contain maps of the towns they discuss, drawn from the memories of the survivors.

major emphasis of the Memorial Books is the fate of the town during the Holocaust, the books also contain some of the finest historical material about the town. It is for this reason that Memorial Books are a good general source, regardless of when a family left a town. Even if your family left the town of Skala in 1901, the Skala Memorial Book would be of interest.

While the Jewish communities of Eastern Europe have been the largest producers of Memorial Books, Jewish communities in Western Europe, especially Germany, have produced many as well. However, a general difference between most of the German works and the Eastern European Memorial Books, is that the German books are usually the effort of one person, while the Eastern European books are collective works.

One of the drawbacks to the use of Memorial Books for many people is that they are written primarily in Hebrew and Yiddish, although many books have English sections which consist of translations of some of the Yiddish or Hebrew, in most cases. However, this should not stop you from examining these books. Certainly, people can be found who can translate the material. In addition, the photographs contained within the books are wonderful to experience. Often, of course, the photographs are hardly "wonderful," however, for they will be of Holocaust atrocities which took place in the locations discussed in the books.

Another feature of a majority of these books is a name index which is of great assistance when doing family history. The indexes are never complete, though, and should not be relied upon as the only thing to check for family history.

Memorial Books can be used in a variety of ways. The most obvious is to read them to find material on members of your family. This is *not* unlikely, particularly since in the case of smaller communities the chances of your being related to many people in the town, through marriage if nothing else, are great. But in addition to personal family research, Memorial Books can provide other information. We have already mentioned the value of the photographs, which are often the greatest source of photographs on particular towns that exists. Memorial Books also often discuss religious life in the towns, and frequently focus in on the rabbis or Masters who taught in the town. The influence of a rabbi on his following was often (and continues to be for many) the most profound in a person's life. There is little question but that knowledge about an ancestor's rabbi or rebbe is knowledge about an ancestor.

Many of the Memorial Books have street maps of the towns as well. These maps range from the most general views to house-to-house detail. Often you can, with the aid of a relative who was from the town, locate the exact place where your family's home stood. These maps can also give you a vivid idea of the size of the town of your ancestral home.

In the same way that you can "enter" the life of an historic figure by reading his or her biography, you can enter the towns of your ancestors by reading the biographies of the towns themselves. Memorial Books are exactly that: biographies of towns which no longer exist, but which at one time were known as home to your ancestors. The following is a country-by-country, town-by-town listing of places about which Memorial Books have been written. This is probably the most complete list in print since it is drawn from what was the most complete list to date plus additions which I have made.

The "Bibliographical List of Memorial Books Published in the Years 1943-1972" by David Bass was published in *Yad Vashem Studies on the European Jewish Catastrophe and Resistance, IX*, Jerusalem, 1973. The Memorial Books in the Bass bibliography plus others which were either left out or published since then make up this list.

Keep in mind that there may still be some additional towns which have books which bear their name and which are not represented.

Note: The towns are to be found under the country based on a 1939 map.

Austria
Eisenstadt
Wien (Vienna)

Bulgaria
Bulgaria

Czechoslovakia
Bratislava
Brezova
Michalovce
Mikulov
Mukocevo (Munkács)
Myjava

Piestany
Podkapatska Rus
(Karpatorus)
Uzhorod (Ungvar)
Vrbove

Germany
Altona
Berlin
Braunschweig
Hagen
Hamburg
Siegen
Wandsbek

Greece
Thessalonica (Salonika)

Hungary
Balmazujvaros
Bethlen
Budapest
Csenger
Debrecen
Derecske
Des
Fehergyarmat
Hajdunanas
Hajdusamson
Konyar
Magyarlapos
Mikepercs
Nagyilonda
Paks
Porcsalma
Retteg
Teglas
Vamospercs

Latvia
Bausk
Daugavpils
Liepaja
Ludza
Riga
Shimberg (Scheinberg)
Ventspils

Lithuania
Alsedziai
Alytus
Aukstadvaris
Birzai
Dusetos
Gargzdai
Janova
Jeznas
Jurbarkas

Kalvarija
Kaunas
Kedainiai
Kelme
Klaipëda
Krekenava
Kudirkos Naumiestis
Linkuva
Lithuania
Marijampole
Merkine
Moletai
Obeliai
Palanga
Panevezys
Pasvalys
Pasvitinys
Pumpenei
Raguva
Ratnitcha
Rokiskis (Rakishok)
Siauliai
Sirvintai
Skaudvile
Skuodas
Taurage
Telsiai
Ukmerge
Vaskai
Vilkaviskis
Virbalis
Vyzunonos

Poland
Aleksandrow (Aleksander)
Andrychow
Augustow
Bakalarzewo
Baranow
Baranowicze (Baranowitz)
Bedzin (Bendin)
Belchatow

Beligrod
Beresteczko
Bereza-Kartuska
Berenzo (Berezne)
Biala Podlaska
Bialystok
Biecz
Bielica (Belitsa)
Biezun
Bilgoraj
Bobrka
Bolechow
Bolimow
Boremel
Borszczow (Borstchoff)
Boryslaw
Bransk (Brainsk)
Brody
Brzesc Kujawski
Brzesi nad Bugiem
Brzeziny
Brzeznica
Bucsacz (Buchacz)
Budzanow
Bukaczowce
Bukowsko
Bursztyn
Busk
Bychawa
Byten
Charsznica
Chelm
Chmielnik
Chodecz
Chorostkow
Chorzele
Ciechanow
Ciechanowiec
Ciechocinek
Cieszanow
Cmielow
Czarnkow

Czerbin
Czestochowa
Czortkow
Czyzewo
Dabrowa Gornicza
Dabrowica (Dombrovitsa)
Daugieliszki
Dawidgrodek (Davidgrodek)
Debica
Deblin (Demblin)
Delatycze
Dereczyn (Deretchin)
Derewno
Dobromil
Dobryn
Dobrzyn
Dokszyce
Drodzyn
Drohiczyn
Drohobycz
Druja
Druzkopol (Droshkopol)
Dubno
Dukszty
Dunilowicze
Dzisna (Disna)
Ejszyszki
Falenica
Filipow
Frampol
Gabin
Galicia
Garwolin
Glebokie
Gliniany (Gline)
Gniewaszow
Golub
Goniadz
Gorlice
Gostynin
Goworowo
Grayevo

Grodek
Grojec (Gritze)
Hoduciszki
Holszany
Holynka
Horochow (Horochiv)
Horodec
Horodenka
Horodlo
Horodno
Horyngrod
Hoszcza (Hoshch)
Hrubieszow
Husiatyn
Ilia
Iwie
Jadow
Janow
Jaworow
Jedrzejow
Jezierna
Jezierzany
Kadzidlo
Kalisz (Kalish)
Kaluszyn (Kalushin)
Kalwaria
Kamien Koszyrski
Kamiensk
Karczew (Kartchev)
Kazimierz (Kuzmir)
Kielce (Kielts)
Kiemieliszki
Kiernozia
Kleck (Klezk)
Klobucko (Klobutsk)
Knihynicze
Kobryn
Kobylnik
Kock (Kozk)
Kolbuszowa (Kolbasov)
Kolno
Kolo

Kolomyja (Kolomey)
Kolonia Synajska
Koltyniany
Konin
Koprzywnica
Korczyna
Korelicze
Korzec (Korets)
Koscow (East Galicia)
Kostopol
Kowal
Kowel
Kozangrodek
Koziany
Kozieniec
Krakow (Cracow)
Krashnik
Krasnobrod
Krasynstaw
Krosniewiec
Krynki
Krzemienica
Krzemieniec (Krenenits)
Ksiaz Wielki
Kunow
Kurow (Koriv)
Kurzeniec
Kutno
Kuty
Lachowicze
Lachwa
Lancut (Lanzut)
Lanowce (Lanovits)
Lask
Leczyca (Lintschits)
Lenin
Lesko
Lezajsk (Lezhensk)
Lida
Lipniszki (Lipnishok)
Lodz
Lomza

Losice (Loshits)
Lowicz
Lobartow (Levartov)
Lubcza (Lubtch)
Lublin
Lubraniec
Luck (Lutzk)
Ludwipol
Lukow
Luniniec
Lutowiska
Lwow
Lyngmiany
Lynki
Lyntupy
Lyskow
Lyszkowice
Makow-Mazowiecki
Malecz
Markuszow
Medenice
Miechow
Miedzyrzec (Mezritch)
Miedzyrzec-Wolyn
Mielnica
Mir
Mizocz
Mlawa
Mlynow
Mszczonow
Murawica
Mysleniec
Myszyiec
Nadarzyn
Naliboki (Nalibok)
Nieszawa
Nowe Miasto
Nowogrod
Nowogrodek (Navaredok)
Nowo-Swieciany
Nowy Dwor
Nowy Sacz (Santz)

Nowy Zagorz
Olkeniki
Opatow (Apt)
Orlowa
Osiek
Ostrog (Ostra)
Ostroleka
Ostrow-Mazowiecka
Ostrowiec (Ostrovtse)
Ostryna
Oszmiana
Otwock (Otwozk)
Ozarow
Pabianice
Parafianowo
Parysow (Porisov)
Piatnica
Pinczow (Pintchew)
Pinsk
Piotrkow Trybunalski
Plawno
Plock (Plotzk)
Plonsk
Poczajow (Pitchayev)
Podbrodzie
Poland
Polaniec
Poligon
Porozow
Postawy
Pruszkow
Pruzana
Przasnyas (Proshnitz)
Przeclaw
Przedborz
Przemysl
Pshitik
Pulawy
Pultusk
Punsk
Raciaz
Raczki

Radom

Radomsko

Radomysl Wielki

Radoszkowice (Radoshkovits)

Radzanow

Radzin

Radziwillow

Rakow

Ratno

Rohatyn

Rokitno

Rowne

Rozana (Rozhinoy)

Rozanka

Rozprza

Rozwadow

Rubiezewicze (Rubizhewich)

Ryki

Rypin (Ribin)

Rytwiany

Rzeszow

Sanok

Sarnaki

Sarny

Schodnica

Semiatycze (Semiatich)

Serock

Siedlce (Shedlets)

Siedliszcze

Sielec

Sierpc

Siniawka

Skala

Skalat

Skierniewice (Skierniveitz)

Skole

Slonim

Slupia

Sluzewo

Smorgonie

Sobota

Sochaczew

Sokal

Sokolka

Sokolow

Sokoly

Stanislawow

Staszow (Stashow)

Stawiski (Stavisk)

Stojaciszki

Stojanow

Stolin

Stolpce

Stryj

Stryzow

Strzegowo

Sucha

Suchocin

Suchowola

Suwalki

Swieciany (Svintzian)

Swierzen

Swir

Swislocz

Szarkowszczyna

Szczekociny

Szczuczyn (District Bialystok)

Szczuczyn

Szereszow

Szransk

Szumsk

Szydlow

Targowica (Trovits)

Tarnogrod

Tarnopol

Tarnow

Tartakow

Telechany

Tluste

Tluszcz (Tlusht)

Tomaszow Lubelski

Tomaszow Mazowiecki

Troki

Trzebinia (Tshebin)

Tuczyn
Turka
Turobin
Tykocin (Tiktin)
Tyszowce (Tishovits)
Uscilug
Ustrzyki Dolne
Wadowice
Warcz
Warszawa (Warsaw)
Wasiliszki
Wasniow
Wegrow
Widze
Wielun
Wieruszow
Wilno
Wiskitki
Wislica (Weislitz)
Wisniowiec Nowy
Wloclawek
Wlodawa
Wlodzimierz (Ludmir)
Wlodzimierzec (Vladimerez)
Wojslawice
Wolborz
Wolbrom
Wolkowysk
Wolma
Wolozyn
Wolpa
Wsielub
Wysock (near Rowno)
Wyszkow
Wyszogrod (Vishogrod)
Wyzgrodek
Zablotow
Zabludow
Zambrow
Zamosc
Zareby Koscielne
Zarki

Zarszyn
Zassow
Zawiercie
Zdunska Wola
Zdzieciol (Zetel)
Zelechow
Zgierz
Zolkiew
Zoludek
Zoludzk
Zloczew
Zychlin
Zyrardow

Romania
Bessarabia
Briceni
Bricevo
Calarasi (Kalarash)
Cernauti
Cluj
Gherla
Iklud
Lipcani
Orhei
Ruskova
Secureni
Soblas

U.S.S.R.
Balin
Baranovka
Bobruisk
Dubossary
Frampol
Glusk
Gomel
Gorodnitsa
Grozovo
Kamenets-Podolskiy
Kammeny Brod
Kitai-Gorod
Koidanovo

Kopin
Kopyl
Lapichi
Lubenichi
Lyuban
Minkovtsy
Nemirov
Nevel
Novogrod-Volynskiy
Odessa
Osipovichi
Palonnoe
Parichi
Pogost
Rachev
Romanova
Shehedrin
Shpola

Slutsk
Smotrich
Starobin
Starye Dorogi
Stavishche (Stavisht)
Timkovichi
Ukraine
Urechye
Vinitsa
Vitebsk
Vizna
Yampol
Yanovichi
Zamekhov
Zinkov

Yugoslavia
Sombor

Memorial Books: Where to Find Them

Locating Memorial Books is a two-stage process. The first is finding an institution which owns a copy of the book for your examination. The second is purchasing a Memorial Book for your home library if you find that it is of relevance to you. By the way, if you locate a Memorial Book on your family's town and there is nothing specifically on your family, it would still be worth having in my opinion. A history of the town where your family once lived is a special item for your personal library.

Examine the list; if your town appears, you are in luck. If it does not, there are two possibilities. One is that either I missed it or that its Memorial Book was published after my list was compiled (there are Memorial Books *still* in production!). The second is that a Memorial Book was *not* published about your town. In that case, it would still be worth your while to look at a map and to see which towns were in the nearby area. Then check the list for those locations. Often a book will include information about neighboring villages and towns.

Institutions Which Collect Memorial Books. Several libraries and archives collect Memorial Books. While these institutions *cannot* check the books for you for family or other information, they can, of course, tell you if they have them in their collections. They are:

YIVO Institute for Jewish Research
1048 Fifth Avenue
New York, N.Y. 10028

The New York Public Library
Jewish Division
42nd Street at 5th Avenue
New York, N.Y. 10018

Jewish Theological Seminary Library
3080 Broadway
New York, N.Y. 10027

University of California Library
UCLA
Jewish Studies Collection
Los Angeles, California 90024

Yad Vashem
P.O. Box 3477
Jerusalem, Israel

While there are other Jewish institutions which have collections as well, these are the best. None of them will loan the books to you, but they will let you read the books and photocopy material from them at the institution. They would also answer a written inquiry as to whether they have a certain book in their collection.

How to Obtain Copies for Yourself. Once you have located a Memorial Book for yourself, you will undoubtedly want to own a copy. A Memorial Book is not the kind of publication you would find in a local bookshop, nor can a local store order a copy for you. In almost all cases, Memorial Books have been privately published and are distributed by the people who had the book printed—usually a landsmannschaft. Therefore, what you have to do is either track down the individuals (or organization) which had the book published, or find someone who will track them down for you. It is this second option which is the easier, and fortunately there are organizations which will do just that!

Shefa Press
Personal Services Division
19 Heleni HaMalka Street
P.O.B. 7782
Jerusalem, Israel

Shefa Press is the publisher of a fine journal called *Shefa Quarterly*, aimed at a general Jewish audience. The Personal Services Division of Shefa Press will help to locate for you any book either on a Jewish subject or printed in Israel. They are *excellent* in tracking down landsmannschaften and locating Memorial Books. I have personally ordered many books (Memorial and others) from them and their batting average is almost 100 percent. Their current search fee for each title is $5.00. This is added to the cost of the book and the postage from Israel. I would suggest when ordering through them that you request surface mail and not airmail. It will take longer that way, but airmail will have you paying more for the postage than for the book. Shefa Press is the *best* way I know of locating Memorial Books.

> CYCO Publishing House & Book Distribution Agency
> 25 East 78th Street
> New York, N.Y. 10021

CYCO is a Yiddish publisher and bookstore. One of their specialties is Memorial Books; they have more than seventy different titles in stock there. You can visit this bookstore or send for their catalog. Specify whether you want the English catalog or the Yiddish one.

> Moshe Schreiber
> Mea Shearim Street, 16
> Jerusalem, Israel

Moshe Schreiber's is a well-known bookstore in the famous section of Jerusalem, Mea Shearim. He has many Memorial Books in stock and will also try to order others for you. He will, of course, ship them to you.

A final way of locating Memorial Books, and one which is both the most rewarding as well as the most difficult, is to track down the people or landsmannschaft which published the book in which you are interested. In this way you will also have personal contact with interesting people—and that is what it is all about. (See Landsmannschaften, page 207.)

> A scattered nation which remembers its past and connects it with the present will undoubtedly have a future as a people and probably even a more glorious life than the one in the past.
>
> —Lev Levanda

Memorial Books as Unexpected Treasures

As I mentioned at the beginning of this book, a spark that fired my interest in family history was the day I discovered a picture of my great-grandfather, a tinsmith in the tiny shtetl of Dobromil, Poland, in a Memorial Book. I've told the story of that discovery many times, and have often invited people to look for Memorial Books for the towns of their ancestry and attempt to do the same.

One day I was showing a student of mine the wonderful book collection in the New York Public Library Jewish Division—which is the place I originally found my great-grandfather's picture. When we entered the room I asked my student to tell me the names of the towns where her ancestors were from. She looked at me knowingly, and said, "It's not going to happen to me. Don't be funny."

I insisted that we look anyway, and we found several photographs of members of her family, as well as an essay written by her grandfather!

I could tell many other true stories just like this one. The moral: Look for Memorial Books of your towns!

> Remember the days of old.
> —Deuteronomy 32:7

Memorbuchs

As we have said, Memorbuchs are different from Memorial Books. They exist for many towns, and the best source is:

> The Central Archives for the History of the Jewish People
> The Hebrew University Campus
> Sprinzak Building
> P.O. Box 1149
> Jerusalem, Israel

In general, it would be best to write to this archive, which is the largest Jewish archive collecting world-wide Judaica in the world, and ask them for a listing of their holdings for specific locations. For example, if you are interested in Minsk, write to the archives and ask for a listing of material in their Minsk holdings.

> To preserve the past is half of immortality.
> —B. D'Israeli

Memorbuch page from Goch, Germany. (Courtesy of Leo Baeck Institute, New York)

Beginning to Discover Your Ancestral Homes

If you are not familiar with *Encyclopedia Judaica*, you should be. This sixteen-volume, beautifully produced set of books is a well-spring of Jewish knowledge. Though various criticisms have been lodged against the encyclopedia, it remains the finest source, in my opinion, to begin research on most Jewish subjects.

While the smallest of villages and towns will not appear in the *EJ* unless something quite unusual happened there, you can find brief articles about hundreds of Jewish settlements throughout the world here. Volume I is the encyclopedia's index: Always check the index because you might find references to subjects which do not have their own articles.

Each article in the encyclopedia has a bibliography as well, which is useful in sending you off to more information.

> There is an uninterrupted chain of generations which makes it possible for us to regard ourselves as having descended from Abraham, Isaac, and Jacob. We may question this statement biologically; nevertheless, they were our ancestors to all intents and purposes. We are members of one mishpahah, even though our cosmology, our conception of the universe, our way of living, our whole heirarchy of values, may differ radically from theirs. Our relationship to our earliest childhood as a people is analogous to the relationship we have to our own childhood. We think and live differently from the way we did when we were children. Yet, when we think of our childhood, we maintain that we are the same persons we were before, even though there may not be a single cell in our body that has remained unchanged since we were children; but there is a continuity of personality which consists of memories, associations, and habits.
>
> —IRA EISENSTEIN, rabbi

Locating Landsmannschaften

Before explaining how to track down a landsmannschaft, I want to explain the usefulness in doing so.

If your family came from a certain town which still has a landsmannschaft, there is a good chance that members of the organization knew your family and could tell you about them. In addition, landsmannschaft members can give you another perspective on the European town of your ancestors. They might also have pictures of the town.

I have tracked down the landsmannschaften of two towns of my ancestors and I've gone to their meetings. In one case, I was able to purchase a copy of the town Memorial Book as well as to meet people who knew my family. In the other case, my luck was far better. I met a man, as noted in Chapter 3, who had photographs of family members of mine who were killed in the Holocaust! If not for that man and his photographs, my family would never have known what those cousins looked like. I also met a man at a landsmannschaft meeting who was a musician. He was about ninety years old, charming, and friendly. He played the fiddle at my grandparents' wedding in Europe! From members of this landsmannschaft I learned the names and addresses of landsmen in Israel who knew my family from Europe. I wrote to them and received letters with still more stories about my family and their life in the shtetl.

It is difficult, but not impossible, to locate a landsmannschaft. YIVO Institute for Jewish Research has a listing of many of them though it is far from complete. But you might begin your search by inquiring there. Under the direction of Rosaline Schwartz, YIVO has established a Landsmannschaften Project devoted to identifying, locating, and preserving the records of landsmannschaften in the New York City area. If you are interested in learning whether a particular landsmannschaft exists, whether YIVO has any of their records, or if you know of the existence of any landsmannschaften, you should contact Rosaline Schwartz, Director, Landmannschaften Project, YIVO Institute for Jewish Research, 1048 Fifth Avenue, New York, New York 10028; (212) 535-6700.

It is also known that UJA-Federation has information on current landsmannschaften because they solicit money from them and also get contributions. While UJA-Federation will not issue a list of these organizations, they will tell you if they have current information about specific landsmannschaften. Contact:

> UJA-Federation Joint Campaign
> 220 West 58th Street
> New York, N.Y. 10019

A final and more ambitious method of locating landsmannschaften, or even landsmen, is to place an ad in a Jewish newspaper. People have been known to take out an ad in a big city Jewish paper saying, "Anyone belonging to or having knowledge of a *(name of town)* landsmannschaft, please write or call: ———." An ad like this can bring interesting results.

There is an excellent article on the subject of landsmannschaften in *Toledot* (see page 101). Written by Zachary M. Baker, assistant librarian at YIVO Institute for Jewish Research, the article is titled "Landsmannschaften and the Jewish Genealogist" and appears in the summer 1978 issue.

> The past is our cradle, not our prison, and there is danger as well as appeal in its glamor. The past is for inspiration, not imitation, for continuation, not repetition.
> —ISRAEL ZANGWILL, *Fortnightly Review*, April, 1919

Your Shtetl or Town During the Holocaust

Earlier in the book I mentioned the International Tracing Service (ITS) in West Germany. Another very important source of Holocaust information is Yad Vashem.

Yad Vashem in Israel is publishing a series of books called *Guide to Unpublished Materials of the Holocaust Period*. Volumes III and IV offer a town-by-town listing of the towns which are represented in the Yad Vashem archives. Usually this material is taken from post-War testimony offered by survivors. You might find some moving and fascinating information about your towns here.

The Black Book

In 1965, Yad Vashem (see page 141) published the *Blackbook of Localities Whose Jewish Population Was Exterminated by the Nazis*. This book contains a list of almost 34,000 localities in Europe with Jewish residents. Some of these localities contained thousands of Jews, and others contained just one or two Jews living among non-Jewish neighbors.

During the Holocaust, almost every town, city, and village listed in the *Blackbook* was purged of its Jewish population.

The reader of the *Blackbook* will find listings of the most minute hamlets in Europe. If your ancestors came from small villages which have long disappeared from the face of the earth and which no contemporary maps indicate, the *Blackbook* will probably list them. Often you will be told the names of towns lived in by your family and you will be unable to find any reference to them. The *Blackbook* would be your best source to verify the existence of these towns—and the book will give you the number of Jewish residents in that town sometime before the War. The book will tell you the date of the census on which the population figures were based.

If your local Judaica library does not have this book, it should.

Poland

SERIAL NUMBER	LOCALITY	NUMBER OF JEWISH RESIDENTS
6	Dąbrowica gm.pow.Nisko	6
7	!Dąbrowska Starzeńska	9
8	Dąbrówka Polska	15
9	Dąbrówka Ruska	19
800	Dąbrówka Starzeńska	12
1	Dąbrówki	12
2	Delawa	7
3	Dembno	73
4	Demidów	23
5	Derewnia ob.dw.	7
6	Derewnia gm.	19
7	Dereżyce	45
8	Deszno	21
9	Deutschbach	9
10	Dęba	3
1	Dębina	21
2	Dębna	11
3	Dębów	43
4	Długie gm. pow.Sanok	19
5	Długie gm.pow.Krosno	2
6	Dłużniów ob.dw.	12
7	Dłużniów gm.	19
8	Dmytrowice gm. pow.Lwów	18
9	Dmytrowice gm. pow.Mościska	16
20	Dmytrowice ob.dw.pow.Mość.	38
1	Dmytrowice ob.dw.pow.Lwów	6
2	Dmytrowice gm.	6
3	Dmytrze	16
4	Dobcza	49
5	Dobieszyn	20
6	Dobkowice ob.dw.	4
7	Dobkowice gm.	22
8	Dobra	25
9	Dobra Rustykalna	34
30	Dobra Szlachecka	30
1	Dobraczyn	17
2	Dobrohostów ob.dw.	21

SERIAL NUMBER	LOCALITY	NUMBER OF JEWISH RESIDENTS
• 3	Dobrohostów gm.	27
4	Dobromil	2119
5	Dobrosin ob.dw.	7
6	Dobrosin gm.	26
7	Dobrostany ob.dw.	6
8	Dobrostany gm.	20
9	Dobrowlany gm.pow.Drohobycz	54
40	Dobrowlany ob.dw.	8
1	Dobrowlany gm.pow.Bóbrka	20
2	Dobrzanka	23
3	Dobrzany gm. pow.Lwów	7
4	Dobrzany ob. dw.	7
5	Dobrzany gm. Gródek Jagiell.	32
6	Dobrzechów	6
7	Dolina	15
8	Doliniany	5
9	Dołhe Modenickie	8
50	Dołhe Podbuskie	144
1	Dołhomościska	8
2	Dołobów	11
3	Dołżyca	22
4	Dołżyce	4
5	Domacyny	18
6	Domaradz	123
7	Domaszów gm.	40
8	Domaszów ob. dw.	5
9	Domatków	25
60	Domażyr gm.	25
1	Domażyr ob. dw.	7
2	Domostawa	4
3	Dornbach	6
4	Dornfeld	18
5	Doroszów Wielki	8
6	Dorożów	92
7	Drabinianka	44
8	Drohobycz	11833
9	Drohobyczka	17

A page from the *Blackbook of Localities,* published by Yad Vashem, listing the thousands of Jewish cities, towns, villages, and hamlets in Europe along with their last known Jewish populations before the Holocaust.

Unfortunately, it is currently out of print and Yad Vashem seems to have no plans to re-issue it. Perhaps you could arrange to see if your local Judaica library would be able to photocopy the book for its collection. It would be worth it.

I once gave a lecture in which I mentioned the *Blackbook*. I rather boldly stated that the book listed *every* Eastern European town. A young woman raised her hand and said, "The town my family was from, in Hungary, had only four people in it. They were all my family. That town will not be listed!" Well, the book, as we said, lists town names and their pre-War population figures. We looked up the town which the woman had in mind—and we found it! And the population *was* four!

A skeptic was suddenly a believer.

> No individual can be constructed entire without a link with
> the past.
>
> —AHAD HA'AM

The Leo Baeck Institute

If any of your ancestors came from Germany, the Leo Baeck Institute at 129 East 73rd Street, New York, N.Y. 10021 should be of interest. The institute includes a 50,000+ volume library, an archive, and is a publisher of books in the field of German Jewry, and an academic center.

While the entire collection of the Leo Baeck Institute is fascinating and important, a few items in particular should be noted. The institute has a large collection of family trees of German Jewish families, many of which are a few centuries old. German Jews have been known to have a keen interest in genealogy, and this is reflected in the outstanding collection of material of this kind at the Leo Baeck Institute.

In addition, the institute has a collection of family histories and community histories pertaining to German Jewry, as well as a large number of unpublished memoirs.

While the Leo Baeck Institute specializes in German Jewry, its collection also contains material related to other countries with German-speaking Jews before the Holocaust.

If you have located the town or region in Germany from where your ancestors came, you should check the institute for background information. A review of their family tree collection might also be worthwhile. Do not assume, however, that finding a family tree with a familiar surname means that it is your family, however tempting this might be.

See *Toledot: The Journal of Jewish Genealogy*, Volume 2, Number 4 (Spring 1979), for an excellent article on the genealogical resources of the Leo Baeck Institute. The article was written by Dr. Sybil Milton, Chief Archivist of the institute.

> Man lives not only in the circle of his years but also, by virtue of the subconscious, in the provinces of the generations from which he is descended, and Jewish life, to a very great extent, is based here.
>
> —LEO BAECK, *The Jew*

How to Locate Your Shtetl

It is not always easy to locate a shtetl, town, village, or city. There are several possible problems.

1) The location might no longer exist, having been wiped off the map with its inhabitants during the Holocaust.

2) The name might have changed since your family last resided there.

3) You may know the location by a name in a different language from one currently used.

4) You may know the location by its Jewish name, but not by its more commonly used name.

5) Often a locality will be spelled the way it sounds, but this is not necessarily the way it is spelled on maps.

6) Since borders change throughout history, you may be looking for your town in the wrong country.

7) The town may have been hardly a town at all, and may simply not be found on most maps. Frequently, a town was no more than a few houses.

If you have tried, without success, to locate a particular town, do not give up. There are several possibilities, some of which might prove to be fascinating.

Most libraries have an atlas collection and large public and university libraries often have extensive map departments. One of your first steps to locating your towns and shtetlach is to consult a gazetteer. A gazetteer is a geographical dictionary. You use it just like a dictionary by looking up the word by the various ways you think it would be spelled. A gazetteer will provide the "definition" of a location. It will tell you the country that it is in, its proximity to other well-known locations, the longitude and latitude, and even a little about the current and historical situation.

Perhaps the finest gazetteer available is *The Columbia Lippincott Gazetteer of the World*. This book was published after World War II so it will often not be helpful for towns which were completely wiped off the map. In that case, you should check their earlier edition, known as *A Complete Pronouncing Gazetteer or Geographical Dictionary of the World* published by J. B. Lippincott Company in 1906.

A gazetteer in the German language which is also excellent is *Ritters Geographisch-Statistisches Lexikon*.

One problem which is difficult to solve is spelling. Often you will only know the pronunciation of a location and not the spelling. Your best bet would be to get a dictionary in the language of the name of the location and figure out how that pronunciation is spelled. Also, a good map librarian would be familiar enough with foreign pronunciations to be able to help you. A final suggestion is this: whenever you learn the name of a town, try to find out where it was near. If you can locate, on a map, a familiar spot, then you can examine a detailed map of the area and try to locate the place by scanning the map. One of my ancestral towns is Przemysl. However, I was first introduced to the town by hearing its name—which is pronounced Pahshemishel. It took me a while to find it on a map, but after using some of the resources just mentioned, I was able to do it rather quickly. My one key was that I knew its general vicinity. From that point on, it was simple.

When you have exhausted the few sources pertaining to geographical locations mentioned here, as well as the many others discussed elsewhere in this book (a good example is the *Blackbook* on page 209), I would urge you to read an article published in *Toledot: The Journal of Jewish Genealogy*, Volume 2, Number 3 (winter 1978–79). Zachary M. Baker, as assistant librarian at the YIVO Institute for Jewish Research, has written the finest study I have seen on the question of how to locate Eastern European towns. Titled "Eastern European 'Jewish Geography': Some Problems and Suggestions (Or, How to Get From Amshinov to Mszczonów without Moving an Inch)," Baker's article is essential if you are having difficulty spelling, pronouncing, or locating your ancestral towns.

> Tradition must be a springboard into the future, not an armchair for repose.
>
> —BEN-GURION

European Sources

Frequently, you can find published genealogical material on the subject of European archives and libraries which may have information on your family. Unfortunately, the books which list these sources do not also warn that it is often doubtful that you will get a response. Too many "how-to-do-it" genealogy books generate lots of mail and lots of disappointment as well.

It is for this reason that I hesitate to describe the possible sources available in Europe or generally outside the United States. While each country in Europe has its own archives, libraries, and public records, various problems arise:

1) Because of the history of the country, Jewish records may not have been included or even kept.

2) Wars, pogroms, and other human-made disasters have destroyed much material.

3) Many European archives claim to have certain holdings but will not release them.

4) Many of the same archives make material available but do not have the staff or the set-up to answer genealogical inquiries.

This leaves us in the position of not knowing how much time and effort to put into attempting to find European records. Some generalizations can be made:

1) The chances of getting information or records about your family from Eastern European countries are slim. I know personally of many cases where either the request was never answered or it was answered in the negative.

2) Western European sources have much more potential, but your hopes should still not be raised too high. Some people have had remarkable successes with German records. Others have been able to find useful information from Italian, British, and French records, as well as others.

3) A negative response (or no answer at all) does *not* necessarily mean that the records do not exist, but merely that they are unobtainable by mail. Often a visit to Europe will result in major family history finds. Again, Germany is a good example of this. While most local German record halls are not set up to do research for people, a visit there can turn up a lot of material—if you are willing and able to work your way through the files. (See "Visiting the Old Country," p. 222.)

4) There are several "how-to-do-it" genealogy books with material on European archives and sources. I know of no good one, so rather than recommend one, I will simply suggest that you try to find them in your library and take them with the necessary grain (or more) of salt.

5) The rule of thumb is always to go to the source rather than write, but this is not always possible when it concerns far-away places.

6) The Mormon Church continues to be the best source for world-wide records, and I have seen startling success with their Jewish Eastern European material—which proves simply that this information is available but you must have personal access to it in order to make it useful.

7) Be wary of genealogy books which sound too easy and are filled with sources. Too often the sources fill up the book but amount to very little.

> "Why are you crying, Mother? Because the house is burning?"
> "Yes."
> "We shall build another, I promise you."
> "It's not the house, son. If I cry, it is because a precious document is being destroyed before our eyes."
> "What document?"
> "Our family tree; it is illustrious, you know."
> "Don't cry. I'll give you another. I'll start anew, I promise you."
>
> At the time, Dov-Ber was five.
>
> —ELIE WIESEL, telling of The Maggid of Mezeritch, a Chassidic master, in Souls on Fire.

The Mormon Church and Jewish Genealogy

The Mormon Church administers what is perhaps the most ambitious genealogy archive and library in the world. The Genealogical Society of Utah, which is the genealogical arm of the Mormon Church, has a granite mountain in Salt Lake City, Utah, which has been carved out and has a capacity for housing six million reels of microfilm. The archive in the mountain is carefully controlled for temperature and other climate variations, and is also supposed to be able to withstand nearly every possible disaster, man and nature made.

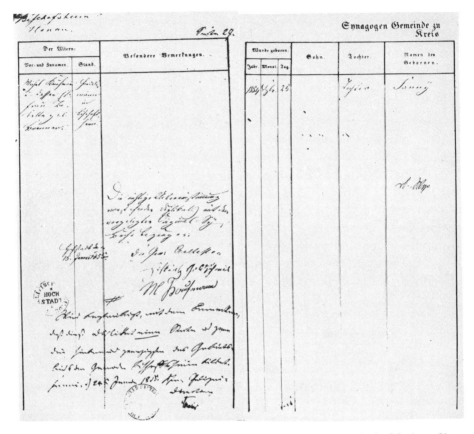

Birth register from 1854 of the Jewish community of Bischofsheim, district of Hanau, in Hessen, Germany. (Courtesy of Genealogical Society of Utah)

To understand the Mormon interest in genealogy, one must know something about their religious beliefs. Let it be sufficient to say that the Mormons believe that people who are no longer alive can be baptized and that genealogy research uncovers unknown people for this purpose. As a religion dependent on and interested in converts, the Mormon Church is interested in *all* genealogical records.

For the Jewish researcher, there are several points of interest relating to the Mormon genealogical facilities. Simply put, the Mormons have been able to gain access to Eastern European records, including Jewish records. The result of this is that the Mormon Church has acquired and continues to acquire Eastern European

Birth register from
1877 of the Jewish
community of Ujpest,
Budapest, Hungary.
(Courtesy of
Genealogical Society
of Utah)

(and other) Jewish records, including census material, synagogue and Jewish communal records, and other documents. Their collection already has some fascinating Polish, German, and Hungarian records of Jewish interest, and they are continuing to gather more documents all of the time.

At the present time, the Mormons have research projects going on in the U.S.S.R., Romania, Bulgaria, Poland, Hungary, Austria, Czechoslovakia, Germany, and all of the other European countries.

To gain access to the material gathered by the Mormons you need not travel to Salt Lake City. Rather, you must locate a branch library (there are many throughout the country) of the Church. Check a phone book for a branch library in your area. Look under "Church of Jesus Christ of Latter Day Saints." There you will find a microfilm copy of the index to their holdings. When you find what you want in the index, you can send for the material through the branch library at a nominal price per reel of microfilm. The index is arranged by country. If you are interested, for example, in seeing what Polish records they have, you must look up "Poland—Jews." I have also found material under the heading "Poland—Minorities—Jews" which means that their indexing system could use improvement. You might also seek material of a general nature. For example, a census taken in Hungary might have included Jews and non-Jews. Again, locate what you want by location—first by country, then by county or city.

Note: I have used the Mormon library for years and have never been approached to join the Church or to read a pamphlet. They seem to separate their religious work from their genealogical work. I would recommend using their library, but I would also suggest that you protest strongly if someone approaches you on a religious matter. The central address for their organization is:

> The Genealogical Society of Utah
> 50 East North Temple Street
> Salt Lake City, Utah 84150

Toledot: The Journal of Jewish Genealogy (see page 100) has been publishing an inventory of all of the Jewish holdings at the Mormon library. The editors of *Toledot* have gone through all of the indexes in Salt Lake City and have produced a country-by-country, town-by-town listing of all the specifically Jewish records which the Mormons have microfilmed and now make available. *Toledot*'s publication of these inventories has made things quite

"		B M D	1847-1858	807,756
Izbica	Po	B M D	1810-1835	741,831
Kujawska		B M D	1836-1852	741,832
"		B M D	1853-1865	741,833
Iłża	Ki	B M D	1850-1861	714,995
"		B M D	1862-1865	714,996
Jabłonka				
Kościelna	Bi	B M D	1827-1865	747,702
Jabłonka				
Świerczewo	Bi	B M D	1838-1888	1,046,484
Janów	Lu	B M D	1826-1839	807,766
Podlaski		B M D	1840-1843	807,767
"		B M D	1844-1865	807,768
"		B M D	1866-1869	937,498
Janowiec	Lu	B M D	1817-1841	813,880
"		B M D	1842-1857	813,881
Jarczów	Lu	B M D	1827-1850	813,882
"		B M D	1851-1865	813,883
"		B M D	1866-1870	937,498
Jaroszyn	Lu	See Góra Puławska		
Jędrzejów	Ki	See Sobków		
Jeżów	Łó	B M D	1826-1860	723,535
"		B M D	1861-1865	723,536
"		B M D	1866-1870	767,101
Józefów	Lu	B	1810-1818	813,884
(Biłgoraj)		M	1810-1818	813,885
"		B M D	1810-1825	813,886
"		B M D	1823-1826	813,887
"		B M D	1826-1843	813,893
"		B M D	1844-1863	813,894
Józefów	Lu	B M D	1826-1845	813,895
(Opole Lubelskie)		B M D	1846-1862	813,896
Józefów	Lu	B	1863	905,146
nad Wisłą		B M D	1866-1868	905,146
Kalisz	Po	B M D	1809-1820	743,141
"		B M D	1821-1828	743,142
"		B M D	1829-1837	743,143
"		B M D	1838-1845	743,144
"		B M D	1846-1851	743,145
"		B M D	1852-1857	743,146
"		B M D	1858-1861	743,147
"		B M D	1862-1865	743,148
"		See also Błaszki, Stawiszyn		
Kałuszyn	Wa	B M D	1826-1832	702,435
"		B M D	1833-1840	702,436
"		B M D	1841-1846	702,437
"		B M D	1847-1852	702,438
"		3 M D	1853-1859	702,439
"		B M D	1860-1863	702,440
"		B M D	1864-1865	702,441
Kamionka				
Lubartów	Lu	B M D	1826-1865	813,843
Karczew	Wa	B M D	1826-1841	702,442
"		B M D	1842-1864	702,443
"		B M D	1842-1872	702,444
Kartuzy	Gd	Recs-1	1848-1873 G	475,222
Kazimierz	Lu	B M D	1826-1841	813,859
Dln.		B M D	1842-1863	813,860
Kępno	Po	B M D	1825-1835 G	742,975
"		B M D	1836-1841 G	742,976
"		B M D	1842-1847 G	742,977
Kielce	Ki	See Chęciny		
Klimontów	Ki	B M D	1826-1839	809,129
"		B M D	1840-1853	809,130
"		B M D	1854-1861	809,131
"		B M D	1862-1865	809,132
Kłobuck	Ka	B M D	1826-1860	879,546
"		B M D	1856-1864	879,547
"		See also Krzepice		
Kłodawa	Po	B M D	1826-1831	743,000
"		B M D	1832-1858	743,001
"		B M D	1859-1865	743,002
Klwów	Ki	B M D	1851-1860	718,961
Kock	Lu	B M D	1826-1842	813,989
"		B M D	1843-1858	813,990
"		B M D	1859-1865	813,991
Kodeń	Lu	B M D	1826-1841	813,999
"		B M D	1843-1854	814,000
Kołaki	Bi	Recs-5	1808-1869	
Kołbiel	Wa	B M D	1826-38,1854	702,445
Koło	Po	B M D	1825-1840	741,979
"		B M D	1841-1854	741,980
"		B M D	1855-1865	741,981
"		See also Babiak, Dąbie, Sompolno		
Komarów	Lu	B M D	1826-1842	813,874
"		B M D	1843-1860	813,875
"		B M D	1861-1865	813,876
"		B M D	1866-1870	905,158
Koniecpol	Ki	B M D	1826-1842	730,078
"		B M D	1844-1855	730,079
Konin	Po	M	1815	741,998
"		B M D	1826-1845	741,998
"		B M D	1846-1853	741,999
"		B M D	1855-1865	742,000
"		See also Golina, Skulsk, Ślesin, Wilczyn		
Końskie	Ki	B M D	1826-1836	716,412
"		B M D	1837-1845	716,415
"		B M D	1846-1859	716,416
"		B M D	1857-1863	716,413
"		B M D	1864-1865	716,414
"		B M D	1860-1865	716,607
"		See also Gowarczów, Przedbórz		
Końskowola	Lu	Recs-5	1826-1863	
"		B M D	1866-1870	905,160
Konstantynów				
nad Bugiem	Lu	B M D	1826-1854	715,358
Koprzywnica	Ki	B M D	1857-1858	809,133
Kórnik	Po	B M D	1817-1847 G	742,003
Koronowo	By	B	1847-1874 G	813,169
Kościerzyna	Gd	B M	1847-1865 G	742,795
"		Recs-1	1847-1873 G	474,721
"			1873-1919 G	474,715
Kosów	Wa	B M D	1827-1844	808,908
"		B M D	1845-1862	808,909
Koszalin	Ko	B M D	1812-1846 G	896,086
Kozienice	Ki	See Magnuszew		
Koźmin	Po	B M D	1811-1812	742,946
Kożuchów	Zi	M	1849-1873 G	896,080
Krajenka	Ko	Recs-1	1812-1833 G	495,964
"		"	1833-1841 G	495,965
"		"	1834-1854 G	495,966
"		"	1846 G	495,967
Krajenka				
Chełmno	By	Recs-1	1829-1832 G	495,967
Kraków	Kr	B D	1798-1819	718,912
"		B	1820-1829	718,913
"		B	1830-1836	718,914

Page from extensive catalog of German, Polish, and Hungarian Jewish vital records in the Genealogical Society of Utah collection. Published by *Toledot: The Journal of Jewish Genealogy*, this catalog page is of Polish-Jewish records.

convenient for the researcher wanting to know what Jewish material is in Salt Lake City. First of all, for certain countries you now need not locate a branch library of the Mormon Church and sit for hours with their microfilm machines; *Toledot*'s editors have done it for you. You can, at a glance of the pages of *Toledot*, see if your towns are among the Mormon holdings. Secondly, not all of the branch libraries even have the complete indexes of the Mormon holdings. For example, since Polish material is rarely used, it is only upon special request that branch libraries receive the Polish indexes. Finally, the Mormon indexes are difficult to use. You cannot always find Jewish material easily. For example, while the Polish-Jewish material is listed under "Jews in Poland," the Hungarian-Jewish material is not under "Jews in Hungary." Believe it or not, staff members of the Mormon library were not even aware of much of their Hungarian-Jewish material for this reason. *Toledot*'s editors brought this to their attention.

Back issues of *Toledot* contain these inventories. They have published the material as follows:

> Hungarian-Jewish records: winter 1977-78
> Polish-Jewish records: spring 1978
> German-Jewish records: summer 1978

Back issues of *Toledot: The Journal of Jewish Genealogy* are available for $2.50 each from

> Toledot: The Journal of Jewish Genealogy
> 155 East 93rd Street
> Suite 3C
> New York, N.Y. 10028

One of the early rabbis, Ben Azzai, translated the words of Genesis 5:1, "This is the book of the generations of man," and declared them to be "a great fundamental teaching of the Torah." As all human beings are traced back to one parent, he taught, they must necessarily be brothers.

—Dr. J. H. Hertz, in the Soncino
Pentateuch

The Central Archives for the History of the Jewish People

In 1969, the Central Archives for the History of the Jewish People was established by the Israeli government, the Jewish Agency for Israel, the Historical Society of Israel, the Israel Academy of Sciences and Humanities, the Hebrew University of Jerusalem, Tel Aviv University, and Bar-Ilan University.

The archives are in possession of "the most extensive collection of documents, pinkassim (registers), and records concerning Jewish

From civil register of Jewish community in Tarlow, Poland, the record of marriage of Gecel Maierowicz Rotman and Ryfka Maierowiczowna Geilman, 19 February, 1826. (Courtesy of Genealogical Society of Utah)

history in the Diaspora from the Middle Ages to the present day."
While the archives staff attempts to collect original documents, it is
also involved in the microfilming of historical records around the
world. A unique aspect of the archives is the fact that while other
Jewish archives specialize in one region or period of Jewish history,
the Central Archives collects material from every Jewish community
in the world.

The collection at the Central Archives is arranged by country
and town. If you want to know what they have of interest to you, it
would be best to send them a letter asking for an inventory of their
holdings for a specific town or region. In their reply, they will tell
you what they have. It might be a marriage register from the 1840's
or a mohel book from 1909, or a record book from the community,
or they might not have anything for your community. However,
if they do, you can arrange to purchase microfilm of other copies of
the material.

The address of the archive is:

> The Central Archives for the History of the Jewish People
> Hebrew University Campus
> P.O. Box 1149
> Jerusalem, Israel

It would also be worthwhile to write to them asking for their
guide to the collection.

> I never realized, when I was very young, how much I missed
> by never having met either of my grandfathers . . . Not
> having known a grandfather, I had to go out looking for
> him, and what I will try and set out here is simply the story
> of the search. The trouble is that, given my own type of
> mind, this is bound to take me further than a few nostalgic
> family tales. However, if it is a little grown up for the
> einiklach (grandchildren) at this stage, they'll get round
> to it one day. Above all, they will understand, I think, that I
> was not just looking for my grandfather but for myself.
>
> —CHAIM RAPHAEL, "Roots—Jewish Style,"
> Midstream

Visiting the Old Country

Sooner or later, every Jewish family historian considers planning
a trip to the places in the Old Country whence they or their ancestors
came. For years, I had the fantasy of walking the same streets in

Poland that my great-grandfather walked as a child and as a young married man. I wanted to see the shops which were once ours; I wondered if the Jewish cemetery still existed. Were there any Jewish records in the town? were there any Jews still there? did the citizens of the town remember my family? These questions and others ran through my mind hundreds of times.

I eventually made the trip to Poland and did visit my great-grandfather's town. But before I share that experience and discuss the things that you ought to consider before making such a trip, it would be best to explore the "cons" of the argument as to whether or not to travel to the Old Country.

Several family members were upset with me for considering and planning such a trip. "How could you even step foot on the places where our people were murdered?" they asked. Other people said, "You have better things to do with your money than support those countries." Still others said, "If you want to go to find your roots, go to Israel!" People used all kinds of reasons to dissuade me from making the journey. "What do you expect to find there?" many asked. "Everything was destroyed." Or, "They won't let you see anything. You are wasting your time." Or, "I know someone who was there shortly after the War. Nothing is left."

I've heard all the arguments, and while I can appreciate them all, I nonetheless had my own private reasons for going. I had to see for myself.

Let me try to answer all of the above questions and objections as best as I can. While I know that the decision of whether to travel to the Old Country is a personal one, I think it would be useful to share my own feelings on the subject.

I try to understand the bitterness felt by survivors toward the non-Jewish population in the countries where our people were murdered. I can understand them not wanting to have contact with people, many of whom just stood by watching while Jews were killed. Others, of course, did not just stand by, but participated. But I was born after the War, and as a new generation I feel I must have faith in humankind. I cannot harbor the same feelings as the generations before me. While I am, for example, quite suspect of Germans who were adults in Germany during the War, I cannot declare them all guilty, and I surely can hold nothing against their children. The same is true for other countries in Europe.

As for the comment (which I have heard several times) that my "roots" are really in Israel so therefore I should go there instead, I have two responses. One is that I have visited Israel and feel that every Jew who has the opportunity should do the same. But my "roots" do not lie only in Israel. Maimonides was from Spain, Rashi from France, the Baal Shem Tov from Eastern Europe, and even the Babylonian Talmud was not written in Israel. Certainly my roots go *back* to Israel, but they travel far and wide outside of Israel as well. I want to discover *all* of my past.

I was quite influenced before my trip to Eastern Europe by those people who told me that everything was destroyed and that there was nothing left to see. If this was true, I thought to myself, then surely I would be wasting my time and money. I thought about it for a long time. What if the town was completely leveled and a new town built on top of it? What would be the point of seeing this? But finally I decided: I was going to Eastern Europe not only to see what was left but also what was no longer left! I had done enough research about the town, I had seen enough photographs of the places where my ancestors lived to know what it looked like when they were there. I wanted to see what had stayed the same and what had changed. Seeing *nothing* would also be important to me.

There was one additional factor in my decision to visit Eastern Europe: I have cousins who live there. My father's cousin, Josef Schlaf, lives in Warsaw, and my mother's first cousin, Gyorgy Barta, and his family live in Budapest. I wanted to visit them. This was the most important element in my decision. I finally decided to go.

While I was planning our trip, one book excited me the most. It was *Traveler's Guide to Jewish Landmarks of Europe* by Bernard Postal and Samuel H. Abramson (Fleet Press, New York, 1971). This volume is a country-by-country, town-by-town guide to Europe—and it includes Eastern Europe. While far from complete, it is a gold mine of information for anyone planning a trip to Europe. When you are in the major cities of Eastern and Western Europe as well as smaller localities, the *Traveler's Guide* will inform you of many Jewish historical and current sights of interest.

When I checked the book, I was startled to find the name of my great-grandfather's town, Przemysl. To my surprise, I read that the Jewish cemetery still existed! How much I wanted to see that cemetery, to search for the graves of my family members, to walk through the paths and feel the Jewish history which took place there. I thought to myself that even if there were no Jews there, even if nobody remembered my family, even if everything else was destroyed—as tragic as it all would be—I would still be able to touch my past through the graves of the Jewish community. How many times my family must have stood in that cemetery to bury our dead.

The day finally came. I arrived in Warsaw. After spending a few days in that historic Jewish city with my cousin who lives there, I went to Przemysl. One of the first things I wanted to see was the Jewish cemetery. Everyone knew where it was. When I saw it, I was astounded for opposite reasons. I was shocked at how bad it looked and by how good it looked. It was interesting to learn that the major problem with Jewish cemeteries in Poland is *not* vandalism. It is neglect. The stones were not toppled over and crumbling from deliberate desecration. It was the seasons of bad winters, the overgrown trees and bushes, the tall growth of weeds and roots, and the total neglect of the whole area which caused the cemetery to look so bad. On the other hand, there it was, sitting there peacefully. Many of the stones could be read with ease. Others were quite worn but could still be made out. Still others were not visible at first, but after we pulled out giant weeds and pushed aside bushes and overgrowth, they too appeared! Some of the stones were 150 years old. Others were certainly older, but a good percentage of the old stones were totally illegible. Some were just slabs of rock with no inscription. Obviously, they once had words engraved on them, but time has worn them clean. I stayed in the town for five days. Three times I visited the cemetery, taking photos on each visit, recognizing names each time I uncovered new tombstones under the overgrowth. Visiting that cemetery was one of the most moving moments of my life. Each time I went, I prayed, and somehow felt the presence of a Jewish community which once was so filled with life, and now is present only in the remains of the cemetery.

One of the many surprises in Przemysl was the number of people whom I found to speak English. English is taught in the schools and is apparently a popular subject. I had almost no problem communicating with people. The people who spoke English were happy to show me around and serve as my interpreters.

I was anxious to see where the synagogues were. I knew from my research that there were several synagogues before the War. Today, two of the buildings still exist. One is now the Przemysl Public Library. The other is a bus garage. This was obviously an upsetting discovery. While I did not expect the buildings to still be synagogues (there are but a handful of Jews still in Przemysl), it was horrible to see this beautiful building turned into a bus garage. Somehow the library did not bother me as much. Actually, the reason is evident. While I visited both buildings, I was most interested in the one which is now the library. This synagogue was a short distance from where my family in Przemysl lived, so I was fairly certain that it was in this synagogue that my family prayed. Walking into the library, I was obviously a stranger. Only one member of the library staff spoke English and I was introduced to her. She was a young, pretty woman, very bright and warm. After an interesting conversation and a glass of tea which I was served right in the middle of the library, the young librarian invited me to her home for that evening. I had a wonderful time, learned a lot about Przemysl from her and her husband, and I still write to them. They send me information about Przemysl and I send them magazines about tennis, their favorite pastime. They are, by the way, always on the lookout for Jewish items of interest to send me.

I could go on for pages about my trip to Eastern Europe. Suffice it to say that it was a deeply moving and profound experience for me. Again, both what I saw and what I knew I could never again see had a great impact on me. I visited concentration camps and former ghettos. I visited synagogues which were hundreds of years old and cemeteries even older. I met Jews who survived the Holocaust and stayed in Eastern Europe and I met some of their children. They are all eager to make contact with American Jews and in this way I think my trip served a valuable purpose in showing a few lonely Jews that they are not totally alone.

Did I discover anything of specific genealogical value in Eastern Europe? I certainly did. When I was in Przemsyl, the city of my great-grandfather's birth, I went to the city hall and asked the man (through the aid of a Jewish man who still lived in Przemysl and spoke some English) behind the counter if he had my great-grandfather's birth record. He asked me when my great-grandfather was born. I said 1867. The man climbed up a tall ladder and reached up to grab a volume which was covered with dust. When he set the book down on the counter, I saw that it was a birth register of Jews from the 1800's! This particular volume was dated 1860-1870. Within a few minutes I found the name of my great-grandfather, along with his parents' names, their address in Przemysl, and other information as well. It was the birth record from more than 100 years ago of my great-grandfather, Abusch Kurzweil.

The myth that I was told so many times was that all Jewish records were destroyed. The fact of the matter is quite different. There, in Przemysl, Poland, was the birth record of the man after whom I was named. It was waiting for me all these years.

How to Plan Your Trip

The first piece of advice that I can give you is to see a travel agent who specializes in Eastern European travel if it is Eastern Europe that you want to visit. If you are visiting a different part of the world, find a travel agent who knows about that area. In this way you will be getting the most up-to-date information regarding travel conditions at your destination.

Specifically relating to Eastern Europe, be aware of the fact that every country is different. Each has a different attitude toward travel inside its borders. In the Soviet Union, for example, special permission is needed to travel anywhere other than the official list of approved locations. In Poland and Hungary, on the other hand, you can rent a car and travel anywhere in the country without special permission. All the other Eastern European countries are also more liberal toward tourists.

Again, the best thing to do is to check with a travel agent. Visa requirements are different for each country as are accommodations.

Of course, you should not travel to your ancestral hometown without having done your homework. You must learn about the general and Jewish history of the places you intend to visit. Otherwise you will not be able to appreciate fully your visit. (See page 191.) Try to locate as many photographs of the towns as possible so that you can recognize the places when you get there. Make copies of your family history notes and papers to bring with you. You might meet someone with whom you can have a rewarding famliy history conversation.

Often I am asked, "For how long should I visit my ancestors' town?" That depends upon how big the town was. If it is Warsaw or Prague, you can stay for days. If it is the average little village, one day is more than enough time (after which you will want to explore other places in the area, and so on). A small city might interest you for a few days. But do not think that your visit to a tiny old shtetl need take a week. Chances are you can walk every street and take every photograph and talk to every person within a few hours. Most of these places are rural and there is not much to see. On the other hand, your day or two might be among the most memorable moments of your life.

There are several sources that you will want to check for information about the locations to which you want to travel. The first is the *Traveler's Guide to Jewish Landmarks of Europe* already described. Once again, the book is far from complete. If you do not

Four generations in present-day Radauti, Romania. Child at his circumcision, held by his grandfather; his father behind his grandfather; and portrait of his great-grandparents on the wall. (Photographed and courtesy of Laurence Salzmann)

find your town, it does not necessarily mean that the town no longer exists. I visited many towns in Galicia which were not mentioned in the book but which had Jewish cemeteries still intact as well as other sites of Jewish interest. Of particular interest for me, in each town I visited, were three things: Where is the Jewish cemetery? where are the buildings which used to be synagogues? are there any Jews still in the town? Often I found cemeteries, buildings which were once synagogues, and sometimes even Jews. None were listed in the *Traveler's Guide* or in any other source I could find, yet there they were.

Memorial Books (see page 192) are a must to check before your trip. If there is a Memorial Book for your town, it will provide you with pictures, names, history, and sometimes even a map of the town! With a map, you can more easily find sites of interest. For example, since the synagogues have almost all since been converted into other kinds of buildings, an old map from a Memorial Book can serve as your guide to finding it. By the way, there are four things which most synagogue buildings are now used for: libraries, warehouses, garages, and movie theaters.

The *Encyclopedia Judaica,* mentioned often throughout this book, can be a good source of information about the current situation in the town of interest.

Landsmannschaften might also be a good source of information (see page 207) but I must make the following warning: I have found that members of the landsmannschaften that I have encountered were both the first ones to discourage me from making the trip as well as the most interested in hearing about my experiences and seeing my photos when I returned.

Speaking of your return, when I returned from my trip, I did two things: I wrote an open letter to family and friends describing my trip. I could not write a separate note to each person, but I found it useful to write up a letter that I photocopied and sent around to interest people. The second thing I did was to make slides of my photographs (in some cases I took slides too) and invite the family to see them while I narrated. I did *not* put in all of my tourist shots—I did not want to bore my family with one more travelogue—but only the photos relating to the family history (along with a few general shots of Eastern Europe to put it into context). It was a very successful "party" when these slides were shown and it was appreciated by the family. Through my trip, they received a better sense of the family history. And that was my whole purpose.

If you are planning a trip to Poland, you will want to first examine a book called *Scenes of Fighting and Martyrdom Guide; War Years in Poland, 1939-1945*. This book is a town-by-town guidebook describing Holocaust monuments throughout the country (not necessarily all Jewish) and how to find them. There is a description of the monument or location, a brief passage about what happened on that spot, and directions on how to get there. YIVO (see page 191) has a copy of this book.

If you are traveling to Czechoslovakia, you might want to send for a somewhat useful booklet put out by Cedok, the Czechoslovakian Travel Office, 10 East 40th Street, New York, N.Y. 10016. The booklet is called "Jewish Monuments—Czechoslovakia."

Many people have traveled to the Old Country and have written about their journey. It would be useful for you to read some of these accounts to prepare you additionally for your trip. These are among the best I've encountered:

"The Last Return" by Elie Wiesel, in *Legends of Our Time*, Holt, Rinehart and Winston, 1968.

"Journey to Istanbul" by Raquel Sinai, in *Ke Xaber? A Newsletter from Adelantre!*, issue 5-6. (See page 255.)

"A Visit to the 'World of our Fathers'" by Gloria L. Freund from *Passover with Newsday,* April 9, 1978, *Newsday,* Garden City, New York.

"The Last Jews of Radauti" by Laurence Salzmann from *The Jewish Exponent,* April 28, 1978, Philadelphia, Pa.

Remove not the ancient landmark which the fathers have set.

—Prov. 22:28

With the present-day Jewish community of Radauti, Romania, ca. 1975. (Photographed and courtesy of Laurence Salzmann)

Hebrew Subscription Lists

In the past (and sometimes even today), Jewish scholars who wanted their books published would do it themselves. They or their representatives would go from town to town trying to sell "subscriptions" to a forthcoming book. The potential reader would pay in advance to support the publication of the volume. In return, the author of the book would usually publish the subscriber's name in the book—for two reasons. First, as an incentive to subscribing. After all, if your name was to appear in a scholarly Jewish text you might be more apt to invest. Secondly, in order for the "publisher" to know who ultimately gets the book, a list of towns and names must be produced for distribution purposes.

The result of all this is that within thousands of rabbinic and scholarly books which have survived until today we can find lengthy lists of towns and individuals in those towns. The persons listed are the ones who subscribed, pre-publication, to the book.

Berl Kagan, a scholar to be admired who is affiliated with the Jewish Theological Seminary in New York, has put together a magnificent book on the subject. The remarkable task which Kagan set for himself and which he completed is the indexing, by town, of thousands of subscription lists in Jewish books.

Hebrew Subscription Lists, with an Index to 8,767 Jewish Communities in Europe and North Africa (the Library of the Jewish Theological Seminary of America and KTAV Publishing House, Inc., New York, 1975) is the result of Berl Kagan's efforts.

What Kagan has done is to go through the thousands of books published during the last few hundred years which had subscription lists in them. Every time a town name appeared, he noted the name of the town, the name of the book, and the number of people who subscribed to the book. In other words, for you to use Kagan's book genealogically, you would look up the name of a town in your family history. Under the listing of that town you would find the titles of Jewish books and a number following the title. The number would indicate how many people in that town subscribed to that book.

Once you discover that a particular book was subscribed to by certain people in your town, you can go to the original book (to be found at the Jewish Theological Seminary library or in other good Jewish libraries) and examine the subscription list. What you just might find is a name familiar to you.

What would such a discovery mean? Well, if you found an ancestor of yours on a subscription list in an old Jewish text, you would now know nothing more—but nothing less—than that your ancestor helped to support this particular book in which his name appears. It would not offer you any great new discovery of an unknown ancestor, but it would tell you something somewhat significant about that individual.

By the way, the whole process of checking Kagan's book and then checking each old text is a very long one. This step of your research should be saved for a time when you have just about reached dead ends with everything else. But it is a fascinating and educational process.

Chapter 6

The History of Your Family Is Chiseled in Stone

Apart from the personal significance that a cemetery has for the survivors of someone who has died, cemeteries also represent the history of people. There is something special, something strange yet basic, that you feel when walking among the graves in a cemetery. I have said this to people who have responded by calling me morbid. But a cemetery is not morbid. On the contrary, somehow a cemetery, on a quiet day, is filled with life. Scanning the stones, you can read: "Died at age 87," "Died at age 68," "Died at age 74" and you begin to have the sense that each of the stones which surround you represents lives which were filled with complexity, love, struggle, hardship, pleasure, celebration, faith, pain, and exploration of life. Each stone is a lifetime, a family, a world.

In a cemetery, you cannot escape facing your own life. You are alive. This is what each stone says to you. You are alive. You are able to read the words engraved in the rock. You can read the names, the dates, the epitaphs. In fact, those words on the monument were put there for you, for that very moment when you wander over to it and wonder what this person's life was really like.

I would like you to go to a cemetery at a time other than when you must for a funeral because I want you to know what it is like to walk between the paths of graves in silence, with no one near you to distract your thoughts. I want you to know, as I have known, what it is like to read gravestone after gravestone, wondering about each person and the lives that they led.

But how can you know, from a few words chiseled on a stone, what the person was like? And what would it mean if you could? These people are strangers.

I cannot answer that in full; but in part, what a cemetery affords you the opportunity of doing is to see the world, for just a moment, frozen in time. Outside, in the busy streets and noisy rooms, the world seems to move too fast. It is difficult to see that this planet of ours is made of individual lives, each of whom has feelings, sensitivities, and his own concerns. But in a cemetery, the lives are still, and each grave stands there to be witnessed, each representing the

232

end of time for an individual. Standing in front of the grave of a stranger—the same kind of stranger whom you pass on the street each day—the vivid sense has come over me that we are all so mortal, so unique, so special in our ways. Individual lives—this is what our world consists of.

But walking through a graveyard must be more than that, more than simply the ideas which I have been trying to express. Otherwise, it would be enough to read this—and it surely is not.

Some people make sure to visit a cemetery when they go for a vacation. It is on the sight-seeing list with the museums, parks, and historic spots. How can a graveyard be a place to visit on a vacation? How can one visit it when sight-seeing? Again, it has to be experienced to be known. But in part, a cemetery is a symbol (and the reality) of the history of a community and a people. When you stand on a piece of ground and read a stone which says "1803," you suddenly know, perhaps more than if you were told it or read it, that life went on at that very spot generations ago. And you know, as you stand before each grave and read the date of death, that it was just a day or two later that a group of people stood where you are standing, to bury a loved one. Each grave represents a life and the world left behind. A cemetery contains the monuments representing the people who made history; not just the famous individuals who make the history books and the headlines, but also each person who, in his or her way, brought Time forward a few more years, to this very moment.

But this still is not all that a graveyard represents. There is more to this custom that we have of burying those who have died. The custom itself goes back to the earliest days of human history. The particulars have changed, but the custom and its importance have been a part of humankind and the Jewish people since the beginning. The Bible records burial customs as does the Talmud and other writings. Sometimes the burial was done in caves, other times in scattered graves, but always there was a great concern for this point in our lives.

Our cemeteries, as sacred as they are to us, have often been desecrated. History records the desecration of Jewish cemeteries as early as the Middle Ages, and today we still hear of Jewish graveyards attacked by vandals.

During the Middle Ages, when Jews were forced out of a community, the cemetery was frequently destroyed, the tombstones used for other purposes. Some old buildings in Europe can still be found with slabs of stone taken from Jewish cemeteries. In more recent times, such desecrations in Israel by Arabs have been witnessed on a large scale. Jewish tombstones have been stolen and used for a variety of calculated purposes.

We know that the desecration of Jewish cemeteries has always been widespread. It is important to note that there are no ancient Jewish burial grounds in existence, save for a few scant traces. Furthermore, an old Jewish cemetery such as the Prague Cemetery contains no graves earlier than the fourteenth century since the Jewish cemetery before that time was totally destroyed in April of 1389. In addition, it is tragic to note that Popes Calixtus II, Eugenius III, Alexander III, Clement III, Celestine III, and Innocent III had to specifically protect Jewish graveyards by means of Papal declarations. Also, Duke Frederick II of Austria declared in July of 1244, "If a Christian attempts to destroy a Jewish cemetery or to break into it, he shall be put to death after the manner of the law, and all his property, no matter what it may be, shall be confiscated by the Duke."

There were other rulers who also extended protection, for a time at least, to Jewish cemeteries, including Frederick the Great of Prussia (1786-1840) who put up a sign at the entrance of the Jewish burial grounds warning that anyone who harms the cemetery would have his head chopped off with an ax.

Unfortunately, these attempts at protection of the Jewish graves were few and far between. Desecration of Jewish cemeteries coincided throughout history with the persecution of living Jews as well. Neither the living nor the dead were left in peace.

auf
Das erste Blatt ist mit der Vorderseite überklebt,die etwa 20 Einträge
enthalten mag.Vorerst hat man sie noch nicht losgelöst,um das an sich schon
so wurmstichige Buch nicht weiter zu schädigen.Vielleicht wird diese Los=
lösung mit aller Vorsicht noch erfolgen können,nachdem der übrige Inhalt
durch diese Abschrift sicher gestellt sein wird.

```
 1)Iöser שׁעדריגאן (kaum=Dittingen),st.in Höchberg        27.Tebet 539,15.1.1779
 2)Nefel e.Orach,                     "    "    "          4.Sch'vat " ,21.1.
 3)Frau e.Orach (des Jakob,Metz) "    "    "    beerd. 7.  "     " ,24.1.
 4 )Wwe.des Vorbeters Iob in Mainstockheim,st.im Hause
     ihres Schwiegersohnes,Gem.Dieners Seckel in Höch=
     berg                                                 am selben Tag.
 5)S'chen e.Orach,st.in Acholshausen                      8.Sch'vat " ,25.1.1779.
 6)Nefel T.des Josef Hirsch in Sommerhausen              28.   "     ,14.2.  "
 7) Nefel desselben                                       2 Tage später.
 8)Tochter des Jona Iob,Heidingsfeld                      6.Adar 539,22.2.1779.
 9)Eine Orach-Frau,st.in Heidingsfeld                    12.  "     ,28.2.  "
10 )Nefel T.des Mosche levi,     "                        24.  "     ",12.3.  "
11)S'chen des Hirsch,Kirchheim                            26.  "     ",14.3.  "
12 )Frau des Josef Hirsch in Dittigheim                   29.  "     ",17.
13 ) S'chen des Benjamin (Gau=)Königshofen                1.Nissan " ,18.
14 )T'chen des Hirsch,Bütthart                            12.  "     ",19."
15 )T'chen des Iob kohen,Giebelstadt                      13.  "     ",20."
16 )Nefel eines Orach,st.in Höchberg                      18.  "     ",24.4.
17 )Frau e.Orach aus Kleinsteinach,st.in Giebelstadt      14.Ijar " ,10.4.
18 )Iöb kohen,Giebelstadt                                 am selben Tag
19 )S'chen e.Orach,st.in Höchberg                         16.Ijar 539 ,11.5.  "
        Hier offenbar ein Blatt (oder mehrere)ausgerissen.
20 )S'chen des Jakob,Allersheim                           4.Siwan 540 ,7.6.1780.
21 )Sohn eines Orach,st.in Kirchheim                      11.  "     " ,14.6.  "
22 )Nefel S.des Iob,Rottenbauer                           19.  "     " ,22.6.  "
23 )Sohn des David,Rottenbauer                            2.Tammus " , 5.7.  "
24 )S'chen des Ahron ben 'א ,Heidingsfeld                16.  "     " ,19.7.  "
25 )Meir kohen,Höchberg                                   2.Av     "  ,2.8.  "
26 )Nefel T.des Vorbeters Ioser in Allersheim             9. "     "  ,9.8.  "
27 )Nefel S.des Scholem levi,Grünfeld                    10.Menachem" ,11.8.  "
28 )Unverheir.S.des Abr.kohen,Heidingsfeld               16.  "     " ,17.8.  "
29 )T'chen des Vorbeters in Sommerhausen                 27.  "     " ,28.8.  "
30 )Nefel S.eines Orach,st.in Giebelstadt                28.  "     " ,29.8.  "
31 )S'chen des Iöb,Fuchsstadt                            28.Elul     " ,28.9.  "
32 )Nefel e.Orach,st.in Rottenbauer                      Anfang Tischri,anf.  "
33 )Frau des David,Fuchsstadt                            19.Tischri 541,18.10."
34 )T'chen des Mordechai,Giebelstadt                     25.  "     541,24.10.80.
35 )T'chen des Bendit,Sommerhausen                       27.  "     " ,26.10.80.
36 )Parnos Josua,Heidingsfeld                            am selben Tag.
37 )Frau des Vorbeters Iippmann kohen,Königshofen        28.Cheschvan,18.10.80.
38 )Tochter des Michael kohen,Reichenberg                am selben Tag.
39 )Nefel S.des Simeon levi,Höchberg                     5.Kislev 541,3.12.780
40 )Frau des Lehrers Rafael kohen in Heidingsfeld        9.  "     " ,7.12.  "
41 )Eine Frau aus Niederwerrn,st.im Hause ihres
     Schwiegersohnes Bendit,Sommerhausen                 15.  "     " ,13.12.  "
42 )Frau eines Orach,st.in Impfingen                      1.(?)Tebet" ,29.12."
43 )  "    "    "    "   "  " Geroldshausen               Um dieselbe Zeit (un
                                                              leserlich).
44 )  "    "    "    "   "  " Kirchheim                   16.Tebet 541,13.1.1781
45 )Wwe.des Iob aus Obernbreit,st.im Hause ihres
```

Cemetery list for Jewish cemetery, Allersheim, Bavaria. (Courtesy of Leo Baeck Institute, New York)

After the First World War, desecration of Jewish cemeteries was widespread in Germany, and continued until the Holocaust. During and after the Second World War, Jewish graveyards continued to be desecrated, and the destruction of Eastern European Jewry resulted in the absence of Jewish communities who could even maintain these sacred spots. While many Jewish cemeteries in Europe have Holocaust memorials placed in them, the task of maintaining these sites becomes a greater and greater problem every day.

Cemeteries as Family Bonds

Often we will go to a cemetery on the sad occasion of a death and we will see members of our family and friends of the family whom we have not seen for a long time. We sometimes think to ourselves that it is odd to see these people at graveyards and nowhere else. But, in fact, the cemetery and the funeral is not just an occasion to bury the dead, but also to renew our ties with the living as well as to our past and tradition.

When we attend a funeral, we have the opportunity to reflect upon the past and upon the people in our families who were members of past generations and whose lives were the links between our own and history. Funerals are a time to go to a cemetery, to read the epitaphs of family members who have departed from this earth, and to remind ourselves of who we are and from where we have come.

Ironically, funerals and burial grounds often serve to renew our relationships with those people whom we perhaps have not seen since the last funeral. There may have been no contact since the last death in the family, but maybe this time there will be future contact "at happier occasions." While a funeral is a time of sorrow, it is not inappropriate or irreverent to think of the funeral or the presence at the cemetery as a deeply important opportunity from which to reap benefits. It is a time to think about one's childhood, to remember the last generations and their contributions to our lives, and to see the people whom we have not seen in a long time. Often those people remind us of happy times in our past and offer us a strong sense of who we are.

It is for these reasons, in part, that graveyards and funerals are so important in the Jewish Tradition. Cremation (forbidden by Jewish law) or other methods of treating the dead often prevent the coming together of people at a funeral, unveiling, or cemetery. Even when there is a funeral, the absence of a grave means the absence of the opportunity for a visitor at a grave who can read the words on a tombstone.

Standing before the grave of an ancestor or a relative and reading the words on the stone is a unique and priceless experience. One has to stand in silence among the silent graves of a burial field to be in touch with a sense of one's own history in such a vivid way.

In my family, my father and his brother and sister come together to visit the graves of their parents at least once a year. While the three of them see each other often during the year, there is something special about the annual visit they make. If they went separately it would be different. If there was no grave it would be different. If they got together and spoke about their deceased parents for hours it would be different. By coming together and in silence amidst the grave of their parents—and their grandfather, who is buried in the same family plot—they share moments that could never be replaced or equaled. Their silence at the graves says more than words could ever express. When the three children stand as grown adults at the grave of their parents, it is as if, in a sense, their family is together again. And, of course, it is not imagination, but reality, for their family *is* together for those moments at the graves. As they leave until the next time, they know that they come from the cemetery with much more than they arrived.

A Walk Through a Jewish Cemetery

A walk through a Jewish cemetery is a walk through Jewish history. Find the Jewish graveyard closest to your home or travel to one that has members of your family within its gates, and spend an hour or two wandering up and down the paths, comparing the monuments, reading the inscriptions, and absorbing the decades (or perhaps centuries) around you.

You will encounter, on your walk, the brief though often moving personal histories of many people. You will notice children who died before reaching their first birthday and great-grandparents who left this world after ninety-five years. Be on the lookout for unusual or instructive items. Perhaps you will wander over to a family plot and notice the more recent generations shortening the European last name. Speaking of names, a cemetery is an excellent place to observe the different naming customs from era to era. Names which were common sixty years ago will hardly be familiar today.

Do not think it bizarre to walk through a burial ground. The stones were engraved with words for people to read. The monuments were chosen to keep a memory alive. Certainly the family of the deceased would not mind if you stopped at a grave, read the inscription, and wondered about the person.

Notice the different shapes and sizes of the gravestones. Some will be tall and massive, others will be smaller and more modest. Some will be lavishly engraved with Jewish symbols and decorations and others will be simple, without any frills. The inscriptions, too, will be quite different. Some will be entirely in Hebrew, others totally in English. Some will include just the name of the person and the dates of birth and death, and others will include lengthy sayings and quite a bit of information about the person. Many Jewish gravestones even include photographs which are imbedded in the monument.

Read the inscriptions carefully. You will usually find the name of the deceased and then, in Hebrew, the name of the person's father. For the family tree researcher, this is, of course, an excellent source of genealogical information.

An inscription on a gravestone can offer more information about the life and the time of the people buried in the graves. You can discover the length of the person's life, for example. Often on a double gravestone, where there is room for a husband and a wife, one side is still empty, telling you that a spouse is still alive. Or both sides might be filled and you will know how long one person was alive while his or her spouse was deceased. You cannot help but wonder what the survivors of the family must be feeling when these graves are visited.

Family plots are a popular custom and you will surely find one which will tell a story about several generations of a family. You will find the graves of the great-grandparents, their children—the grandparents and their children. It is easy to pick out family plots, not only by the family name being repeated, but also by studying the inscriptions carefully. Since gravestones of Jews usually provide the name of the father of the deceased, it is a rather simple task to pick out the relationships, both by the names and by the positions of the stones. In this way, you can visualize entire families, imagine the lives of these people, study the names and see who was named for whom, who carried on the tradition in whose name, who lived to a ripe old age and who died tragically in his or her youth, who never married and who had many children.

A cemetery is rich in tradition and history. Jewish symbols abound on the stones which memorialize simple, common people. Their ancient names inscribed in stone stand as a tribute to lives of happiness, sadness, struggles, and celebrations. You look at a stone and read a few words about a man; when he was born, when he died, what his name was, and what his father's name was. You glance to the right and see his wife's name and her father's name. You see how long they lived and wonder whether they were born here or were they born across the ocean in a Jewish community that no longer exists. You look to see where the graves are located and notice that this is not a family plot but the plot of a landsmannshaft, consisting of people from the same town who are now "resting in peace" among people from their community, their lifelong friends who journeyed to America too and established their families here. Suddenly, this is not the grave of one person at all, but it is, rather, a brief history. It is the history of a man, his family, his community, and his beliefs. He was born a Jew and he died a Jew. He was born within his community and he lies at rest in his community. He lived with his wife and now, as the inscription on the grave itself says, He is with his beloved forever.

As you walk through the narrow paths of the Jewish graveyard, the names and the lives of the people who a few moments ago were strangers are no longer foreign. By stopping by a grave and reading the few words on the stone, you touch the life of the person who is represented to you by the inscription. A moment ago you did not know her name; now you know her name. A moment ago you did not know her father's name; now you know this too. A brief moment ago you did not know her husband's name, or her age, or her English and Hebrew names or the fact that she died a wife, mother, grandmother, and great-grandmother. Now you know that too. Next to her grave you notice the grave of a child. The first name is the same as her father's, so you know that the child was named for a great-grandfather. Then you realize: the child is the grandson of the woman. She was to her grandson's funeral.

A walk through a Jewish cemetery is not an unusual or futile effort. It is an encounter with lives and generations. You will not learn about Kings and battles, you will not encounter politicians and political upheavals. But you will meet the people who made Jewish history—by living and dying as Jews.

A TIME TO BE BORN, A TIME TO DIE

Tombstones

Tombstones offer a variety of information. Some include lengthy epitaphs, others have photographs imbedded in the stone, and still

Yahrzeit (anniversary of death) calendar from Hungary, in Hebrew and German, indicating name of deceased and of deceased's father, and date of death. (Courtesy of Gyorgi Barta, Budapest, Hungary)

From the Jewish cemetery of Mannheim, Germany. (Courtesy of Stadtarchiv Mannheim)

others include biographical information about the person.

Since the Jewish Tradition includes a father's name along with a person's name (and sometimes includes a mother's name, though not often), tombstones can help you to go back on your family tree an additional generation.

You may find that a tombstone offers differing information from what you have learned from other sources. Keep in mind that tombstones are often inaccurate. This is so for a few reasons: 1) Often there is no one available to give accurate information to the engraver, 2) when a mistake is made in the engraving, it is often not corrected, and 3) false information is sometimes given deliberately (to make a person seem younger, or older, at the time of death). Many people approach the question of age with peculiar biases. In any case, do not be surprised if you find a tombstone with conflicting information on it.

No monument gives such glory as an unsullied name.

—ELEAZER B. JUDAH, *Rokeah*, 13c

Cemetery Plots

There are several different types of cemetery plots.

1) Some plots are owned by entire families and contain the graves of family members. Often a large stone or archway can be found at a family plot with the name of the family on it. Family organizations such as cousins' clubs or Family Circles will own a plot. This would obviously be helpful to a family historian.

2) Synagogues often have plots for their members, or for those members who have purchased a plot.

3) Landsmannschaften and other fraternal organizations have cemetery plots. In fact, many of these organizations originally formed for the very purpose of buying a plot for its members.

4) Some people have individual plots with no affiliation or special location among other plots.

Walk reverently in a cemetery, lest the deceased say, "Tomorrow they will join us, and today they mock us."

—HIYYA RABBAH
Talmud: Berakot, 18a

Tombstone Transcribing

When you visit a cemetery for family history purposes, make sure that you transcribe all the information on the tombstone to your paper or notebook. Don't just jot down the names and dates, but rather record the inscription in its entirety. While you should seriously consider photographing the stones as well, sketches of the tombstones are also worthwhile.

If you are visiting a family plot containing many tombstones of personal interest, you should draw a map of the entire plot and note the location of each stone with its inscription. Finally, do not forget to label your notes, indicating the exact location of the plots within the cemetery. Cemeteries are often quite large, and an exact record of the plot location may be helpful in the future.

After every funeral I used to stay on at the cemetery and copy tombstone inscriptions.

—Jacob Shatzky, Jewish historian,
in memoirs about his youth

How to Read a Jewish Tombstone

If a tombstone of interest is written in Hebrew (as most Jewish tombstones are—in part, if not completely), a few pointers will be helpful if you cannot read the language.

At the top of most Jewish tombstones is the abbreviation פ״נ for a man and פ״ט for a woman. פ״נ stands for פֹּה נִקְבַּר meaning "here lies." פ״ט signifies פֹּה טְמוּנָה, meaning "here is interred."

At the close of most Jewish tombstone inscriptions you will find the abbreviation תנצב״ה , which stands for תְּהִי נַפְשׁוֹ צְרוּרָה בִּצְרוֹר הַחַיִּים This is a verse from I Sam. 25:29, "May his soul be bound up in the bond of eternal life."

The tombstone may contain an epitaph in Hebrew, in which case you would simply have to copy the letters or take a clear photograph of the inscription and get it translated.

Calculating a date from the Hebrew on the tombstone will also be necessary. Actually, it would be useful for you to learn how to convert a Hebrew date into an English date for tombstones as well as any other Jewish document written in Hebrew. The system is quite simple.

The letters of the Hebrew alphabet each have a numerical value. They are:

א —1	ז — 7	מ —40	ק —100
ב —2	ח — 8	נ —50	ר —200
ג —3	ט — 9	ס —60	ש —300
ד —4	י —10	ע —70	ת —400
ה —5	כ —20	פ —80	
ו —6	ל —30	צ —90	

When a Hebrew date is written, you must figure out the numerical value of each letter and then add them up. This is the date. But remember that this is the Hebrew date and not the date we use in daily life. In other words each Rosh Hashanah, which appears on the calendar in September or October, we add a year to the Jewish date. In September, 1979, for example, the Jewish year was 5740. With this information you need only do a little arithmetic to change a Hebrew date to a secular date.

There is just one minor complication. Often a Hebrew date after the year 5000 on the Hebrew calendar will leave off the number 5 in the thousands column. In other words, taking the example of 1979 being 5740, you will usually see the Hebrew date written as 740 rather than 5740. To arrive at a Common Era date simply add 1240 to the shortened date. Therefore, 740 plus 1240 is 1980. Why 1980 rather than 1979? Because the Jewish date changes, as I have said, in September or October. Most of the year 5740 will be in 1980, not 1979.

Of course a tombstone as well as other documents will have the month too, probably the Hebrew months. Here is a list of them:

תשרי	Tishre	September
חשון	Heshvan	October
כסלו	Kislev	November
טבת	Tevet	December
שבט	Shevat	January
אדר	Adar (Adar II	
אדר ב׳	in leap year)	February
ניסן	Nisan	March
אייר	Iyar	April
סיון	Sivan	May
תמוז	Tamuz	June
אב	Av	July
אלול	Elul	August

Since the Hebrew calendar is not the same as the calendar which we use in secular life, the months indicated above do not correspond exactly. In a given year the corresponding months can be off by several days or even weeks.

Here is one example of how to convert a Hebrew date into an English date: If the year is תרפ , the letter ת is 400, the letter ר is 200, פ is 80. In total 680. As I pointed out, the 5000 is usually left off, so actually the date would be 5680. But using our formula, 680 plus 1240 is 1920. That is the date we are familiar with.

Tombstone Rubbings

Tombstone rubbing is the art of transferring the design and inscription of the surface of a tombstone to a piece of paper or fabric, using a special wax or crayon. The procedure is simple, does not harm the tombstone, and allows you to end up with an exact, life-size reproduction of the stone.

While the art of rubbing is used to reproduce other images besides tombstones, old graveyards are probably the most popular sites for this ancient pastime. Rubbing tombstones is particularly effective for old stones with unusual shapes and lettering styles.

To obtain the supplies you need to practice this art, write to Oldstone Enterprises, 77 Summer Street, Boston, Mass. 02110. They are the largest suppliers of rubbing materials in the U.S.

> Perfect love, brotherhood and mutual assistance is only found among those near to each other by relationship. The members of a family united by common descent from the same grandfather, or even from some more distant ancestor, have toward each other a certain feeling of love, help each other, and sympathize with each other. To effect this is one of the chief purposes of the Law.
>
> —MAIMONIDES, *Guide III,* 49

Photographing Tombstones

It is not in bad taste to photograph tombstones. A photograph of a tombstone or a cemetery can be meaningful and moving.

If you are visiting cemeteries for your family research, it would be a good idea to photograph the stones as well as to transcribe the engraved message. Pictures of your family's tombstones would be a significant addition to your family history collection.

Of course, taking photographs should not prevent you from visiting the graves again, for personal reasons as well as to make sure that the graves are in good condition.

> We always found out at a funeral whoever was great or distinguished in Jewish Warsaw. I used to attach myself to every funeral procession that seemed to me important—according to the number of mourners. Often I did not even know who the deceased was, but hearing the eulogies at the cemetery, I felt that it was a privilege to be there in such lifeless proximity to a living past. Instinctively I inherited that impersonal attitude toward one whose life had graced Warsaw's Jewish life, a life which first revealed itself to me at the cemetery.
>
> —JACOB SHATZKY, Jewish historian

Locating Cemeteries

If no one in your family knows where a burial plot is located, try to obtain a copy of the person's death certificate. A death certifi-

Grave of Nathan, son of Benjamin, Mintz, visited by his son Abraham, in Oshmana, Russia. (Courtesy of Bertha Mintz)

cate usually gives the location of the cemetery. When you arrive at the graveyard, inquire at the office for the exact location of the plot.

While all burial offices will tell you the location of a specific plot, they vary when it comes to giving you additional information about the individual and his or her family. They also have information in their files which might be helpful (such as the name of the spouse, address at time of death, etc.) but cooperation varies from office to office.

> A generation goes and a generation comes, but the earth stands forever.
>
> —Ecclesiastes 1:4

Death Certificates

While the registration of deaths varies from place to place and year to year, there is usually a death certificate on file for deaths which have occurred within the United States. A death certificate can be helpful in your family history research because most of them include information such as full name, name of father, maiden name of mother, name of spouse, date of death, place of death, cause of death, place of burial, name of funeral home, place of birth, address at time of death, and number of years in the United States.

Any one of these pieces of information can lead you to more information. For example, if you know how many years a person was living in the U.S., you can narrow the field when searching for immigration papers and steamship passenger lists. If you know an ancestor's mother's maiden name, you can begin a new branch of your family tree. If you know the place of burial, you can locate the grave and obtain more information from the gravestone.

The U.S. Government Printing Office sells a pamphlet called "Where to Write for Birth and Death Records." It costs 70¢ and can be obtained from the U.S. Government Printing Office, Washington, D.C. 20402, or from any of their local offices throughout the country. While you are sending for this pamphlet, you might also send for two others: "Where to Write for Marriage Records" and "Where to Write for Divorce Records," each costing 70¢, and each being helpful for your family history research.

> Happy is he who grew up with a good name and departed this world with a good name.
>
> —JOHANA, Talmud: Berakot, 17a

Wills

A last will and testament that is filed with the state is usually a public record and is often filled with family history data. In many cases, wills include names of children, grandchildren, and other relatives. Also, you can learn a lot about a person by what he or she is giving to others in a will, as well as to whom the gift is being given. I have found wills indicating sums of money to go to yeshivas and other religious organizations, for example, which give me an insight into the religiosity or affiliations of the deceased.

Wills are located in a variety of places. Sometimes they are kept in Surrogate's Court, Probate Court, or elsewhere. You should check the county clerk office for whatever location interests you and see where the wills are kept. Keep in mind that you are entitled to see these documents, except in specific cases for various legal reasons. I mention this because I have often gotten the feeling that wills are confidential. I have also met with resistance on the part of some clerks in a few places. Be insistent. You have a right to examine most wills.

> Cemeteries must not be treated disrespectfully. Cattle may not be fed there, nor a watercourse turned, nor grass plucked.
>
> —Talmud: Megilla, 29a

Obituaries

Newspaper obituaries can often be key sources of family history information. The difficulty with them, however, is that there is no systematic way of finding an obituary for several reasons:

1) There are no indexes to obituaries which would be useful to the general population. (*The New York Times* issued an index but it is selective.)

2) There are two kinds of obituaries: the articles written by the newspaper, and the announcements provided by individuals. In order to find an obituary of a specific individual, you must first be able to locate the right newspaper. Then you must know the day or the approximate day of death. Then you must hope that either an article was written or that an announcement was published.

3) Back issues of newspapers are often available on microfilm in the geographic area where the newspaper is published. This is true for defunct newspapers as well as those which are still publishing.

4) Do not forget to consider Yiddish papers. Again, this can present a problem since there were many Yiddish newspapers circulating at times, and you may not know which paper was read by the people who might have published a death announcement. Check with the YIVO Institute for Jewish Research regarding how to locate back issues of Yiddish newpapers.

The American Jewish Periodicals Center, Hebrew Union College, 3101 Clifton Ave., Cincinnati, Ohio 45220, also has an excellent collection of Jewish newspapers.

With all of the problems surrounding obituaries, they can still be of great use and should be considered when you are doing your research.

> Moses received the Torah at Sinai and handed it down to Joshua; Joshua to the elders; the elders to the Prophets; and

the Prophets handed it down to the men of the Great Assembly.

—Talmud, Pirke Avot, 1:1

European Jewish Cemeteries

Many Jewish cemeteries in Eastern Europe were partially or entirely destroyed during the Holocaust. Yet, a surprising number of them have survived and are intact. Some are quite old and are filled with family history.

Old Jewish cemeteries in Western Europe are also good sources of information, and a trip to ancestral locations should include such research.

If the town you are interested in has a landsmannschaft (see page 207), its members will usually know the fate of the town Jewish cemetery. A good, though incomplete listing of European Jewish burial grounds can be found in *Traveler's Guide to Jewish Landmarks of Europe* (described on p. 224).

When I visited Poland, one of my main interests was locating old Jewish graveyards. Often as I entered a town which we knew once had a Jewish population I asked people if they could direct me to the Jewish cemetery. Those whom I asked were always quite helpful and usually knew where it was located. Sometimes it was difficult to find the cemeteries because they had been left alone for more than three decades and were now totally covered with weeds and overgrowth. Yet, as I pulled away and pushed aside the growth, I found well-preserved gravestones, some more than 150 years old. (See "Visiting the Old Country," page 222.)

My greatest success in searching for family tombstones came the second time I visited Hungary. I drove several hours from Budapest to a small town in the northeast corner of Hungary called Mátész-alka. After locating the old Jewish cemetery in the typically over-grown, run-down condition that I had come to expect, I searched the graveyard for a few hours. Finally, after almost giving up, I discovered the tombstone of my great-great grandmother. Not only was it a moment of excitement as I was able to look at and touch the tombstone, but it also gave me the name of her father, my great-great-great grandfather. Suddenly I was back one more generation.

Chapter 7

In 1492, the Jews Were
Expelled from Spain

If you ask the average person to tell you what happened in the year 1492, he or she will probably say that in that year Columbus discovered America. While it is true that in 1492 Christopher Columbus did land in what would eventually be called America, the year has a greater significance for Jews. It was in that year that the Jewish population of Spain was presented with a decree of expulsion. Jews in Spain were given a choice: either convert to Christianity, or leave.

The Jewish community in Spain at that time dated back 1,500 years, and legend holds that there were Jews in Spain in King Solomon's day. One particular period in the history of Spanish Jewry was from 900 to 1200 C.E. and is known as "the Golden Age." It was during this time that several generations of Jews enjoyed peace, tranquility, and a rich atmosphere of intellectual stimulation almost without interruption. This era produced such great Jewish names as Judah ha-Levi and Maimonides, as well as some of the finest examples of Jewish scholarship ever created.

While the Spanish Inquisition was not specifically aimed at Jews but rather at heretical Christians, the presence of Jews in Spain was nevertheless not desired, so Queen Isabella and King Ferdinand, the same individuals who sponsored the voyage of Columbus, signed the order to expel the Jews. This was done in the same month that Columbus received his orders, and in fact Columbus set sail on the very day that the Jews had to leave.

It is estimated that there were more than 150,000 Jews in Spain at that time. Some estimates run as high as 250,000. Of this, some sources estimated that 50,000 Jews converted and remained in Spain. One wonders how many Christians in Spain today descend from converted Jews of the late 1400's (and earlier). Of the Jews who left, estimates have been made that about 45,000 went to Turkey, 15,000 to North Africa and Egypt, 10,000 perished, 10,000 went to Southern France and Holland, another 10,000 went to Italy, 5,000 settled in scattered areas and 5,000 eventually went to South America and were among the first European settlers there. These figures are based on the estimates that the Jewish population of Spain was 150,000 at the time of the expulsion.

The Golden Age of Spanish Jewry was then over, but communities of Sephardic Jews developed in other areas and locations. (The term "Sephardic" refers to Jews whose ancestors lived in Spain and Portugal before 1492.) The largest group of expelled Jews appears to have settled in Turkey, and the seaport of Salonika became a great center of Sephardim. Many other cities throughout Europe, the Middle East, and Northern Africa also developed Sephardic communities.

The trauma of the expulsion might best be imagined by comparing it with a present-day expulsion from the U.S. Think for a moment of what it would be like if the United States government suddenly issued such a decree to American Jews, many of whom have been in the country for generations and who have lived and prospered in many ways for years. Imagine yourself faced with the choice: Convert to Christianity or leave. What would you do? Where would you go? The situation in Spain in 1492 was compounded, of course, by there not being too many other governments who welcomed Jews with open arms.

In 1654, twenty-three Jews from Brazil fled Portuguese repression and landed in New Amsterdam, which later became New York. The Jews established a congregation there. Other Sephardic communities also appeared along the east coast of North America, and the Sephardic population of the Colonies in America constituted about 1,000 individuals, or half of the Jewish population in colonial America. From that time to the present, the Sephardic community in the United States has increased significantly. From 1908 to 1925, between 50,000 and 60,000 Sephardim arrived in the U.S., coming largely from the Balkans, Asia Minor, and Syria. The economic and political situation in the Ottoman Empire was deteriorating, and the forces of natural disasters as well as nationalism on the part of the Balkan People all contributed to this migration. After the Holocaust, several thousand Jews from Morocco, Iran, Iraq, Syria, Israel, and Egypt also came to the United States.

In the early twentieth century, many Sephardic Jews migrated to the United States from the Middle East. For obvious reasons they did not join up with the Sephardim who had been on the continent from before the founding of the country. The descendants of the original Sephardic settlers were either quite assimilated or radically different from the new arrivals. These new immigrants were themselves divided into three groups: Judeo-Spanish, Greek, and Arabic. This caused an additional lack of congruity among Sephardim in this country. Many Sephardic communities did establish themselves throughout the U.S., however, and were found in Rochester, Philadelphia, Cincinnati, Chicago, Atlanta, Portland (Oregon), Los Angeles, and most notably New York City.

Sephardic Jewry is often neglected in histories of the Jewish People, and this is unfair. However, it can be understood, in part, by understanding the history of Ashkenazi Jewry and its relation to Sephardim. A simple population count illustrates the point: Before the Holocaust there were approximately 16,500,000 Jews in the world. About 15,000,000 were Ashkenazim and 1,500,000 were Sephardim. Not only was the number of Ashkenazi Jews overwhelming, but the customs of the Ashkenazim thereby had more widespread acceptance. Generally, the power of influence of the Sephardim had been small in recent centuries, while as we said earlier, the impact of the Golden Age has had an indelible effect upon world Jewry.

Sephardic influence has perhaps been most prevalent in Israel. When the Jews left Spain in 1492, and then subsequently in the following two centuries, the Ottoman Empire, which included Eretz Israel, accepted Jews freely. Therefore, Sephardic Jews established settlements and became the predominant element in many towns throughout the country. The city of Safed became the spiritual center of world Jewry by the sixteenth century, populated mostly by Sephardic Jews, among them being Joseph Caro (author of the *Shulhan Aruch*). In the 1950's and 1960's, large numbers of Jews from Arab countries, most of them Sephardic, migrated to Israel, increasing the Sephardic population significantly.

The term "Sephardic" has been misused countless numbers of times and it would be appropriate here to clear up this misunderstanding. As we have stated, Sephardim are descendants of Jews from Spain and Portugal who lived there before 1492. It is erroneously assumed that there are but two groups of Jews, Sephardim and Ashkenazim. Ashkenazim are generally defined as Jews from Central and Eastern Europe. However, these two groups do not comprise all of world Jewry, nor is it proper to assume that all non-Ashkenazi Jews are Sephardim. There are two additional groups of Jews, often referred to as "Oriental Jews," who are neither Ashkenazi nor Sephardic. These Jews come either from North Africa, and are Arab-speaking Jews who have been there since the beginning of the Diaspora, or they are Jews whose families have been in

Eretz Israel since the Jewish People was born.

The history of Sephardic families makes it ofttimes difficult to trace. Countries which have been the homes of Sephardic Jews are not generally cooperative when it comes to examining records of Jews. Nonetheless, the history of Sephardic Jewry is a fascinating one, and a Sephardic Jew will have little difficulty in learning about the communities from which he or she came. The procedure for doing this kind of research would be the same as for any other Jewish community and we have dealt with this in other places in this book.

The history of the Sephardic Jew should be of interest to all Jews, not only because of its effect and influence on world Jewry as we have mentioned, but also because the migration patterns of Sephardim make it likely that many Ashkenazi Jews are descendants, in part, of Sephardim. In my own case, my father's family comes from a town in Galicia and no Sephardic community is recorded there. On the other hand, there has been a legend in my family that we descend from Sephardim who fled Spain after the Inquisition. While our name is Ashkenazi and we look Eastern European, the legend has been passed down to us nonetheless. Through my research I have discovered that in the city of Przemysl, which is where my father's family originates, the first synagogue on record was built in the 1500's by two Spanish immigrants! So, Sephardim did indeed come to my ancestral home centuries ago and I might very well descend from them. Suddenly, with that knowledge, the expulsion of the Jews in 1492 becomes something of a family experience for me. While I can empathize with an oppressed people, Jew or non-Jew, the very possibility that my ancestors were among the Jews who were thrown out of Spain puts a very different light indeed on the year 1492 for me.

SEPHARDIC RESEARCH

How to Research Sephardic Family History

Approaching the history of a Sephardic family is not unlike researching any Jewish family. First, you must begin at home, gathering whatever leads and clues you can from relatives. An important fact to investigate is where the family came from *before* arriving in the U.S.

The history of the immigrants in the family would then be the next step. Searching for passenger lists of steamships, early census records, citizenship papers and so on is similar in the case of

Sephardic Jews to any other immigrant group.

Finally, the locating of sources which can tell you about the histories of the Sephardic communities in the Old Country is the same process as all other Jews would use—but it is here where the availability of those sources changes dramatically.

For Eastern European Jews, there are archives and libraries which have huge collections of materials. If you are a German Jew you have a similar situation. There are also thousands of sources in English which discuss Ashkenazi Jewry in detail. But the same thing does not exist in such great quantity for Sephardim.

The reason for this is somewhat reasonable. As we have seen, there are many more Eastern European Jews in the world than Sephardic Jews and there have been for a long time. It is understandable therefore that more sources exist for Ashkenazim than for Sephardim.

What this all means is that Sephardim will have to make a greater effort to track down sources of interest to them. It is unfortunate that there is no excellent and thorough bibliography on Sephardic culture and communities. However, as of this writing, the finest bibliography of this nature is about to appear. Compiled by David Bunis, an expert in Sephardic language and culture, the work will probably be the single most useful source for Jewish genealogists when they approach the scholarly stage of their research. David Bunis is a founder and editor of "Ke xaber?" which is described in this chapter. Write to him c/o the newsletter for more information on his work.

You will then have to visit the major Jewish libraries and investigate what materials they have on general Sephardic culture and on specific Sephardic communities. One library of particular note is at Yeshiva University in New York City, which has a special Sephardic division with one of the finest collections available.

How can you get access to vital records in the countries from where your families have come? One approach is to see whether the Central Archives for the History of the Jewish People has anything on your specific communities (see elsewhere in this chapter and book). Then check a good genealogical "how-to" book for your countries. (I have recommended a volume by Timothy Field Beard on page 282.)

After this, it's hit or miss—but you might discover something important if you try. For example, I teach a course in Jewish Genealogy and Family History Research at Queens College. All of my students, one particular semester, were originally from Eastern Europe (their families, of course) except for two. These two students were from families originally from Salonika. Most of the semester I spoke about Eastern European Jewry and felt bad that I had very little to say about Sephardic Jews in general or Jews from Salonika in particular. In addition, the other students in the class were generally successful in finding good sources for their Eastern European ancestral homes. This situation caused me to do a little checking on sources for Salonika.

My first discovery was a Memorial Book on Salonika! Though I had worked with the bibliography of Memorial Books hundreds of times, I had never seen the book listed. In fact, I was under the impression that Memorial Books were an Eastern European phenomenon exclusively.

My second discovery was even more surprising. I was at the YIVO Institute for Jewish Research which is known for its Eastern European slant (in particular Russia and Poland as well as anything in Yiddish). In the archives there I was told about the Jewish vital records from the 1920's in Salonika which are a part of the collection! Jewish records from Salonika at YIVO? It's a very unlikely place to find them, but there they were. The experience was just one more which underlined the principle that if you look hard enough, you will find valuable material tucked away somewhere.

In *Toledot: The Journal of Jewish Genealogy* (Volume 2, Number 3; Winter 1978–79) there is an article titled "In Search of a Sephardic Tradition" by Dr. David Sheby. In the article, Dr. Sheby explores the process he has gone through to trace his own Sephardic family. He includes several uniquely Sephardic sources. The article would be an excellent introduction for anyone with similar interests.

Adelantre!

A few years ago, two young scholars—Stephen Levy, who is a Sephardic Jew and a poet, and David Bunis, a linguist and expert in the Sephardic language of Judezmo—founded an organization called Adelantre! The Judezmo Society. The major effort of the society is the publication of its newsletter called "Ke xaber?" which means "What's new?" in Judezmo.

The newsletter is filled each issue with material of importance to anyone wanting to know more about Sephardic culture and history: historical pieces, book announcements, and many other subjects. Levy, one of the co-editors, who is well respected as a translator from Judezmo to English, often publishes his excellent work, especially Judezmo poems and ballads, in the pages of "Ke xaber?"

Of particular note are the articles of genealogical value. In issue

5-6, for example, there is a moving account by a young woman who visited the place of her mother's childhood in Turkey. The title of the article is "Journey to Istanbul."

"Ke xaber?" will also publish your genealogical inquiries. "Ke xaber?" is a good place to meet other Sephardic Jews.

Write to: Adelantre! The Judezmo Society
4594 Bedford Avenue
Brooklyn, N.Y. 11235

Children constitute man's eternity.

—I. L. PERETZ

The Grandees
The popular author Stephen Birmingham has written a book called *The Grandees* based largely on the genealogies available in Rabbi Malcolm Stern's book *Americans of Jewish Descent* (see page 186). What Birmingham has done is to track down many of the present-day descendants of early Jewish Americans and to retell some of their stories. As in the case of Rabbi Stern's book, many of the families discussed in Birmingham's book are Sephardic. It must be noted that while this book was quite popular, it is not viewed too highly by scholars involved with Sephardic heritage.

A good name is better than precious ointment.

—Ecclesiastes 7:1

Archives of the Sephardic Community
The contents of this archive relates to the Sephardic community that has been located in Palestine. Material relating to Sephardic communities elsewhere in the world will not be found here, but their collection is of significance if your family is of Sephardic background and has lived in Palestine or Israel. Some of the documents in this archive are quite old. Their address is Hahavazelet Street 12 A, Jerusalem, Israel.

The Central Archives for the History of the Jewish People
This archive, which we have mentioned several times throughout this book, should be noted in reference to its material from Sephardic communities. While the archive collects material from any Jewish community in the world, it is perhaps the finest source for Sephardic historical items. In general, there are few sources for Sephardic material, so we have singled this archive out in order to call your attention to its Sephardic collection. (See page 220.)

Chapter 8

These Are the Generations

As we continue to travel backward in time through Jewish history, we find it increasingly difficult to discover our individual ancestors and the lives they led. Some of us will find it impossible to trace branches of our family histories farther back than three generations. In part, this is because of the recent adoption of fixed surnames as we have discussed in Chapter 4. In part, your inability to find people who remember the histories of your families will also contribute to the difficulty of the task. But it is important that we continue to see Jewish history in terms of individuals and families. Jewish history is the story of individual Jews, not simply the "important" people. While those "important" people had sweeping effects upon our Jewish ancestors, we want to continue to examine the lives of our ancestors and how they might have lived them.

Jewish history can be seen as several overlapping layers. First there are the individuals. Individuals are connected to each other through their immediate families. Immediate families are actually small parts of larger families. The larger families come together to form the Jewish People, and if we take our progression one step farther, the Jewish People belong to the "family of humankind."

It is easy for us to view the first stage of our progression. Each of us is an individual, as are our parents and so on. We want to view the lives of as many persons as we can and to see how their lives fit into Jewish history. For example, when we view the life of your grandmother who journeyed to America in 1908, we see her as a significant part of Jewish history. When we learn about a cousin of ours who was murdered in the Holocaust, we see that as a significant part of Jewish history. Despite the fact that those experiences happened to millions of people, we enter those experiences ourselves through the lives of the people in our families.

We can also observe the history of our families. Since we, ourselves, are a part of many families, we can see the differences among them. One of our families might be more religious, another might be more Zionist, another might be more literary, and so on. Our purpose is not to generalize about people, but rather to see where they fit into the larger story of Jewish history. In my father's family, for example, there is one branch of the family tree almost all of whom went to Israel when it was still Palestine. Another branch, almost in its entirety, stayed in Europe and was killed in the Holocaust. Hardly a representative of that branch left Europe. In still another branch, nearly the whole family escaped the Holocaust and came to America. It is fascinating to examine these family branches to see how differences and decisions just like these resulted in modern Jewish history.

Can you make these same kinds of observations in your families? Can you see certain entire branches of your family tree having gone in one general direction while others have taken different courses? What about your branch? When viewed from the outside, what choices have been made with your family during the last several generations which have affected you and your life—as a Jew?

There are countless stories of American families who have discovered family in Israel whom they never knew existed. Sometimes branches of a family traveled to Israel a few generations ago. In other cases, survivors of the Holocaust went to Israel and their American cousins did not know that they survived. There could be branches of your family in other countries as well. In my own family, there are branches in Israel, Australia, Poland, Hungary, South America, and the United States.

Again, however, there will come a point when it will be impossible for you to trace the tracks of your early ancestors, in which case you can focus in on the history of their community. Let us say, for example, that your family (a branch of it) can be traced to the town of Jaroslaw in Galicia. Perhaps you can even trace a few generations back in Jaroslaw with names, dates, and stories. But then you can go no farther; no one remembers anyone that far back and no research was able to turn up anything about your specific family. This should not stop you from continuing to understand the Jewish community of which your family was a part. Where is Jaroslaw? What was it like? When did the Jewish community establish itself there? What is its history? Although you cannot trace individual members of your family in Jaroslaw, you can certainly begin to get an idea of Jewish community life there, and in that way enter Jewish history.

To continue with our example, we have to remember that the history of Jaroslaw had to have affected the lives of your Jaroslaw ancestors. As a part of the community, its history, its events, touch its members' lives. By quickly checking a source such as the *Encyclo-*

pedia Judaica, we can get a glimpse of the history of Jaroslaw back to the 1600's. We learn about the famous fairs which took place there, and the meeting of the Council of the Lands of Poland which met there frequently. These meetings were important for all of Polish Jewry. We also learn that in 1738 there were 100 families living in Jaroslaw. If this was a town of yours, perhaps one of those families was yours as well. In 1737 a "blood libel" case occurred, giving us a further idea of the history of this town. This is just the beginning of the history of the Jewish community of Jaroslaw—but if it was a town of yours, you would be able to continue to learn about it and thereby enter Jewish history.

In other words, when you have traced back in your family history as far as you can go, continue to understand your history by examining the towns and regions whence you have come. If you know that your family came from Germany in the 1840's, an understanding of Germany in the decades before that date will contribute to your sense of the history of your ancestors.

While it is not possible for everyone to take his family histories back through the Middle Ages, it is possible to begin to understand the history of the Jewish People through a history of a particular Jewish community. Again, let us take the example of the town of Jaroslaw. Two items in the brief history which we mentioned are of particular interest. The first is the Council of the Lands of Poland, and the second is the "blood libel." In order to understand the history of your ancestors' community, you will need to know about the Council of the Lands of Poland and also the history of "blood libel." In both cases, these questions will take you to other aspects of Jewish history, and again, you will find that you have entered Jewish history through the history of the community of your ancestors. This method of understanding Jewish history can be compared to setting up a long row of dominoes and then tipping over the first one. Step by step the entire row of dominoes will fall over. In the same way, once you have touched any piece of Jewish history, you will arrive quickly at the next step, until you have gone through history yourself, and begun to understand the experiences of your family. Your family is the focus of this process; in tracing their steps, you are tracing the steps of the Jewish People. In tracing the steps of the Jewish People, you will eventually arrive at the beginning of time, and also you will arrive back in the present—at yourself.

A next step would be to begin to get an understanding of the migration patterns within Jewish history. Again, if your family came from Jaroslaw, they were certainly not there since the beginning of time. The Jewish community in Jaroslaw had a beginning before which time there were no Jews there. Whence did the Jews of Jaroslaw come? There are general answers to this type of question, and a familiarity with migration patterns—that is, the routes taken by Jews throughout Jewish history—allows us to get a better idea of where our families came from. For example, we know that in 1492 the Jews of Spain were expelled from that country. Historical research informs us of many places where Spanish Jews fled. If the places where they fled included areas which we know our families to be from, it is reasonable to assume that parts of our families may have originated in Spain. While we cannot be sure of this, it is reasonable speculation, and we can continue to enter Jewish history from that perspective. A branch of my family, as I mentioned earlier, whose earliest known location in Europe was the city of Przemysl, claims a family tradition that had us originate in Spain. While our names are not Spanish (we were probably in Przemysl when surnames were first required) and we do not look Spanish, it is interesting to note that the first synagogue in Przemysl was built by two Spanish immigrants in 1560. This means that Spanish Jews did reach the east end of Galicia at that time, and that our family tradition is conceivable. Suddenly, the expulsion of the Jews from Spain in 1492 becomes a real part of my history.

The detail of Jewish history, from the destruction of the Second Temple to modern times, is filled with tremendous variety and complexity. While short histories of the Jewish People have been written which include the major events and areas of our history, they cannot, by definition, tell the stories of individuals and their communities in the detail that they deserve. And it is the detail which is often the most colorful, the most instructive, and the most interesting.

It is a curious fact that most of us have a good idea as to the events of Biblical history, a familiarity with the Talmudic era, and a general knowledge of recent Jewish history during the last century or so. But in between those eras, from the early days of the Diaspora to the 1800's, most of us have no more than a vague idea of Jewish life. We are familiar with Biblical personalities, dramas, and heroes, as we are familiar with the Holocaust and the birth of the state of Israel, but what was life in Prague like in the 1600's? How did our ancestors in Germany live in the 1700's? What was life for our forebears in those centuries between the Talmud and the present?

We have already attempted to approach those centuries by looking at the histories of specific Jewish communities in which we know our ancestors lived. Another way of entering these centuries is by looking at a few of the artifacts of family interest which our ancestors left for us.

Torah Curtains and Ceremonial Objects

One of the most fascinating of these artifacts is the Torah curtain. At first, the idea of Torah curtain (parochet) seems to have little to do with history, let alone Jewish family history. Yet, Torah curtains historically contain quite a bit of genealogical information and frequently offer interesting insight into the lives of the people who presented these curtains to a synagogue. This, in fact, is exactly what was done with Torah curtains; they were usually presented to a synagogue by a member of its community. It is known that synagogues owned many Torah curtains in order to continue to redecorate the Ark as nicely as possible. Because of this, many individuals in communities presented Torah curtains to the synagogue. The genealogical significance of these curtains is that the curtains usually had the name of the presenters embroidered on them, and often also included genealogies. One can easily understand the great honor it was to be able to see the curtain with the names of one's loved ones sewn into it covering the holy Ark.

An exciting aspect of these curtains is the large number of them from centuries ago which are available for us to examine. The Jewish Museum in Prague, for example, has a collection of 2,800 Torah curtains. That same collection contains 1,000 top draperies, 4,800 Torah mantles, and many other artifacts as well.

Not only Torah curtains, but also other synagogue and ritual items have names inscribed on them. Often these inscriptions are all we know about the many obscure members of old Jewish communities. Had they not decided to invest in these inscriptions, their names would be lost to us. But to the contrary, we can gain insight into these people largely by the messages which they chose to immortalize. A typical example of an inscription on a Torah curtain reads, "Gifted by Juda Leb, son of Aaron of blessed memory, and his wife, the virtuous Zirl, long may she live! with their son Falk and his virtuous wife Feile. In the month of the new moon Sivan 1746." This curtain is one of the many in the Prague Museum. Other museums around the world with Jewish collections have similar items.

Curtain for the Torah Ark from Germany, 1752/3 with Hebrew inscription, "This was given by Abraham, son of Leib Katz, the son of Jacob Katz . . . and on the other side grandson of Meshullam Zalman Mirels . . . and Abraham's wife, Raina, daughter of Jacob, son of A . . ." (Courtesy of the Jewish Museum, New York)

Mohel Books

The Mohel book is another Jewish phenomenon which helps us to view Jewish history through individuals. A Mohel book is a record book kept by the mohel, or circumciser, listing each boy whom he circumcised. These books, many of which still exist from old communities, are an intriguing and unique record of Jewish male births in communities.

Finding a Mohel book for a particular community, and then finding a reference to someone in your family is a long shot, but it would be worth checking by more ambitious family researchers. The Leo Baeck Institute, 129 East 73rd Street, New York, N.Y. 10021 has a collection of Mohel books of German origin. The Central Archives for the History of the Jewish People in Jerusalem also has Mohel books for scattered communities around the world.

Ketubot

The ketubah, or marriage document, is still another custom in Jewish history which underlines the individuals who are a part of it. Very often ketubot will be handed down from generation to generation within a family. Ketubot record the names of the individuals being married and often include other family names as well. In the seventeenth and eighteenth centuries illuminated ketubot were popular, making the documents attractive as works of art.

While the possibility is remote that you will be able to find a Torah curtain or ritual object, a Mohel book, or a ketubah from a few hundred years ago with reference to your family, I have mentioned them for two reasons. The first is to present these customs to you in an attempt to illustrate how Jewish ritual can be seen from family perspectives. But the second reason is more important. I would like to see a revitalization of these customs on the same personal level which they once attained.

In other words, it would be important for us to think in terms of personalizing ritual objects. If you can, donate a Torah curtain to your shul with an inscription in reference to a loved one. Or donate another type of ritual object. An alternative is to engrave the ritual objects which you use at home. The pair of candlesticks which you use on Shabbas would have increased meaning if they were not only inscribed, but also passed down to children with names on them. Perhaps the names of your ancestors.

You could do this for any number of items: a kiddush cup, a

Page from Mohel (circumcision) book, Munich. (Courtesy Leo Baeck Institute, New York)

seder plate, a Chanukah menorah, a talis bag. To engrave or inscribe a brief family tree on any of these items would do wonders
in helping to insure that they will be used and respected in future
generations. Again we can imagine that the power of names is
dramatic. While a kiddush cup used each Shabbas becomes special
in its own right, how much more special does it become when it
contains the names of beloved ancestors. And if your children know

stories about the names engraved on the cup, how much more meaningful will the use of the cup be. There is always the problem that the object will get more respect than the act of the ritual itself, and this is something that we have always to be wary of. But done in the right spirit, the personalizing of Jewish ritual objects can help to pass Jewish Tradition from generation to generation through the use of the names of ancestors inscribed on them.

The same idea can be used in connection with a Mohel book. It is rare today not only for there to be Mohel books, but also for there to be a mohel performing a bris. Again, I would suggest that this ritual be returned to its proper place—in a Jewish setting—and a way to "underline" this would be to reinstitute the use of Mohel books. Appropriate birth rituals exist for males and females. When the rituals are performed, the names of the children should be inscribed in a record book in order to record the birth in a Jewish setting and not simply a secular setting, that of the birth certificate. Presently, when we seek proof of birth, we go to a secular agency, usually a Bureau of Vital Statistics. This is an example of one more phase of life being taken over by the secular. In order for us to be "rooted" in our Jewish lives, I think it is necessary to revitalize the use of the Mohel book and an equivalent for girls, in order to have a birth recorded within the Jewish community.

Finally, the ketubah is a document which is widely used but which is often not given the attention that it should receive. The use of the ketubah stretches back hundreds of years. Jewish marriages in your family for centuries usually used a ketubah. Again, while you will not have much luck in locating old ketubot in your family, you should inquire as to whether any were saved. Finally, when you are married, you should take care to find an attractive ketubah, fill it in with accurate genealogical information (perhaps even adding as many generations as you know), and use the ketubah as a record of family interest. The ketubah will stay in your family as an important document for your descendants to view.

There is opportunity in many aspects of our lives not only to make them Jewish, but also to inject a sense of family and generations in them. If you are getting married, try to locate a yarmulke which was used at some other important occasion in your family. If you lay tefillin, try to locate an ancestor's pair. Express an interest in your family to use those Jewish objects which have been used before.

You may not be able to reach back to the Middle Ages, but in symbol (and so in your soul) you will be a part of our long tradition which does indeed go back for centuries.

Coats of Arms

The question is often asked as to whether Jews have had coats of arms. While it is true that some families were granted these signs of heraldry, the vast majority of Jewish families in history do not have coats of arms, and any claim to the contrary (for most families) is fraudulent. There are companies today, for example, which offer to research your family coat of arms for a fee. The "fine print" on these offers indicates that the coats of arms offered are not necessarily real. For Jewish families they are certainly not real in most cases. Many Jews have surnames which are shared by families who are not Jewish. Many of these same surnames have coats of arms which correspond to them. However, this does not even mean that the family which is not Jewish actually has claim to the coat of arms offered by these companies. A coat of arms is issued to a specific family and not to anyone with a particular family name. Again, while it is true that your family could possibly have a coat of arms, you should be on the alert for this kind of fraud.

Seals

Often a family seal is mistaken for a coat of arms. Seals have been known to exist among Jews since Biblical times and were used for a variety of reasons, from identification on documents, to sealing bottles with an official insignia. At times in Jewish history there have been bans on the use of seals, both from outside and within the community. When the ban was placed on the use of seals from within the community, it was a question of idolatry or of mimicking a non-Jewish practice that raised the issue. There have also been varying opinions concerning the wearing of signate rings on the Sabbath.

Seals have been known to exist for individuals, families, guilds, and communities, and the designs often looked similar to a coat of arms. But there is a distinct difference between them.

Rabbinic Descent

It is not impossible, of course, to trace your family back into the early centuries of this millennium. This depends, however, upon the possibility of finding a link between a branch of your family and a rabbinic or well-known family. While you may have doubts as to this being possible, I need only refer you to my own story in the first chapter to illustrate the point that a most unsuspecting family might descend from illustrious rabbinic lineage.

Among the English, old genealogies are most often available for royal families. In the case of the Jews, our royal families have been those of the rabbis. It is the genealogies of the rabbis throughout the centuries which in hundreds of cases still exist in great detail, and which go back to the Middle Ages.

Again, the point should be stressed that the possibility that you descend, in at least one branch, from a rabbinic family, is not that remote. The mathematics of it explain it best. In the Kurzweil family, I have traced all of the descendants of my great-great-great-grandparents. They lived in the beginning of the 1800's. In all, their descendants number close to 500 people. In other words, from two people in 1800 have come 500 people. It is easy to see that with each additional generation the number will increase greatly. Or we look at it from the other direction: If each of us counts the number of direct ancestors we have up to our great-great-great-grandparents, we each count 62 people. One more generation and we each have 126 direct ancestors. One more generation and we have 254 direct ancestors. In other words, each of us has 254 direct ancestors and we are not even past the 1700's for many of us. Either way we look at it, from the past forward, or from the present backward, we can come up with a large number of relatives. It is not a far-fetched possibility to think that in just one of those cases, an ancestor of ours was either a rabbi or someone who married a rabbi.

Of course, it is not our goal to try to find a rabbi in our family tree. But if we *happen* to find such a case, it is much easier to trace our own families, generation to generation, back through the centuries. Again, the warning must be stated: *Do not* try to pick a rabbi and prove descent. This is non-kosher genealogy! But if a family tradition says that you were a descendant of someone who might be more well known than the average person, it would be worthwhile to follow up that clue.

Yichus

Why is it easy to trace the families of rabbis? There are a few reasons, one of which is known as "yichus." "Yichus" is the Biblical word meaning "genealogy," but the term, in more common usage, has come to mean "family background." It was the custom for many centuries (and still is among some) to try to arrange marriages between one's children and a learned family, or a family with a fine reputation as scholars. To marry into a family with this kind of reputation is to marry a family with yichus. While at the root of this custom there is the recognition of the importance of scholarship and reputation, the dangers are obvious: There is the development of social classes based on the achievements of others, as well as the attempt to marry for self-serving motives.

The result of this custom has been for families to go to the trouble of documenting their lineage to prove illustrious descent. While the accuracy of these documents, many of which are in the possession of families, is generally reliable, many families went to great lengths to try to document their descent back to King David, which was traditionally the finest lineage a person could have.

There is a fine line beween claiming something you do not deserve based on the achievements of your ancestors, and recognizing the influence of your ancestors and their achievements upon you. This distinction must be made when discussing another source of early rabbinic genealogies. It was often the custom, among rabbis and their families, to make it known that they were the descendants of earlier rabbis of fine repute. While this would certainly have some effect upon the way they were treated by the community, it is safe to say that a rabbi who did not earn his own reputation did not achieve great heights. So, while a rabbi had to stand on his own, it was nevertheless the custom to make it known that he was a descendant of someone of high esteem if this was the case. Very often in a document written about a rabbi, or more often in a book written by a rabbi, an introduction will be written which will include the highly respectable lineage of the author. Since many works by rabbis were published posthumously, there were many opportunities to include introductions containing praises for the author. These introductions, usually written by the children or disciples of the rabbi, included biographies of the author. These biographies will often include genealogical information.

Approbations

Another part of these published works are "approbations." An approbation is a "seal of approval" which was written by a rabbi who either knew the author or had read the manuscript and recommended it as a document of worth. While the approbations were supposed to serve almost as a "book review," they often contained a great deal of information about the author. It is not unusual for an approbation to give additional genealogical and biographical information about the author. Very often an approbation of one book will lead the reader to a second book where he will discover a marriage in the rabbi's family to another famous rabbinic family which further extends the genealogy.

Let us assume, for example, that you are able to document descent from a rabbi who lived in the nineteenth century. It is not unlikely that he wrote a book, or wrote a manuscript that was later published as a book. The book would certainly have his name on it, and this alone would take you back at least one more generation since Jewish names include the name of the person's father. It is likely that the book contains one or more approbations (often there are several). A reading of the approbations might enable you to find biographical remarks about the rabbi/author tracing his descent from another rabbi in an earlier generation. In this way, multi-generational genealogies can be created by combining the information found within rabbinic approbations.

A brilliant example of the use of approbations and other similar sources is a book titled *The Unbroken Chain* by Dr. Neil Rosenstein (Shengold, New York, 1976). In this book of more than 700 pages, Rosenstein has pieced together genealogical information included in approbations and additional biographical sources and has created a genealogy extending from the fifteenth century to the present. The remarkable part of this piece of research and scholarship is its presentation of the dramatic way in which the generations since the family's beginnings in the fifteenth century have gone their separate ways. In this huge work, Rosenstein has been able to trace hundreds of contemporary families back through the centuries. While his book is quite large, Rosenstein admits that it is not nearly complete, which indicates that many more contemporary families stem from the same lineage. It must also be remembered that Rosenstein's work is one small part of Jewish family history and that there is room for the same kind of work to be done among the vast number of other families in Jewish history.

There is an important precedent being set by Rosenstein. While the author himself is a descendant of the original family, his research goes far beyond the documentation of his own lineage. Rosenstein has constructed an enormous Jewish genealogy which includes hundreds of other branches. If more of this kind of research would be done, it would be easier for contemporary families to make connections with families of earlier centuries. While it is absurd for any of us to pick a family in the sixteenth century and hope that if we research the genealogy we will make a connection with our own, it is not a far-fetched idea to do the kind of general Jewish genealogical research as Rosenstein has done in an effort to help countless numbers of people to trace their family history.

One further point must be made regarding the possibility that

הסכמת

הרב הגאון האמיתי מופת הדור רשכבה"ג בוצינא קדישא חסידא
ופרישא ע"ה פ"ה קדוש יאמר לו מוה' **חיים האלבערשטאם** יצ"ו
נ"י אב"ד דק"ק **צאנז** יע"א

הנה יד שלוחה אלי מבני חרי אחי אחי הרבני המופלא מוהר"ר **מנשה** נ"י.
והרבני המופלא מוהר"ר **אפרים** נ"י בניס לאחתו לדיק המנוח הרב
המאוה"ג בו"ק חו"פ מוכ' **חיים יוסף** זלה"ה שהי' אב"ד בק"ק סטראפקוב,
והלך למנוחות וקמו בניו בנ"ל ונתעודדו לעשות נחת רוח לאביהם הלדיק
ז"ל שיסי' שפתותיו דובבות ולהוליא לאור מיבור יקר אשר פעל ועשה אביהם
המנוח ז"ל וידיו כי' רב לו **בטיב גיטין וקידושין**. ובקשו ממני הסכמה
על החיבור הזה ונרליתי לדבריהם ואף ידי תכון עמהם להוליא לאור חיבור
יקר כנ"ל. ומלוה גדולה להיות בעזרתם. והמסייע להם יתברך בכל טוב
כה דברי המדבר לכבוד התורה ולומדי'.

יום ד' ע"ו מרחשון **ברכות** לראש לדיק לפ"ק.

פה לאמז.   בק' **חיים האלברשטאם**

An "Approbation," known in Hebrew as a Haskamah. These "introductions" to rabbinic texts usually have genealogical information about the
author, as this one does. This approbation indicates that Rabbi Chaim
Yosef Gottlieb had at least two sons, Ephraim and Menashe.

a branch of your family might have members in it whose genealogies can be traced for centuries. It is not being suggested that any more than one of the countless number of branches of your family tree might contain such a person. All you need is one to be able to connect with an ancestry which might be well documented. Given the number of ancestors we each have, the possibility is not remote. The difficulty is in trying to establish that link.

Of course, if you cannot find this link with such a documented family, there are other ways to make your connection with Jewish history as we have already discussed. The purpose of this discussion is not to encourage illustrious-ancestor hunting, nor is it to have you feel at a loss if your family cannot make a link with such a rabbinic or famous family. It is merely an interesting aspect of Jewish family history research, and a rather effective means of once again entering Jewish history.

The farther we travel back in time, the more remote our sense of family and community becomes. Eventually, regardless of how illustrious our ancestors were, or how much we know about the communities in which they lived, we arrive at the point where Jewish history becomes the story of our past in general terms. While some of us may come from Western Europe and some from Eastern Europe, while some of us may be Sephardim and others Ashkenazi, while some of us may be "cohanim" and others may be "Yisroals," while some of us may be from Iraq and others from Italy, we all eventually arrive at the same places as we reach back into our early history.

There is no way of knowing from where we originate, nor does it matter much, for our tradition says that all the Jewish People, regardless of when they lived, stood at Sinai to receive the Torah. This much is true: the Jewish People stood at Mount Sinai, and we all stem from there. Whether all of us have ancestors who actually stood at Sinai with Moses is impossible to say. There have been times in Jewish history when individuals and families have converted to Judaism, and we might be descendants of theirs. It is not our purpose to attempt to calculate who is somehow more "pure." The very notion is abhorrent to Judiasm. A person who converts today is as much a son or daughter of Abraham and Sarah as any Jew in history. Our purpose in looking at Jewish history through one's family is simply to open a different kind of door to our heritage.

When we arrive in the early centuries of Jewish history, we are unable to speak in terms of our families. We have to discuss the history of the Jewish People as a whole. But, there is not a moment in Jewish history that we, ourselves, as contemporary Jews, cannot enter. There is not an episode of Jewish history of which we are not a part, if we only attempt to share those moments with our history. Just as the Passover Haggadah instructs us to feel as if we ourselves were freed from bondage in Egypt, so too can we be at Mount Sinai, so too can we be among the discussions in the Talmud and Midrashim, so too can we be at the destruction of the Temple, so too can we feel expelled from Spain, so too were we expelled from the countless other communities which oppressed the Jews, and so too do we share in every moment of Jewish history.

When we see our own lives and the lives of our families actually involved in those events, they become a part of our experience. But when the years are too far in the past for us to connect our own families with the events which took place then, we see equally how those times and those events are a part of our history. Just as we have stressed that we can look at the recent centuries of Jewish history as having happened to our families, so too must we see the experience of the Diaspora as our own history. We, as Jews, are in galut. Our Temple was destroyed and we have spread across the earth, living our Jewish lives, struggling and celebrating. We are members of our families, but we are members of the Jewish People. We are individuals, but we are part of a group. As we reach back in history, losing our specific families, we then enter our larger family, the Jewish People.

And as we reach back before the beginning of the Jewish Family, we find ourselves a part, as we have said, of another group: the Human Family.

TRADITIONAL JEWISH SOURCES

God created Adam rather than creating the whole human race together for the sake of peace among mankind, so that no one could say, "My ancestor was greater than your ancestor."

—Mishnah, Sanhedrin 4:5

Rabbinic Texts

If you have located an ancestor who may have written a Jewish text, there are several libraries which should be checked to see if those books are available. They are:

YIVO Institute for Jewish Research
1048 Fifth Avenue
New York, N.Y. 10028

Jewish Theological Seminary Library
3080 Broadway
New York, N.Y. 10027

Mendel Gottesman Library of Judaica and Hebraica and Archives
Yeshiva University Library
Amsterdam Avenue and 185th Street
New York, N.Y. 10033

Klau Library
Hebrew Union College
Cincinnati, Ohio 45220

The New York Public Library
Jewish Division
Room 84
42nd Street and Fifth Avenue
New York, N.Y. 10018

There may be a large university library near you with a good Judaica collection. It would be worthwhile to check there as well.

God prefers your deeds to your ancestor's virtues.

—Midrash, Genesis Rabbah, 74

The ancestors of the arrogant never stood at Mount Sinai.

—Talmud: Nashim, 20a

Descent from King David

I once had a conversation with a Chassidic rabbi about genealogy. He had done some research regarding an ancestor of mine and I visited with him to get some information. After working on my family history for about an hour, I asked him if he had ever done research on his own family history. He nodded casually and encouraged us to get back to my family. But I stopped again and asked him what he found about his own lineage. He continued to seem uninterested in talking about it.

At first I thought he might have found something that he wasn't proud of, but I decided to ask again in any case. So once more I asked him, this time questioning how far back in history he had traced. Finally, I got an answer, albeit a brief one. "Far," he said, in a blase voice.

"How far?" I asked.

In a tone not more than a whisper he said, "David ha Melech" (King David).

Many people have made claims of descent from King David. Accurate documentation simply does not exist to substantiate such claims, though oral tradition does say, for example, that Rashi, the eleventh-century Biblical and Talmudic scholar, is a descendant of David. For this reason, you will find many people claiming descent from Rashi. While I am not questioning the validity of such claims, it is wise to avoid falling into the tempting trap of trying to make them yourself. If you find that your family descends from Rashi, then you should be aware of this tradition. But don't work too hard at attempting to make this claim. The most "famous" claim of Davidic descent is to be found in the New Testament, which goes to great length to "document" the line from David to Jesus.

> If a man casts aspersions upon other people's descent—for instance, if he alleges that certain families and individuals are of blemished descent and refers to them as being bastards —suspicion is justified that he himself may be a bastard.
>
> —MAIMONIDES, *Mishneh Torah*

Rabbinic Dynasties

It is not redundant but, rather, important to stress once again the dangers of going ancestor hunting. It is *not* acceptable to assume that since your last name is the same as that of a famous rabbinic family (or anyone else for that matter) that you are related.

On the other hand, if you do trace descent, *accurately*, from a rabbinic family, you will probably be able to accumulate a great deal of information. Many rabbinic genealogies have been documented, and a thorough check at the major Jewish libraries is suggested to locate such material.

The Index volume of *Encyclopedia Judaica* contains genealogical charts for the major Chassidic dynasties from the founder of Chassidism, the Baal Shem Tov, to the present (pp. 160-167).

If three consecutive generations are scholars, the Torah will not depart from that line.

—JOHANAN B. NAPPAHA, Talmud:
Baba Metzia, 85a

Is There a Rabbi in the Family?

Often people assume that an ancestor was a rabbi simply because they were told by a relative who remembers somebody with a long beard. Long beards have been known to grow on people who were not rabbis.

On the other hand, if you were told that your great-great-grandfather was a rabbi, there is no reason to immediately assume that it is impossible. However, even if it is true, it doesn't mean that the rabbi was famous or even that he worked as a rabbi. A traditional ordination or "smichah" was given to many people who simply graduated from a rabbinic course of study. They may have gone on to become merchants or innkeepers.

Most often, when a tradition which claims a rabbi in its past is passed to you, the claim is a specific one. For example, "We descend from the Dobno Maggid" or "We descend from the Stropkover Rebbe." When you are searching for information about a certain rabbi, you need to know some clue which you can pursue. Generally, this is either a name or a place. If you know the rabbi's name, you will have to use the following biographical directories by looking for the rabbi's name. If you know the name of the town, then you will have to do town history research, obviously.

The following are the best rabbinic biographical sources. Keep in mind that not every rabbi will appear in them. The local rabbi of a small Polish town might or might not be listed. If not, there is still the strong possibility that he will show up in a history of the town.

1. *Otzar Harabanim; Rabbis' Encyclopedia*, by Rabbi Nathan Zvi Friedman, Bnei-Brak, Israel. This volume is a biographical directory of 20,000 rabbis from the year 970 to 1970. There is a name index, a town index, a book index, and cross references to the rabbis' father, father-in-law, sons, and students, if any of them were also rabbis. The book is a fantastic piece of scholarship. Many Jewish bookstores carry this volume. It is written in Hebrew.

2. *HaChasidut* by Yitzchok Alfasi. This book devotes itself exclusively to Chassidic rabbis, from the Baal Shem Tov, founder of

Chassidism, to the present. The book was published in 1977. The volume includes a name and town index, but the name index is a bit difficult to work with since it is by first name. This might seem impractical, but in fact it is the bast way to index a book in which many of the individuals simply do not have last names. The book is organized by Chassidic dynasty, giving the reader a good idea who the teachers and students of the rabbis were. The book is also well illustrated with photographs and drawings of many of the rabbis. Facsimiles of the rabbis' signatures are also reproduced when available. This book also is in Hebrew.

3. Ohole-Schem by Scholom N. Gottlieb, published in Pinsk, 1912. This was a directory, with addresses, of rabbis throughout the world in 1912. It is written in various languages, but the names of the rabbis are almost always in roman alphabet. The YIVO Institute for Jewish Research has a copy of this book and of all the other rabbinic biographies mentioned here.

4. Bet Eked Sepharim; bibliographical Lexicon by Ch. B. Friedberg, published by Baruch Friedberg, MA Bar-Juda, 49, Sheinkin St. Tel Aviv, 1951. This four-volume work is a massive bibliography of rabbinic literature from 1474 to 1950. If a rabbi wrote a book, it is likely to appear here. The set of books includes an index of rabbis.

5. Meorei Galicia; Encyclopedia of Galician Rabbis and Scholars, Vol. 1, A-D, by Rabbi Meir Wunder, Institute for Commemoration of Galician Jewry, 1978. While only the first volume from the letters A to D has been published so far, this is the beginning of a very important series of books. The book is in Hebrew.

6. Atlas Eytz Chayim by Raphael Halperin, Department of Surveys, Tel Aviv, 1978. Through a series of 70 chronological, genealogical, and synchronical maps, tables, diagrams, and graphic illustrations, the author has documented brief biographical information on more than two thousand rabbis and scholars from the years 940 to 1492. The unique aspect of this book is the way the author has shown the relationships between the individuals mentioned. The diagrams, charts, and illustrations indicate teacher-student, father-son, and colleague relationships. Included with the book is a huge folded poster literally mapping in time the lives of 2,091 individuals in Jewish history. This entire volume is an important addition to the field of rabbinic genealogy.

While all of these books are in Hebrew, even a knowledge of the Hebrew alphabet will allow you to use the indexes in search of names of individuals and towns.

If and when you find something of interest, someone with a knowledge of Hebrew can help you.

If these books are not available in local libraries, once again you must do your best in locating them. YIVO Institute for Jewish Research has all of these books. So does the Jewish Theological Seminary Library. Many good Jewish bookstores carry some of them. If not, they may be able to order them for you. As a last resort, you can purchase them for yourself through Shefa Press (see index).

There are other ways to track down information on rabbis. As noted, *Encyclopedia Judaica* is always a source to check; Memorial Books for specific towns are also fine sources.

> A man must not rely on the virtues of his ancestors: if he does not do good in this world, he cannot fall back on the merit of his fathers, for in the time to come no man will eat off his fathers' works, but only of his own.
>
> —Midrash Psalms, 146:3

Jewish Genetic Diseases

One of the more tragic subjects in the field of Jewish family history and genealogy is Jewish genetic diseases. There are several genetic diseases which Jews are more prone to than other ethnic groups. In the past several years there has been an increased awareness of these diseases, and research on the subject is also increasing.

It is my prediction as well as my hope that one day soon Jewish family historians will join forces with research scientists in an effort to combat these diseases. It seems obvious that the amateur family historian collects a lot of data that would be of great interest to many different kinds of researchers. Medical science, ethnography, linguistics, anthropology, history, economics, political science, and other fields could certainly benefit from information about Jewish family histories. In one branch of my own family, heart disease seems to be very common. I am sure that the right medical researcher could use this family history collection in important ways.

I am often asked about the field of Jewish genetic diseases when I lecture. Many people see the link between family history and this subject. There is an organization that attempts to educate the public on this subject, the National Foundation for Jewish Genetic

Diseases, Inc., 609 Fifth Avenue, New York, N.Y. 10017. If you request, they will send you a free pamphlet about their work and the diseases they are researching.

Two books on the subject that are quite technical in nature but should be of interest to laypeople are *Genetic Diseases Among Ashkenazi Jews,* edited by Richard M. Goodman, M.D., and Arno G. Motulsky, M.D., Raven Press, 1140 Avenue of the Americas, New York, N.Y. 10036 (470 pages, $36.00); and *Genetic Disorders Among the Jewish People* by Richard M. Goodman, M.D., The Johns Hopkins University Press, Baltimore, Maryland 21218 (560 pages, $32.50).

> If a man's relative is rich, he claims kinship; if poor, he disowns him.
>
> —D'varim Rabbah 2

SOME FINAL COMMENTS AND SOURCES:
A Jewish Genealogical Miscellany

It is surely worth repeating that there is no perfect system for doing Jewish genealogical research. There is no simple, step-by-step list of guidelines for every researcher. There is no complete list of books and resources to help everyone. It is just impossible to gather every source for everyone.

When I was in Library School, studying for my master's degree in library science, I was taught that there are many ways to find the answer to a research question, and that one of them was to walk down an aisle in a library and have a book fall off the shelf onto your head. That book will have the answer to the question in it. As absurd as that sounds, it has happened! One day, you will just be flipping through a book, looking for something else, and suddenly the answer to a different question will appear.

Of course, those kinds of moments cannot be planned. They just happen. What you have read up to this point in this book are the major techniques and sources for doing Jewish family history and genealogy research. Each researcher will have his or her own path to explore since every family is different. But the general categories of Jewish family history, such as immigration, the Holocaust, cemeteries, the Old Country, names, and family stories will apply to almost every Jewish family. These categories have been dealt with in depth up to this point.

What I have tried to do is to explain and explore those Jewish genealogical sources which have been tried and which are effective. The fault of so many genealogy books is that they are filled with so much useless material. To list the names and addresses of archives and libraries around the world which will probably never answer your letters is somehow dishonest. It would raise false expectations and would frustrate more than help you.

On the other hand, there are sources which I have discovered and used over the years which have been useful in a limited (but at times special) way. It is these sources which I would like to discuss now.

Let it be known at the start that this material which I am about to present does not attempt to be a complete and exhaustive list of Jewish genealogical sources. Far from it! Tucked away in the libraries and archives around the United States and the world are sources waiting to be discovered. Some will be of great use to you and not to me. Others will turn up great discoveries for me and be useless to you. What you need to learn as a Jewish family historian is to be an explorer. You need to go to libraries looking for that special source which will help you. Here are some of mine:

1. MAJOR ENCYCLOPEDIAS

Encyclopedia Judaica, Keter, New York and Jerusalem, 1971, 16 vols.

Universal Jewish Encyclopedia, New York, 1939, 10 vols.

Jewish Encyclopedia, New York and London, 1901-1906, 12 vols.

Any or all of these major Jewish encyclopedias can be found in libraries with medium-size collections. Each of the three is valuable in its own way, although my favorite is *Encyclopedia Judaica*. I have seen fit to invest in the set of books for my home. I am constantly referring to it for one reason or another.

These encyclopedias are useful for general background to any Jewish subject, but are of particular use to us for articles on specific Jewish communities and individuals. Speaking of individuals, an important note should be mentioned. If you have an unusual surname or if other branches of your family have unusual surnames, you will want to, at some time, check these names in Jewish encyclopedias and other biographical sources. *Even if you find someone with your last name, it does not mean that you are related, but it might be a good lead!*

2. WHO'S WHO

Who's Who in World Jewry, 1955

Who's Who in World Jewry, 1965
Who's Who in World Jewry, 1972
Who's Who in World Jewry, 1978

These four volumes, containing brief biographies of thousands of Jews around the world, can be useful in checking for unusual surnames in your family. To repeat my words of caution, people with the same surnames, regardless of how unique the name may sound, might not be related. But the good detective will want to explore these books.

3. LIBRARIES

Where can you find the books and other items which are mentioned in this book? Where can you find other material which might be of potential use? In libraries, of course. But not all libraries have good Judaica collections. What can you do in that case?

A good researcher will want to locate all of the libraries in the vicinity. This includes public libraries and university libraries. Even if you are not a student at a local college or university, in most cases you can use (but not borrow) the collections by simply walking in. Find all of the libraries in your area.

Secondly, inquire at your public library about its inter-library loan system. Most libraries are part of an inter-library loan network. If you want a book which is not part of the local collection, your library can probably borrow it for you. If you live in a small town with a small library, you still have larger library collections available to you through inter-library loan.

On the other hand, you should also make yourself aware of the libraries throughout the United States which are worth visiting someday. Many research libraries with fabulous collections do *not* loan their materials and must be visited. The following is a listing of the best Jewish libraries in the U.S. Some of them have already been mentioned in this book. In all cases, these libraries are the ones which are apt to have many of the major book sources discussed in these pages:

> Jewish Theological Seminary, New York
> Hebrew Union College (Cincinnati, New York, Los Angeles)
> Yeshiva University, New York
> YIVO Institute for Jewish Research, New York
> Leo Baeck Institute, New York
> Harvard University, Cambridge, Mass.

New York Public Library Jewish Division, New York
Library of Congress, Washington, D.C.
U.C.L.A., Los Angeles
Brandeis University, Waltham, Mass.
American Jewish Historical Society, Waltham, Mass.
Zionist Archives and Library, New York
Dropsie University, Philadelphia
Columbia University, New York
Yale University, New Haven

While these are among the best, they are not a complete list. Various other university libraries and Jewish college libraries have excellent collections as well. Once again, you must locate the best ones nearest you.

Local History and Genealogy. Almost every public library has a local history and genealogy department. They range in size from a shelf of books on local history to a fully staffed department of libraries.

The very best example of a local history department of a library may be the New York Public Library Local History and Genealogy Division. In this case, the library is not only interested in New York history and genealogy but *any* local historical material.

The average library, however, has a modest collection of books on the town's history and on genealogy. There is often a particular staff person in each library who has experience in genealogy research and can direct you as to which "how-to" books are the best. Again, it would be worth your while to familiarize yourself with the resources in your local library.

4. GENEALOGY BOOKS

No "how-to-do-it" genealogy book is perfect or without fault—this one included. On the other hand, there are dozens of worthless ones and they must be avoided. How can you spot a bad genealogy book? First of all, if the author makes it all look easy, it cannot be good. Secondly, if the book is filled with names and addresses of every source in the world, it is also not very good. Just because a book looks complete does not mean that it is useful. So many good-looking sources are actually dead ends!

I would like to recommend two books for your home genealogy shelf. Both are well respected in the field. While both do contain some dead ends, they are generally reliable and useful.

The Researcher's Guide to American Genealogy by Val D. Green-

From Jewish birth record book, Berlin. (Courtesy Leo Baeck Institute, New York)

wood, Genealogical Publishing Co., Baltimore, 1975. This is perhaps the best book on American research. Even if your family has been in America for a generation or two, this book is of value.

How to Find Your Family Roots by Timothy Field Beard, McGraw-Hill Book Company, 1977. Tim Beard, a librarian at the New York Public Library Local History and Genealogy Division, has compiled the most comprehensive genealogy book that I have seen. More than 1,000 pages, the book is an encyclopedic work dealing with almost every aspect of the subject from Black to Jewish to Indian to European to Asian genealogy. He has gathered titles of books, names, and addresses of libraries, archives, and record centers, magazine articles, and other items of interest, by ethnic group as well as by country. He may have covered every country on the planet!

One more time I have to offer a cautionary note. While Tim Beard's book is chock-filled with information, you cannot expect it all to be useful. Just because he offers the name and address of an archive in the Soviet Union does *not* mean that it will locate your great-grandmother's birth certificate for you. Nevertheless, in Beard's book it is all there, and all of potential use. This is a perfect lead-in to my next subject.

Other Jewish Genealogy Guidebooks. As of this writing there are two books in print which deal with Jewish genealogy. Each deserves some mention and comment:

1. *Finding Our Fathers; A Guidebook to Jewish Genealogy* by Dan Rottenberg, Random House, New York, 1977. Rottenberg's book was the first general guide for the beginning Jewish family historian. There is some good, basic information in the book. But there are two major flaws which must be noted. The first is that while the author of this book has gone to great pains gathering the names and addresses of archives and record centers around the world, he seldom alerts his readers to the fact that many of the sources suggested will not answer genealogical inquiries. Sometimes I shudder to think how many people are frustrated by genealogy guidebooks which frustrate the researcher in this way.

The second problem I have with Rottenberg's book is his "Alphabetical Listing of Family Names." More than half the book is filled with this listing in which Rottenberg has gone through the major Jewish encyclopedias, several books, and a few archives, and listed the surnames mentioned in those sources. What could have taken a page or two—to refer the reader to the sources he checked—actually takes well over two hundred pages. The worst problem, however, is not the padding of the book so much as the misleading nature of the lists. Although Rottenberg cautions his readers not to assume that the surnames mentioned are necessarily part of your family if you have the same name, the temptation is there.

One example will suffice to illustrate the problem with Rottenberg's list of surnames. I once received a phone call from a young man who said that he was able to trace his family back to the 1500's. I said that this sounded very interesting and asked him how he was able to do this. He replied, "Rottenberg's book lists a family named Levy which goes back that far. My name is Levy." While the caller was somewhat naive and foolish to assume that such a common name as Levy was related to him, I imagine that the error has happened many times as a result of Rottenberg's book.

Nevertheless, the book did inspire many people to begin their research, and in that regard I applaud it. Again, there is some good basic information in this book, and I suggest that you take a look at it—with my cautions in mind.

2. *My Jewish Roots* by David Kranzler, Sepher-Hermon Press, New York, 1979. In many ways this slim volume is better than the Rottenberg book. There is more practical information, more reliable information, and it is more traditionally Jewish in its tone. I would recommend that you examine this book. It may give you some ideas or inspiration.

5. COUNTRY BY COUNTRY

Often, "how-to-do-it" genealogy books give a country-by-country approach to research. This one has not—and for good reason. Because of frequent border changes, frequent migrations, and most importantly the types of sources available for specifically Jewish genealogical research, a country-by-country method would not be appropriate.

A few examples will make this clear.

As I mentioned earlier, the town my father is from is currently in the Soviet Union. When he was born there, it was in Poland. When his father was born there, it was Austria. And my great-grandfather, who traveled to that town, was from a different town. When he left it, it was in Austria. When he returned to it, it was in Poland.

Which country should I research?

The town my mother's father is from is in Czechoslovakia, but when he was born there, there was no such country. Part of his family was also from Hungary. Again, which country should I research?

One more example should suffice. Let us assume that your family is from Russia—as are so many Jewish families. If I told you that the Soviet government does not cooperate with genealogists and if I added that no Russian records except for a scattered few are available outside the Soviet Union, would you then conclude that you could do no research? Probably you would, but it is far from the truth. And this is why this book is *not* arranged by country.

It is, rather, arranged by period, starting with the present, then immigration, then the Old Country, and so on.

On the other hand, there is *some* value to a country-by-country approach. Many foreign archives do have genealogical material and you can get access to that material. *The problem is that it is not always reliable.* What I mean by that is that too often you do not get any response from a foreign archive or record center. Almost every country has record repositories and the ambitious family historian might decide to write (or visit) them, but it is my belief that listing them here would not prove fruitful. It would simply "pad" this book with useless or questionable material. More importantly, you can get this information elsewhere. This is why I recommend the book by Beard. Each country around the world is a specialty in itself and there are books devoted to research on specific countries. Beard's book can get you started if you need to go in-depth with a particular country. The one final thing to keep in mind is that Jewish communities often kept separate records which are not included in the civil registries. But again, this is not consistent and varies in place as well as in time.

6. COUNTRY BY COUNTRY—PART II

While I just finished discussing how a country-by-country approach to Jewish genealogy is not the best way to do it, I want nevertheless to discuss some special sources which *are* by country. These are scattered items which I have discovered through my own research but are not nearly a complete list of this type of material. Compiling a complete list would be impossible. There is hardly a day I visit a Jewish library that I do not find some potentially valuable Jewish genealogical source. These are some of the best:

Magyar Zsido Lexikon, edited by Ujvari Peter, Budapest, 1929.

This book is written in Hungarian (which I do not read or speak) and is very valuable and useful. It is essentially a Hungarian-Jewish encyclopedia in one volume offering historical as well as contemporary (as of 1929) information about the Hungarian-Jewish community. Hundreds of towns are listed, and the articles usually mention many names of Jews who lived in the towns. I found several references to towns in my family and a few names of relatives as well!

Jewish Deaths in Denmark, 1693-1976 by J. Margolinsky, available from Dansk Historisk Haandbogsforlag, 25 Klintevej, DK-2800 Lyngby, Denmark.

This book contains a listing of 12,500 Jews who died in Denmark

Mitteilungen der Gesellschaft für jüdische Familien-Forschung

INHALT:

Jahrgang XIV 1938   937—960   Heft 50

Front cover of *Mitteilungen der Gesellschaft für Jüdische Familien-Forschung*, a Jewish genealogy journal published in Germany from 1924–1938.

from 1693 to 1976. It is an invaluable source, obviously, for Danish-Jewish genealogy research.

Memorbook; History of Dutch Jewry from the Renaissance to 1940, with 1,100 illustrations, text by Mozes Heiman Gans; Bosch and Keuning n.v., Baarn, Netherlands, 1971.

Of genealogical value if your family was a well-known Dutch family, but generally of interest for all Dutch Jews.

The Jews of Czechoslovakia, Vol. I & II, by the Society for the History of Czechoslovak Jews, New York. Jewish Publication Society of America, Philadelphia, 1968, 1971.

While this historical society cannot give help to individuals doing genealogical research, they have provided two volumes (and a third is in progress) devoted to Czech-Jewish history. Excellent background reading for the researcher.

Hungarian Jewish Studies, edited by Randolph Braham, three volumes. World Federation of Hungarian Jews, 1966, 1969, 1973.

As with the book on Czechoslovakia mentioned above, these three books are issued by an organization devoted to the Jewish history of its country. Genealogical material is not to be found here, but good background data is.

Hugo Gold. Hugo Gold, publisher and historian, has produced several invaluable volumes on the Jewish communities of Central Europe. Through a publishing house which he established called Olamenu, he has issued, over the years, books on Bukovina, Vienna, Burgenland, Austria, Moravia, Bohemia, Czernowitz, and Slovakia. Each of these works offers, in considerable detail, the Jewish histories of communities in these areas. For example, in the book *Geschichte Der Juden In Der Bukowina* which Gold edited, you can find descriptive and biographical information about a few dozen Jewish communities in that geographical area.

Most of the major Jewish libraries have at least some of Hugo Gold's works. But if you are particularly interested in this geographic area, you will want to send to Gold's publishing company for the sixteen-page catalog of books still in print. The address is:

Olamenu Publishing House
P.O. Box 3002
Frischman Street, 7
Tel Aviv, Israel

Lithuania. Two sets of books have been published on the Jewish communities of Lithuania and are indispensable for research on this area.

1. *Yahadut Lita (Lithuanian Jewry)*, Vol. I., Am-Hasefer, Tel Aviv, 1959. Vols. II and III, Association for Mutual Help of Former Residents of Lithuania in Israel, Tel Aviv, 1967.

2. *Lite (Lithuania)*, Vol. I, Jewish-Lithuanian Cultural Society, New York, 1951. Vol. II, Tel Aviv, 1965.

The first set (of three volumes) is in Hebrew; the second set (of two volumes) is in Yiddish. Both have invaluable name and town indexes. If your family comes from a small Jewish community in Lithuania and you have trouble finding *any* reference to it at all, one of these two books may be the only place where you will find a reference to the place.

EUROPEAN JEWRY

Yad Vashem in Jerusalem has undertaken the publication of a series of volumes called "Pinkas Hakehillot." The aim of the project is "to establish a memorial to European Jewry which was destroyed in our lifetime." The subtitle of the book series is "Encyclopedia of Jewish Communities" and the following volumes have already been published:

> *Rumania,* Vol. I, 1969
> *Germany-Bavaria,* 1972
> *Hungary,* 1976
> *Poland,* Vol. I: The Communities of Lodz and Its Region, 1976

Each of these volumes is beautifully produced and excellent for family history purposes when you desire additional information of town histories and perhaps even individuals in some of those towns.

Once again, the above-mentioned sources are simply a smattering of some of the excellent items available. Why not list more? Because in reality, every Jewish book offers a potential source for research. Those just cited are among the best, but the point is that you must begin to explore libraries by yourself. When visiting Jewish libraries, you must begin to ask the librarians for assistance in your research.

I have come to believe that there is a book on every subject in the world—you simply have to find it.

ISRAELI ARCHIVES

In 1973, the Israel Archives Association published a volume, in English, called *Guide to the Archives in Israel.* This 260-page book offers, in good detail, descriptions of the major collections of the archival institutions in Israel. At some time, your research ought to take you to these archives, either in person or by mail, but I must report that I have not received the best cooperation from many of these places either by mail or in person. I have also heard many reports by other researchers regarding the same complaints. It seems that too many archives have a bias against the average researcher. Unless you are a famous writer or serious scholar, many librarians and archivists do not seem to want to help you or let you in to their collections. This is unfortunate—but it also leads me often to suggesting to people that they pretend to be working on an important Ph.D. dissertation when arriving at or writing to an archive.

Be that as it may, many of the Israeli Archives have potentially valuable material. As noted, the Central Archives for the History of the Jewish People in Jerusalem has a fine collection of material from Jewish communities around the world. To obtain a copy of the *Guide to the Archives in Israel*, write to

The Israel Archives Association
P.O.B. 1149
Jerusalem, Israel

Two Interesting WPA Projects

During the Great Depression, the Work Projects Administration in the City of New York sponsored a Yiddish Writers' Group as part of the Federal Writers' Project. Two of their published books are of interest to us.

The Jewish Landsmannschaften of New York, 1938 was a descriptive work on the subject and included a directory, in English, of New York landsmannschaften as of 1938. Needless to say, the directory is hopelessly out of date. But the book may still have some reference value for the eager researcher.

A note of interest regarding landsmannschaften and directories however is that YIVO Institute for Jewish Research in New York has recently received a grant to locate landsmannschaften material. Part of this effort will be to find current names and addresses of landsmannschaften.

Jewish Families and Family Circles of New York is also out of date (1939), but this book lists the names and addresses of about 100 Jewish Family Circles (also known as cousins' clubs or family organizations). A good detective might find this book and its listing very useful if a surname of interest is within it. One of the more amusing listings, which I would love to know more about, is "The Association of Descendants of Rashi," the medieval Biblical and Talmudic scholar.

COMPUTERS AND GENEALOGY

The use of computers in genealogy is a growing field. I am always hearing of new people who have designed a computer program capable of storing millions of pieces of genealogical data in it. I don't doubt it. But what many of these people fail to understand is that genealogy is not meant to turn into an instant printout of your family tree by the push of a button. Nor is it practical to think that a computer can be programmed so quickly as to make the information useful to the average researcher. As talk about genealogy and computers grows, my fear is that more and more people will come to believe that one day it will be possible to ask a computer to "print out" your genealogy. I am not denying that one day this might be so (anything's possible!). But unless people begin to talk to their relatives *today,* vital information will be lost forever. Valuable genealogical data is scattered in thousands of books and in thousands—no, millions—of memories, and computers will probably never be able to tap all of those sources. Finally, the whole point of genealogy research is the *process* of discovery, not just the results.

On the other hand, some computer-related genealogy efforts do serve the purpose of helping to locate material of value to the researcher. The Mormons are putting on computers much of the information they locate, for example.

An ambitious Jewish project which comes out of Israel is also attempting to gather and computerize genealogical data. Under the direction of Professor I. Halbrecht, the Society for Jewish Documentation and Preservation of the Jewish Heritage, Petah-Tikva, P.O.B. 121, Israel, is attempting to do just this. At this point it is unclear whether Halbrecht's efforts will prove worthwhile, but his project is an interesting one to keep an eye on. Halbrecht is trying to obtain the cooperation of various large Jewish organizations to distribute genealogical questionnaires, the contents of which Halbrecht's organization will then put into a computer. The computer will be able to print out the information for others to use. I am somewhat skeptical, but the effort must be admired.

Appendix A

A Jewish Family History Workbook

Emperor Hadrian was walking one day when he saw an old man digging holes to plant trees. Hadrian asked the old man, "How old are you this day?" Said he, "I am one hundred years old." Said Hadrian, "You are a hundred years old and you stand there digging holes to plant trees! Do you expect to eat their fruit?" The old man replied, "I shall eat the fruits if my merits are sufficient. If not, I toil for my descendants, as my fathers toiled for me."

—Midrash, Lev. Rabbah 25

A FAMILY HISTORY WORKBOOK

If any one of your ancestors took the time and energy to record information about his or her family, you would probably now be in possession of a more complete family tree than you would have been able to reconstruct by yourself. Many families own family trees which date back several centuries and which are filled with facts about brothers and sisters, aunts and uncles, cousins and children. How indebted you would be to that ancestor who had the insight to know that if not for his or her effort, so much would be lost to time.

At this very moment, you have the opportunity to *be* that ancestor for a future generation. You have the chance to be the driving force behind the sharing of information, names, dates, stories, and photographs about your family. You can be the one who establishes the link between the present generation and history. You can uncover the names of towns which no longer exist but which were the ancestral homes of your family. You can discover the cemeteries where your relatives are buried, or stories about the immigration of your family to America. In short, you have the chance, at this moment, to preserve the history of a family.

Climbing a family tree is actually building one. The process is a step-by-step effort to collect the information which finally results in the story of your family and its history. On the pages which follow, you will find the charts and forms which you will be able to fill in, sometimes slowly and sometimes quickly. In doing this kind of research, you should start with yourself and build from there, adding the names of your parents, grandparents, and so on. Eventually, you will come to a point where you will not be able, with the information you have, to go farther. You will then have to begin to ask questions of relatives and friends of the family who will be able to give you the clues you need to continue.

This workbook might not be large enough for your family. You might need to add additional sheets to document generations farther back. Also, you might find that some branches within your family had more children than there are spaces on some of the forms. Again, you will have to add more sheets as you need them. But generally, if you can fill the forms on the following pages, you are well on your way to compiling your family history. As you examine each type of form, you will get an idea of the kinds of information which you will be seeking. Keep in mind that this is merely the framework for a more extensive family history. You will want to collect photographs, stories, and documents. These pages do not provide much space for this, so you will have to keep those elsewhere.

You might want to use the workbook as a permanent record, or this might be just a place to record the information before putting it in a separate booklet that you can construct. Either way, the forms will be your first step to becoming a family historian and connecting yourself with Jewish history.

RELATIONSHIP CHART

How many times have you had conversations with relatives of yours when you tried to figure out how you were related? There is often confusion regarding the names of the relationships between people. For example, do you know the difference between a second cousin and a first cousin once removed? What does "once removed" mean? Is it possible for you to be your own cousin? The following chart will clear up any confusion you might have with the definitions of relationships. This is an easy system for you to use to answer the question: How are we related?

First we need to define some terms.

Common Progenitor. The closest ancestor which two people have in common is their common progenitor. So, for example, you and your sister have your parents as your common progenitors. You also have your grandparents and great-grandparents in common, but for the purpose of this chart we are only concerned with your *closest* common ancestor. To give another example, the common progenitor of you and your first cousin is one of your grandparents. In other words, you and your first cousin do not have the same parents, but you have the same grandparents.

Removed. When we speak of a cousin being once removed, we are referring to generations. For example, if you know who your father's first cousin is, then you are that person's first cousin once removed. That is, you are one generation away (or removed) from that person. Subsequently, if you know your grandfather's first cousin, then you are that person's first cousin twice removed. You are two generations from that person.

Cousin. A cousin is a child of your aunts and uncles, great-aunts and great-uncles, and so on.

With those terms understood, you will now be able to understand and determine your relationships with your relatives.

As you see on the chart, there are numbers from 0 to 6 across the top and down the left side. These numbers represent the number of generations from a common progenitor. The square in the upper left corner which says "CP" stands for common progenitor.

The first thing you must do is to figure out who the common progenitor between two people is. For example, suppose you want to know the relationship between yourself and your first cousin's son. The first question to ask is: Who is the closest ancestor to both of us? The answer is your grandfather (or grandmother, but for simplicity, the chart shows only male descent though it is the same for males and females).

On the left-hand column, notice that the square next to number 2 says GS, which stands for grandson. That is *you* (in our example). On the row across the top, you can see that the square below number 3 says GGS, which means great-grandson. That is your first cousin's son. Again, your grandfather and your first cousin's son's great-grandfather are the same person. On the chart, you are number 2 and he is number 3.

The square at which row 2 and row 3 meet tells you the relationship. That is, the square which says "1C1R" is the square where row 2 and row 3 meet. 1C1R means "first cousin once removed." That is your relationship to each other.

By the way, "once removed" works both ways. You are his first cousin once removed and he is your first cousin once removed.

Try the chart with a few examples from your family to get used to determining relationships.

Finally, to the question, "Can you be your own cousin?" the answer is yes. If, for example, your great-grandparents were first cousins when they married, then you are your own fourth cousin!

"HOW ARE WE RELATED?"

Relationship Chart

	0	1	2	3	4	5	6
0	CP	S	GS	GGS	2 GGS	3 GGS	4 GGS
1	S	B	N	GN	GGN	2 GGN	3 GGN
2	GS	N	1C	1C 1R	1C 2R	1C 3R	1C 4R
3	GGS	GN	1C 1R	2C	2C 1R	2C 2R	2C 3R
4	2 GGS	GGN	1C 2R	2C 1R	3C	3C 1R	3C 2R
5	3 GGS	2 GGN	1C 3R	2C 2R	3C 1R	4C	4C 1R
6	4 GGS	3 GGN	1C 4R	2C 3R	3C 2R	4C 1R	5C

CP = Common Progenitor
C = Cousin
B = Brother or Sister
R = Times Removed
S = Son or Daughter

N = Nephew or Niece
GS = Grandson or Grand-
     daughter
GGS = Great-grandson or Great-
     granddaughter

YOUR FAMILY HISTORY WORKBOOK

Direct Ancestor Chart. On the Direct Ancestor Chart, you can record the names of your direct ancestors: your parents, grandparents, great-grandparents, and so on. The Direct Ancestor Chart does not have room for indirect or collateral ancestors such as aunts, uncles, and cousins.

Two Direct Ancestor Charts have been provided for a family to use. One chart can be used by a wife and the other by a husband.

Family Group Work Sheets. Each Family Group Work Sheet will allow you to record information regarding individual branches of your family tree. It is on these sheets that indirect or collateral ancestors can be recorded.

The Family Group Work Sheets correspond to the Direct Ancestor Charts. As you can see on the Direct Ancestor Charts, each individual has a number and every two numbers represent a couple. Each couple should also have a Family Group Work Sheet. For example, on your Direct Ancestor Chart, numbers 4 and 5 are your father's parents. You should then have a Family Group Work Sheet (numbers 4 and 5) on which you can record some details about these people as well as information about their children, grandchildren, and so on.

Cemetery Inscriptions and Notes. When you go to a cemetery, do not just record the information inscribed on the stones. As noted earlier, take down the entire inscription and if you have a family plot, draw a sketch of it, indicating the location of each stone and its inscription. Use the Cemetery Inscriptions and Notes page for this purpose.

Research Calendar. When you do library research on your family history, it is a good idea to keep track of your search. Use the Research Calendar to record your activities. You will be surprised at how useful your notes will be when keeping track of your searches. This is for your own sense of what you have done, as well as to aid you in the future. As you can see from the columns on the chart, there is room for the name of the library or institution, the call number of the item, the name of the source, the purpose of your search, the outcome of your search, and the date.

Correspondence Calendar. If you send for any of the documents suggested in this book, you will have to keep track of what you have sent for and what you are waiting for. Use the Correspondence Calendar for this purpose. Included on this Calendar is the date of your request, the amount of money sent (if any), a space for a follow-up letter if necessary, the date of the reply and refund (if any), the name and address of the place the inquiry was sent, the subject of the inquiry, the results of the inquiry, and a file number— if you keep a file of your correspondence (which is a good idea!).

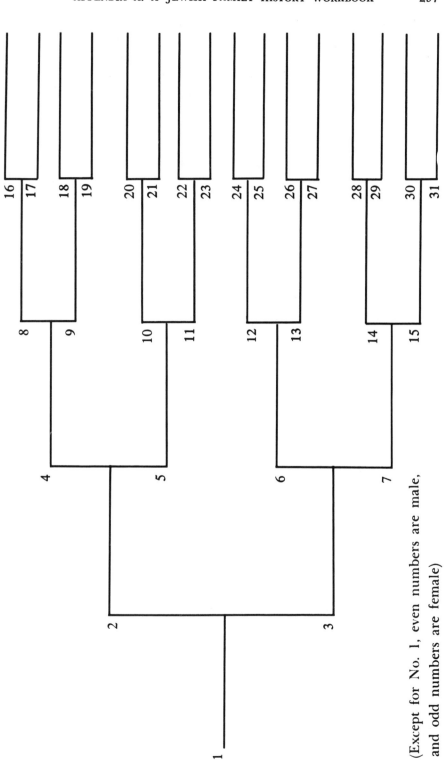

(Except for No. 1, even numbers are male, and odd numbers are female)

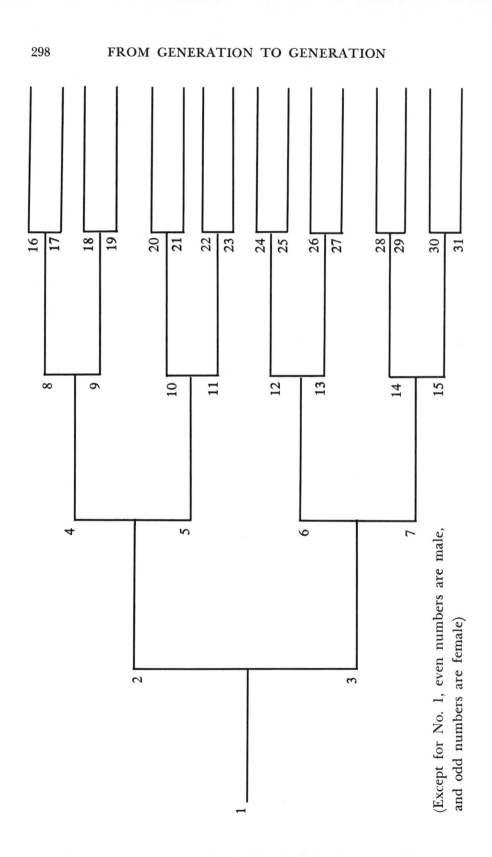

(Except for No. 1, even numbers are male, and odd numbers are female)

Direct Ancestors—Additional Generations:

(If you know information about any ancestors farther back than there is room provided on your Direct Ancestor Charts, record this information here.)

FAMILY GROUP WORK SHEET #'s _____

HUSBAND, Name:
Birth: Place:
Death: Place:
Burial: Place:
Father: Mother:
Occupation:
Notes:

WIFE, Name:
Birth: Place:
Death: Place:
Burial: Place:
Father: Mother:
Occupation:
Notes:

NAME	Date & Place of: Birth	Marriage	Death	Married to:	Date & Place of Birth Death
1.					
2.					
3.					
4.					
5.					
6.					
7.					
8.					
9.					
10.					

FAMILY GROUP WORK SHEET #'s———

HUSBAND, Name:
Birth: Place:
Death: Place:
Burial: Place:
Father: Mother:
Occupation:
Notes:

WIFE, Name:
Birth: Place:
Death: Place:
Burial: Place:
Father: Mother:
Occupation:
Notes:

NAME	Date & Place of: Birth	Marriage	Death	Married to:	Date & Place of Birth Death
1.					
2.					
3.					
4.					
5.					
6.					
7.					
8.					
9.					
10.					

Cemetery Inscriptions and Notes

Research Calendar

Library Call #	SOURCE	PURPOSE	RESULTS	DATE OF SEARCH

Correspondence Calendar

DATE SENT / $$$	FOLLOW UP	DATE OF ANSWER / REFUND	CORRESPONDENT AND ADDRESS	SUBJECT	RESULTS	FILED

Family History
Notes

Family History
Notes

Appendix B

Readings on Jewish Genealogy

1. *Sueños* by James Reiss
2. *Testament of a Jew in Saragossa* by Elie Wiesel
3. *Unto the Fourth Generation* by Isaac Asimov
4. *Family Reunion* by Dr. Leslie Farber
5. *My Grandmother Had Yichus* by May Natalie Tabak
6. *The Crippler* by Danny Siegel
7. *A Worker Reads History* by Bertolt Brecht

With these few lines, the poet James Reiss captures both sides of my relationship with the history of my family: the deep closeness and the vast distance. When I first read this poem, I immediately pinned it to the wall above my desk. It has been there for the last several years and will surely remain there.

SUEÑOS

In my dreams I always speak Spanish.
The cemetery may be in Brooklyn,
and I may be kneeling on a rise
looking out at the skyline of the city,
but I will whisper, *Mira el sol.*

And it is true the late morning
sun will turn that bank of skyscrapers
the color of bleached bone in Sonora,
and all the window washers of Manhattan
will white-out like a TV screen

in Venezuela turning to snow.
But the gray face on the headstone photograph
has a nose like my father's,
and his voice had the lilt of the ghettos
of central Europe.

So I should kneel lower and say something
in Yiddish about fathers, grandfathers,

the hacked limbs of a family tree
that reaches as high as Manhattan.
I should say, *Grampa, I loved those times*

we ran through the underpasses in Central
Park, you with your cane, I with my ice
cream cones, shouting for echoes,
bursting out into sunlight—
if I only knew the language to say it in.

—JAMES REISS

No writer has reached my Jewish soul more often and with
more impact than Elie Wiesel. While Wiesel draws upon
his own family history in most of his writing, "Testament
of a Jew in Saragossa" speaks of another man's discovery.
It is a discovery which every Jewish family historian will
understand at some point in his or her research.

TESTAMENT OF A JEW IN SARAGOSSA

One day the great Rebbe Israel Baal Shem-Tov ordered his faithful coachman to harness the horses as fast as he could and drive him to the other side of the mountain.

"Hurry, my good Alexei, I have an appointment."

They came to a stop in a dense forest. The holy man stepped down, went over to lean against an oak, meditated for a moment, then climbed back into the carriage.

"Let's go, Alexei," he said, smiling. "We can go back now."

Though accustomed to not understanding the behavior of his master, the miracle-worker, the coachman still had the courage to be astonished.

"But your appointment? Did you miss it? You, who always arrive on time, who never disappoint anyone? Did we come for nothing?"

"Oh no, my good Alexei, we did not come so long a way for nothing. I have kept my appointment."

And as happened whenever he banished a bit of misery from the world, the Rebbe's face radiated happiness.

According to Hasidic tradition it is not given to man to measure the extension of his actions or the impact of his prayers, no more than it is given the traveler to foresee his precise destination: that is one of the secrets of the notion of *Tikkun*—restoration—which dominates Kabbalism.

The wanderer who, to purify his love or to free himself from it, travels around the world and does not know that everywhere he is expected. Each of his encounters, each of his stops, without his knowing, is somewhere inscribed, and he is not free to choose the paths leading him there.

Souls dead and forgotten return to earth to beg their share of grace, of eternity; they need the living to lift them out of nothingness. One gesture would suffice, one tear, a single spark. For each being participates in the renewed mystery of creation; each man possesses, at least once in his life, the absolute power of the *Tzadik,* the irrevocable privilege of the just to restore equilibrium, to repair the fault, to act upon the absent. Condemned to go beyond himself continually, man succeeds without being aware of it and does not understand until afterward.

And now let me tell you a story.

Traveling through Spain for the first time, I had the strange impression of being in a country I already knew. The sun and the sky, the tormented lustre in the eyes: landscapes and faces familiar, seen before.

The strollers on the *ramblas* in Barcelona, the passersby and their children in the back streets of Toledo: how to distinguish which of them had Jewish blood, which descended from the Marranos? At any moment I expected Shmuel Hanagid to appear suddenly on some richly covered portico, or Ibn Ezra, Don Itzchak Abarbanel, Yehuda Halevi—those princes and poets of legend who created and sang the golden age of my people. They had long visited my reading and insinuated themselves into my dreams.

The period of the Inquisition had exercised a particular appeal to my imagination. I found fascinating those enigmatic priests who, in the name of love and for the sacred glory of a young Jew from Galilee, had tortured and subjected to slow death those who preferred the Father to the Son. I envied their victims. For them, the choice was posed in such simple terms: God or the stake, abjuration or exile.

Many chose exile, but I never condemned the Marranos, those unhappy converts who, secretly and in the face of danger, remained loyal to the faith of their ancestors. I admired them. For their weakness, for their defiance. To depart with the community would have been easier; to break all ties, more convenient. By deciding to stand their ground on two levels simultaneously, they lived on the razor's edge, in the abnegation of each instant.

I did not know it when I arrived in Spain, but someone was await-ing me there.

It was at Saragossa.

Like a good tourist, I was attentively exploring the cathedral when a man approached me and, in French, offered to serve as guide. Why? Why not? He liked foreigners. His price? None. He was not offering his services for money. Only for the pleasure of having his town admired. He spoke of Saragossa enthusiastically. And eloquently. He commented on everything: history, architec-ture, customs. Then, over a glass of wine, he transferred his amia-bility to my person: where did I come from, where was I going, was I married, and did I believe in God. I replied: I come from far, the road before me will be long. I eluded his other questions. He did not insist.

"So, you travel a great deal," he said politely.

"Yes, a great deal."

"Too much, perhaps?"

"Perhaps."

"What does it gain you?"

"Memories, friends."

"That's all? Why not look for those at home?"

"For the pleasure of returning, no doubt, with a few words I didn't know before in my luggage."

"Which?"

"I can't answer that. Not yet. I have no luggage yet."

We clinked glasses. I was hoping he would change the subject, but he returned to it.

"You must know many languages, yes?"

"Too many," I said.

I enumerated them for him: Yiddish, German, Hungarian, French, English, and Hebrew.

"Hebrew?" he asked, pricking up his ears. *"Hebreo?* It exists?"

"It does exist," I said with a laugh.

"Difficult language, eh?"

"Not for Jews."

"Ah, I see, excuse me. You're a Jew."

"They do exist," I said with a laugh.

Certain of having blundered, he looked for a way out. Embar-rassed, he thought a minute before going on: "How is Hebrew written? Like Arabic?"

"Like Arabic. From right to left."

An idea seemed to cross his mind, but he hesitated to share it with me. I encouraged him: "Any more questions? Don't be shy."

He said: "May I ask a favor of you? A great favor?"

"Of course," I said.

"Come—come with me."

This was unexpected.

"With you?" I protested. "Where to? To do what?"

"Come. It will take only a few minutes. It may be of importance to me. Please, I beg you, come."

There was such insistence in his voice that I could not say no. Besides, my curiosity had gotten the upper hand. I knew that Saragossa occupied an important place in Jewish history. It was there that the mystic Abraham Aboulafia was born and grew up, the man who had conceived the plan to convert to Judaism Pope Nicholas III himself. In this town, anything could happen.

I followed my guide home. His apartment, on the third floor, consisted of only two tiny rooms, poorly furnished. A kerosene lamp lit up a portrait of the Virgin. A crucifix hung opposite. The Spaniard invited me to sit down.

"Excuse me, I'll only be a second."

He disappeared into the other room and returned again after a few minutes. He was holding a fragment of yellowed parchment, which he handed me.

"Is this in Hebrew? Look at it."

I took the parchment and opened it. I was immediately overwhelmed by emotion, my eyes clouded. My fingers were touching a sacred relic, fragment of a testament written centuries before.

"Yes," I said, in a choked voice. "It is in Hebrew."

I could not keep my hand from trembling. The Spaniard noticed this.

"Read it," he ordered.

With considerable effort I succeeded in deciphering the characters, blurred by the passage of some four hundred years: "I, Moses, son of Abraham, forced to break all ties with my people and my faith, leave these lines to the children of my children and to theirs, in order that on the day when Israel will be able to walk again, its head high under the sun, without fear and without remorse, they will know where their roots lie. Written at Saragossa, this ninth day of the month of *Av*, in the year of punishment and exile."

"Aloud," cried the Spaniard, impatient. "Read it aloud."

I had to clear my throat: "Yes, it's a document. A very old document. Let me buy it from you."

"No," he said sharply.

"I'll give you a good price."

"Stop insisting, the answer is no."

"I am sorry."

"This object is not for sale, I tell you!"

I did not understand his behavior.

"Don't be angry. I did not mean to enrage you. It's just that for me this parchment has historical and religious value; for me it is more than a souvenir, it is more like a sign, a . . ."

"For me, too!" he shouted.

I still did not understand. Why had he hardened so suddenly?

"For you too? In what way?"

He explained briefly: it was the tradition in his family to transmit this object from father to son. It was looked upon as an amulet the disappearance of which would call down a curse.

"I understand," I whispered, "yes, I understand."

History had just closed the circle. It had taken four centuries for the message of Moses, son of Abraham, to reach its destination. I must have had an odd look on my face.

"What's going on?" the Spaniard wanted to know. "You say nothing, you conceal your thoughts from me, you offend me. Well, say something! Just because I won't sell you the amulet you don't have the right to be angry with me, do you?"

Crimson with indignation, with anxiety perhaps, he suddenly looked evil, sinister. Two furrows wrinkled his forehead. Then it was he who was awaiting me here. I was the bearer of his *Tikkun*, his restoration, and he was not aware of it. I wondered how to disclose it to him. At last, finding no better way, I looked him straight in the eye and said: "Nothing is going on, nothing. I am not angry with you, know only this: you are a Jew."

And I repeated the last words: "Yes, you are a Jew, *Judeo*. You."

He turned pale. He was at a loss for words. He was choking, had to hold himself not to seize me by the throat and throw me out. *Judeo* is an insult, the word evokes the devil. Offended, the Spaniard was going to teach me a lesson for having wounded his honor. Then his anger gave way to amazement. He looked at me as if he were seeing me for the first time, as if I belonged to another century, to a tribe with an unknown language. He was waiting for me to tell him that it was not true, that I was joking, but I remained silent. Everything had been said. A long time ago. Whatever was to follow would only be commentary. With difficulty, my host finally regained control of himself and leaned over to me.

"Speak," he said.

Slowly, stressing every syllable, every word, I began reading the document in Hebrew, then translating it for him. He winced at each of the sentences as though they were so many burns.

"That's all?" he asked when I finished.

"That's all."

He squinted, opened his mouth as if gasping for air. For an instant I was afraid he would faint. But he composed himself, threw his head back to see, on the wall behind me, the frozen pain of the Virgin. Then he turned toward me again.

"No," he said resolutely. "That is not all. Continue."

"I have given you a complete translation of the parchment. I have not left out a single word."

"Go on, go on, I say. Don't stop in the middle. Go on, I'm listening."

I obeyed him. I returned to the past and sketched a picture of Spain at the end of the fifteenth century, when Tomas de Torquemada, native of Valladolid, Grand Inquisitor of gracious Queen Isabella the Catholic, transformed the country into a gigantic stake in order to save the Jews by burning them, so that the word of Jesus Christ might be heard and known far and wide, loved and accepted. Amen.

Soon the Spaniard had tears in his eyes. He had not known this chapter of his history. He had not known the Jews had been so intimately linked with the greatness of his country before they were driven out. For him, Jews were part of mythology; he had not known "they do exist."

"Go on," he pleaded, "please go on, don't stop."

I had to go back to the sources: the kingdom of Judea, the prophets, the wars, the First Temple, the Babylonian Diaspora, the Second Temple, the sieges of Jerusalem and Masada, the armed resistance to the Roman occupation, the exile and then the long wait down through the ages, the wait for the Messiah, painfully present and painfully distant; I told him of Auschwitz as well as the renaissance of Israel. All that my memory contained I shared with him. And he listened to me without interrupting, except to say: "More, more." Then I stopped. I had nothing more to add. As always when I talk too much, I felt ill at ease, suddenly an intruder. I got up.

"I have to leave now, I'm late."

The car would be waiting for me in front of the cathedral. The Spaniard took me there, his head lowered, listening to his own footsteps. The square was deserted: no car in sight. I reassured my guide: there was no reason to worry, the car would not leave without me.

We walked around the building once, twice, and my guide, as before, told me more about the Cathedral of Notre-Dame del Pilar. Then, heavy with fatigue, we found ourselves inside, seated on a bench, and, there, in that quiet half-darkness where nothing seemed to exist anymore, he begged me to read him one last time the testament that a Jew of Saragossa had written long ago, thinking of him.

A few years later, passing through Jerusalem, I was on my way to the Knesset, where a particularly stormy debate was raging over Israel's policy toward Germany. At the corner of King George Street, a passerby accosted me:

"Wait a minute."

His rudeness displeased me; I did not know him. What was more, I had neither time nor the inclination to make his acquaintance.

"I beg your pardon," I said. "I'm in a hurry."

He grabbed my arm.

"Don't go," he said in a pressing tone. "Not yet. I must talk to you."

He spoke a halting Hebrew. A tourist, no doubt, or an immigrant recently arrived. A madman perhaps, a visionary or a beggar; the eternal city lacks for none. I tried to break away, but he would not let go.

"I've a question to ask you."

"Go ahead, but quickly."

"Do you remember me?"

Worried about arriving late, I hurriedly replied that he was surely making a mistake and confusing me with someone else.

He pushed me back with a violent gesture.

"You're not ashamed?"

"Not in the least. What do you want? My memory isn't infallible. And judging from what I see neither is yours."

I was just about to leave when under his breath the man pronounced a single word: "Saragossa."

I stood rooted to the ground, incredulous, incapable of any thought, any movement. Him, here? Facing me, with me? I was revolving in a world where hallucination seemed the rule. I was witnessing, as if from outside, the meeting of two cities, two timeless eras and, to convince myself that I was not dreaming, I repeated the same word over and over again: "Saragossa, Saragossa."

"Come," said the man. "I have something to show you."

That afternoon I thought no longer about the Knesset or the debate that was to weigh on the political conscience of the country for so long. I followed the Spaniard home. Here, too, he occupied a modest two-room apartment. But there was nothing on the walls.

"Wait," said my host.

I sank into an armchair while he went into the other room. He reappeared immediately, holding a picture-frame containing a fragment of yellowed parchment.

"Look," the man said. "I have learned to read."

We spent the rest of the day together. We drank wine, we talked. He told me about his friends, his work, his first impressions of Israel. I told him about my travels, my discoveries. I said: "I am ashamed to have forgotten."

An indulgent smile lit his face.

"Perhaps you too need an amulet like mine; it will keep you from forgetting."

"May I buy it from you."

"Impossible, since it's you who gave it to me."

I got up to take leave. It was only when we were about to say good-bye that my host, shaking my hand, said with mild amusement: "By the way, I have not told you my name."

He waited several seconds to enjoy the suspense, while a warm and mischievous light animated his face:

"My name is Moshe ben Abraham, Moses, son of Abraham."

*I have often dreamed about meeting my ancestors one day.
I have learned so much about them that in some ways I
know them better than people who are alive today. Once
I dreamed that the first thing you do when you get to
heaven is go down a receiving line shaking hands, hugging
and kissing your ancestors. At those times when I do not
believe in heaven, I imagine a science fiction story along a
similar line. Isaac Asimov, in his own way, beat me to it
with the following story.*

UNTO THE FOURTH GENERATION

At ten of noon, Sam Marten hitched his way out of the taxicab,
trying as usual to open the door with one hand, hold his briefcase in
another and reach for his wallet with a third. Having only two
hands, he found it a difficult job and, again as usual, he thudded
his knee against the cab-door and found himself still groping uselessly
for his wallet when his feet touched pavement.

The traffic of Madison Avenue inched past. A red truck slowed
its crawl reluctantly, then moved on with a rasp as the light changed.
White script on its side informed an unresponsive world that its
ownership was that of *F. Lewkowitz and Sons, Wholesale Clothiers.*

Levkovich, thought Marten with brief inconsequence, and finally
fished out his wallet. He cast an eye on the meter as he clamped
his briefcase under his arm. Dollar sixty-five, make that twenty cents
more as a tip, two singles gone would leave him only one for
emergencies, better break a fiver.

"Okay," he said, "take out one-eighty-five, bud."

"Thanks," said the cabbie with mechanical insincerity and made
the change.

Marten crammed three singles into his wallet, put it away, lifted
his briefcase and breasted the human currents on the sidewalk to
reach the glass doors of the building.

Levkovich? he thought sharply, and stopped. A passerby glanced
off his elbow.

"Sorry," muttered Marten, and made for the door again.

Levkovich? That wasn't what the sign on the truck had said. The
name had read Lewkowitz, *Loo-koh-itz.* Why did he *think* Levkovich? Even with his college German in the near past changing
the w's to v's, where did he get the "-ich" from?

Levkovich? He shrugged the whole matter away roughly. Give it
a chance and it would haunt him like a Hit Parade tinkle.

Concentrate on business. He was here for a luncheon appointment with this man, Naylor. He was here to turn a contract into an account and begin, at twenty-three, the smooth business rise which, as he planned it, would marry him to Elizabeth in two years and make him a paterfamilias in the suburbs in ten.

He entered the lobby with grim firmness and headed for the banks of elevators, his eye catching at the white-lettered directory as he passed.

It was a silly habit of his to want to catch suite numbers as he passed, without slowing, or (heaven forbid) coming to a full halt. With no break in his progress, he told himself, he could maintain the impression of belonging, of knowing his way around, and that was important to a man whose job involved dealing with other human beings.

Kulin-etts was what he wanted, and the word amused him. A firm specializing in the production of minor kitchen gadgets, striving manfully for a name that was significant, feminine, and coy, all at once—

His eyes snagged at the M's and moved upward as he walked. Mandel, Lusk, Lippert Publishing Company (two full floors), Lafkowitz, Kulin-etts. There it was—1024, Tenth floor. O.K.

And then, after all, he came to a dead halt, turned in reluctant fascination, returned to the directory, and stared at it as though he were an out-of-towner.

Lafkowitz?

What kind of spelling was that?

It was clear enough. Lafkowitz, Henry J., 701. With an A. That was no good. That was useless.

Useless? Why useless? He gave his head one violent shake as though to clear it of mist. Damn it, what did he care how it was spelled? He turned away, frowning and angry, and hastened to an elevator door, which closed just before he reached it, leaving him flustered.

Another door opened and he stepped in briskly. He tucked his briefcase under his arm and tried to look bright alive—junior executive in its finest sense. He had to make an impression on Alex Naylor, with whom so far he had communicated only by telephone. If he was going to brood about Lewkowitzes and Lafkowitzes—

The elevator slid noiselessly to a halt at seven. A youth in shirtsleeves stepped off, balancing what looked like a desk-drawer in which were three containers of coffee and three sandwiches.

Then, just as the doors began closing, frosted glass with black lettering loomed before Marten's eyes. It read: 701—HENRY J. LEFKOWITZ—IMPORTER and was pinched off by the inexorable coming together of the elevator doors.

Marten leaned forward in excitement. It was his impulse to say: Take me back down to 7.

But there were others in the car. And after all, he had no reason.

Yet there was a tingle of excitement within him. The Directory *had* been wrong. It wasn't A, it was E. Some fool of a non-spelling menial with a packet of small letters to go on the board and only one hind foot to do it with.

Lefkowitz. Still not right, though.

Again, he shook his head. Twice. Not right for what?

The elevator stopped at ten and Marten got off.

Alex Naylor of Kulin-etts turned out to be a bluff, middle-aged man with a shock of white hair, a ruddy complexion, and a broad smile. His palms were dry and rough, and he shook hands with a considerable pressure, putting his left hand on Marten's shoulder in an earnest display of friendliness.

He said, "Be with you in two minutes. How about eating right here in the building? Excellent restaurant, and they've got a boy who makes a good martini. That sound all right?"

"Fine. Fine." Marten pumped up enthusiasm from a somehow-clogged reservoir.

It was nearer ten minutes than two, and Marten waited with the usual uneasiness of a man in a strange office. He stared at the upholstery on the chairs and at the little cubby-hole within which a young and bored switchboard operator sat. He gazed at the pictures on the wall and even made a half-hearted attempt to glance through a trade journal on the table next to him.

What he did not do was think of Lev—

He did *not* think of it.

The restaurant was good, or it would have been good if Marten had been perfectly at ease. Fortunately, he was freed of the necessity of carrying the burden of the conversation. Naylor talked rapidly and loudly, glanced over the menu with a practiced eye, recommended the Eggs Benedict, and commented on the weather and the miserable traffic situation.

On occasion, Marten tried to snap out of it, to lose that edge of fuzzed absence of mind. But each time the restlessness would return. Something was wrong. The name was wrong. It stood in the way of what he had to do.

With main force, he tried to break through the madness. In sudden verbal clatter, he led the conversation into the subject of wiring. It was reckless of him. There was no proper foundation; the transition was too abrupt.

But the lunch had been a good one; the dessert was on its way; and Naylor responded nicely.

He admitted dissatisfaction with existing arrangements. Yes, he had been looking into Marten's firm and, actually, it seemed to him that, yes, there was a chance, a good chance, he thought, that—

A hand came down on Naylor's shoulder as a man passed behind his chair. "How's the boy, Alex?"

Naylor looked up, grin ready-made and flashing. "Hey, Lefk, how's business?"

"Can't complain. See you at the—" He faded into the distance.

Marten wasn't listening. He felt his knees trembling, as he half-rose. "Who was that man?" he asked, intensely. It sounded more peremptory than he intended.

"Who? Lefk? Jerry Lefkowitz. You know him?" Naylor stared with cool surprise at his lunch companion.

"No. How do you spell his name?"

"L-E-F-K-O-V-I-T-Z, I think. Why?"

"With a V?"

"An F. . . . Oh, there's a V in it, too." Most of the good nature had left Naylor's face.

Marten drove on. "There's a Lefkowitz in the building. With a W. You know, Lef-COW-itz."

"Oh?"

"Room 701. This is not the same one?"

"Jerry doesn't work in this building. He's got a place across the street. I don't know this other one. This is a big building, you know, I don't keep tabs on everyone in it. What is all this, anyway?"

Marten shook his head and sat back. He didn't know what all this was, anyway. Or at least, if he did, it was nothing he dared explain. Could he say; I'm being haunted by all manner of Lefkowitzes today.

He said, "We were talking about wiring."

Naylor said, "Yes. Well, as I said, I've been considering your company. I've got to talk it over with the production boys, you understand. I'll let you know."

"Sure," said Marten, infinitely depressed. Naylor wouldn't let him know. The whole thing was shot.

And yet, through and beyond his depression, there was still that restlessness.

The hell with Naylor. All Marten wanted was to break this up and get on with it. (*Get on with what?* But the question was only a whisper. Whatever did the questioning inside him was ebbing away, dying down. . . .)

The lunch frayed to an ending. If they had greeted each other like long-separated friends at last reunited, they parted like strangers.

Marten felt only relief.

He left with pulses thudding, threading through the tables, out of the haunted building, onto the haunted street.

Haunted? Madison Avenue at 1:20 P.M. in an early fall afternoon with the sun shining brightly and ten thousand men and women be-hiving its long straight stretch.

But Marten felt the haunting. He tucked his briefcase under his arm and headed desperately northward. A last sigh of the normal within him warned him he had a three o'clock appointment on 36th Street. Never mind. He headed uptown. Northward.

At 54th Street, he crossed Madison and walked west, came abruptly to a halt and looked upward.

There was a sign on the window, three stories up. He could make it out clearly: A. S. LEFKOWICH, CERTIFIED ACCOUNTANT.

It had an F and an OW, but it was the first "-ich" ending he had seen. The first one. He was getting closer. He turned north again on Fifth Avenue, hurrying through the unreal streets of an unreal city, panting with the chase of something, while the crowds about him began to fade.

A sign in a ground-floor window, M. R. LEFKOWICZ, M.D.

A small gold-leaf semi-circle of letters in a candy-store window: JACOB LEVKOW.

(Half a name, he thought savagely. Why is he disturbing me with half a name?)

The streets were empty now except for the varying clan of Lefkowitz, Levkowitz, Lefkowicz to stand out in the vacuum.

He was dimly aware of the park ahead, standing out in painted motionless green. He turned west. A piece of newspaper fluttered at the corner of his eyes, the only movement in a dead world. He veered, stooped, and picked it up, without slackening his pace.

It was in Yiddish, a torn half-page.

He couldn't read it. He couldn't make out the blurred Hebrew letters, and could not have read it if they were clear. But one word was clear. It stood out in dark letters in the center of the page, each letter clear in its every serif. And it said Lefkovitsch, he knew, and as he said it to himself, he placed its accent on the second syllable: Lef-KUH-vich.

He let the paper flutter away and entered the empty park.

The trees were still and the leaves hung in odd, suspended attitudes. The sunlight was a dead weight upon him and gave no warmth.

He was running, but his feet kicked up no dust and a tuft of grass on which he placed his weight did not bend.

And there on a bench was an old man; the only man in the desolate park. He wore a dark felt hat, with a visor shading his eyes. From underneath it, tufts of gray hair protruded. His grizzled beard reached the uppermost button of his rough jacket. His old trousers were patched, and a strip of burlap was wrapped about each worn and shapeless shoe.

Marten stopped. It was difficult to breathe. He could only say one word and he used it to ask his questions: "Levkovich?"

He stood there, while the old man rose slowly to his feet; brown old eyes peering close.

"Marten," he sighed. "Samuel Marten. You have come." The words sounded with an effect of double exposure, for under the English, Marten heard the faint sigh of a foreign tongue. Under the "Samuel" was the unheard shadow of a "Schmu-el."

The old man's rough, veined hands reached out, then withdrew as though he were afraid to touch. "I have been looking but there are so many people in this wilderness of a city-that-is-to-come. So many Martins and Martines and Mortons and Mertons. I stopped at last when I found greenery, but for a moment only—I would not commit the sin of losing faith. And then you came."

"It is I," said Marten, and knew it was. "And you are Phinehas Levkovich. Why are we here?"

"I am Phinehas ben Jehudah, assigned the name Levkovich by the ukase of the Tsar that ordered family names for all. And we are here," the old man said, softly, "because I prayed. When I was already old, Leah, my only daughter, the child of my old age, left for America with her husband, left the knouts of the old for the hope of the new. And my sons died, and Sarah, the wife of my bosom, was long dead and I was alone. And the time came when I, too, must die. But I had not seen Leah since her leaving for the far country and word had come but rarely. My soul yearned that I might see sons born unto her, sons of my seed, sons in whom my soul might yet live and not die."

His voice was steady and the soundless shadow of sound beneath his words was the stately roll of an ancient language.

"And I was answered and two hours were given me that I might see the first son of my line to be born in a new land and in a new time. My daughter's daughter's daughter's son, have I found you, then, amidst the splendor of this city?"

"But why the search? Why not have brought us together at once?"

"Because there is pleasure in the hope of the seeking, my son," said the old man, radiantly, "and in the delight of the finding. I was given two hours in which I might seek, two hours in which I might find . . . and behold, thou art here, and I have found that which I had not looked to see in life." His voice was old, caressing. "Is it well with thee, my son?"

"It is well, my father, now that I have found thee," said Marten, and dropped to his knees. "Give me thy blessing, my father, that it may be well with me all the days of my life, and with the maid whom I am to take to wife and the little ones yet to be born of my seed and thine."

He felt the old hand resting lightly on his head and there was only the soundless whisper.

Marten rose.

The old man's eyes gazed into his yearningly. Were they losing focus?

"I go to my fathers now in peace, my son," said the old man, and Marten was alone in the empty park.

There was an instant of renewing motion, of the sun taking up its interrupted task, of the wind reviving, and even with that first instant of sensation, all slipped back—

At ten of noon, Sam Marten hitched his way out of the taxicab, and found himself groping uselessly for his wallet while traffic inched on.

A red truck slowed, then moved on. A white script on its side announced: *F. Lewkowitz and Sons, Wholesale Clothiers.*

Marten didn't see it.

I love reunions: family reunions, class reunions, meeting old friends whom I have not seen for years. I never knew exactly why, but something about the experience of seeing people and renewing our relationships provides me with so much. So much what? Dr. Leslie Farber explained it perfectly in the following essay. Nowhere have I read a more brilliant statement on the subject of the family.

FAMILY REUNION

Social critics often decry the absence of ritual in our culture noting that our hunger for ritual leads us to devise all manner of pomp and circumstance, some of it as foolish as a conclave of Shriners in funny hats, some of it as ominous as a troop of Ku Klux Klanners in hoods. In their headlong rush down this inviting ideological path, however, critics may miss altogether the multitude of pompless rituals that engage us in our ordinary lives. Not merely birthdays and holidays, but such simple festivities (or ordeals) as the evening dinner and the favorite TV program may qualify in this category.

By far the most powerful ritual to celebrate the institution of the family is the family reunion, a gathering of interconnected family units, spanning several generations, related by blood or marriage. The occasion may be a wedding, a birth, a death, an anniversary. Or the reunion may arise out of no impulse other than a mutually felt obligation that the clan should gather again. Indeed, many families have regular, scheduled gatherings, the gathering together itself providing both the occasion and the regularity.

Some years ago I attended a reunion on the occasion of my parents' fiftieth wedding anniversary. In my memory the event has unfortunately merged with an 8-mm movie, which I tend to confuse with my actual recollection. Still, in both the movie and my memory a cousin cradles my infant son and sings "Bill Bailey" to him. In the movie he merely mouths the song, but in my mind his voice is true and confident, not very different from what it was when he was a Dartmouth undergraduate home for the holidays with all the newest songs in his repertoire, and I was only a callow thirteen, dazzled by his sophistication and assurance. I remind myself that he has had two coronaries, three marriages. And I see his father's face hidden in his face. His father, my favorite uncle, my father's oldest brother. If I try hard I can even find my father's face somewhere in his features as I am sure he can find my own father in my features.

This is but a small instance. Actually there is a profusion of small and large family resemblances to be seen in this gathering. There is something unnerving about all this resemblance, as though we all wore masks. Or as though we were science-fiction creatures all of whom developed from the same intergalactic spore.

In watching my cousin, then a man of about fifty-five, singing to my baby, reminding me of the person he had been, or seemed to both of us to have been, so many years earlier, it crossed my mind to wonder at what he was doing. Had it become his habit, at his age, to dandle infants on his knee and croon hits from the 20's to them? Would he, when he left this party, search out someone else's new-born, in order to repeat the performance? Not likely. The performance, and surely that is exactly what it was, was for me, for him. He was performing a version of himself we both remembered and could endorse as genuine, if not to this time and place, then to some other, then to history. He was identifying himself in the group portrait.

I also appear briefly in this movie (my wife and I took turns behind the camera). I appear in a manner that perhaps tends to justify its existence, for what I behold on the screen is not what I would likely have remembered. I am first glimpsed standing in the corner of the patio chatting with a young man, my nephew. My head is slightly inclined toward him as he speaks; I am looking noticeably thoughtful and attentive. Later, the party and the camera move into the house, and I may be seen sitting near my mother as she opens and exclaims and weeps over her anniversary gifts. Despite the extremely dim light of this indoor scene, it is clear that I am still looking noticeably thoughtful and attentive.

Prodded by this pictorial record, I have to acknowledge that a portion of my consciousness on that occasion was occupied with how I appeared, not merely to my nephew, or my mother, or the camera, but to the entire company. I was not dissembling—exactly. I was then and am now a thoughtful and attentive person, as befits my age, profession, and character. On the other hand, I wasn't breezing through the afternoon, looking bored if bored, wandering away if distracted—letting the chips fall as they might.

My wife, too, turns up now and again in this movie, and she offers an entirely different dish, but clearly part of the same banquet. She is seen having a very good time, time after time, talking and laughing animatedly with a number of people, not singing, not looking especially thoughtful, but doing her own little number in her own way. "It's the jolly me," she says. "It didn't feel too bad at the time, but please don't make me look at it again." This movie, by mutual consent, is not shown often at our house.

Yet let me point out, while neither of us relishes witnessing ourselves performing these—or any—versions of ourselves, neither of us felt that he or she—or the other—falsified himself in any important way. What we were attempting—what everyone there was attempting—was to provide a sort of snapshot identity by which the company might refer to us, evaluate us, if they would (and they would, they would); a stereotype, to be sure, yet one that did not, we hoped, deliberately misrepresent our more private conditions.

This matter of stereotypes is worth dwelling on for a moment. We present ourselves and see one another as stereotypes at a family reunion not in order—or not merely—to deceive, but in order both to create and to survive the event.

As for the creation of the event: the purpose of a family reunion, after all, is not to take everyone's spiritual temperature, but to confirm this family, as a family (and through this family all families, Family itself). Naturally, the subject of the occasion is *the family*, and the most significant expression of this subject is the updating, the revising, of the Family Chronicle, for which purpose each individual must be ticked off in time and place and worldly enterprise; his accomplishments must be reviewed and measured against his earlier promise. All this may have relatively little to do with his private, subjective concerns, but the Family Chronicle does not record its members' progress—or lack of it—toward the moral life, and perhaps we should be grateful for that. It does not ask, "Are you a good person?" but "How are you getting on in the world?"; and since that is a question the world often asks us in its own many ways, it need not be considered impudent or unfair. On this great secular Day of Judgment the family seeks to chart its own worldly progress, which is the only progress it can measure or understand. The family is an entity, but it is not a person; it has no collective subjective dimension; its concern, in addition to its history, is with its survival, its prosperity—these being its rough equivalent of moral goals.

So, evaluations are in order, and evaluations are made, usually quite shrewdly, if not harshly. The stereotyping of the individual members is merely a convenience, and usually it is not rigid, but quite responsive to change. Ratings rise and fall as fortunes are made or lost, promising marriages sour and children fall from the fold, or new marriages bring new expectations and new children.

As for surviving the event, the dealing in stereotypes can be a welcome protection against what could amount to a massive personal assault. Can you imagine a houseful or yardful or banquet-hall full of family members all intent on having profound, private exchanges with one another? It could produce mass slaughter. One of the cardinal rules of conduct for the family reunion is: Don't get personal. Nothing must really happen.

Further, the "catching-up" sort of exchange that goes on provides an objectification of one's life that is by and large outside experience—or, at any rate, outside one's customary self-awareness. It may offer a convenient, even a comforting frame for one's own private story.

One's private story *is* separate from the Family Chronicle—surely, at least, they are not identical. The Chronicle, that compilation of events—births, deaths, marriages, divorces, graduations, retirements, promotions, demotions, not to mention moves, accidents, diseases, crises, surprises, tricks and winks of fate—this record constitutes the family story. Few families are without their amateur archivists—those devoted chroniclers whose energetic gift for comprehensive "catching-up" is matched only by their extraordinary powers of absorption and recall. This is probably one of the crudest forms of history ever written—indeed, it is usually never written; it is an oral record, often buttressed with photographs, letters, passports, clippings, and other magical documents; it is also one of the most compelling forms of history we will ever know, for two reasons: 1) It is our first existential experience of history itself; and 2) it is not our own story, but the story to which our lives belong. It is our first experience of history as *story*—how many of us, as children, did not beg our parents, "Tell me a story about when you were little," and how many have not heard our own children repeat the plea? When this tradition of storytelling is once begun, books have a hard time competing—until the children are ready for real books; and even then, they read their books, and still ask an immoderate and unanswerable number of questions about how it was when we were they. Children are passionate historians and "storians." So are we.

Our two accounts—our own story and our role in the family story—will maintain a lively dialectic all our lives. They will seem to merge only to reassert their independence, but this they share: we can no more escape the one than the other.

If, by its stereotyping as well as by its proliferating and disturbing resemblances, the family reunion seems to oppose individuality, so does it also, again with its resemblances as well as with its ruthless Chronicle, oppose anonymity.

When I was a boy I looked upon these reunions with sharp skepticism. Our blood tie, I would complain, was not a sufficient reason for all of us to carry on as though we had things in common—like friends, for example. My experience of the actual occasions was usually bearable—I did have some relatives of whom I was fond—but not joyous; I disliked—perhaps even feared—the judging and reckoning, and I disliked the interminable bragging of parents about their children. They would labor the large and puff up the small accomplishment, or, in the absence of accomplishment, dwell on their children's deference and devotion. A good deal of lying would be necessary to explain away failure and to exalt the minor achievement. Fortunate the parents whose children were both successful and devoted, although seldom fortunate enough to be able to resist a bit of boastful lying themselves.

What I recall most vividly, however, is that the entity of the family, with its uncles, aunts, nephews, nieces, cousins, seemed to obliterate any claim to individuality, no matter how overweening the effort. In the midst of my boredom I thought I would never succeed in escaping or transcending this family, which would continue to multiply and wander even as I would. Even if I were to change my name and settle in Australia, I would eventually be found out by a third cousin who had also ventured to Australia, no doubt for identical reasons. And the one who had fled last could tell the one who had fled first how his departure had been set into the Chronicle, how often the family spoke of him, speculated about him, making him present in his absence. (One reason for the popularity of the movie *The Godfather* was its near sanctification of the family, which was seen to be larger than caste or class or culture or geography.)

For the family is, indeed, inescapable. You may revile it, renounce it, reject it—but you cannot resign from it; you are born into it, and *it* lives within and through you, to the end of your days. This may be inspiring, it may also be very annoying; in either case it is humbling.

Family reunions differ from one another in mood and style (a funeral will obviously not have the same tone as a wedding), and from one family to another, but on the whole I think the similarities, surprisingly, are more striking than the differences.

On the issue of resemblances, more is at stake here than literal facial structure. Families seem to have particular styles and themes that run through them in uncanny variation and repetition, making it possible, for example, immediately to spot a family connection between two remote cousins who hardly know each other and share no physical resemblance at all. And however much the composition of the family may change, and the fates of individuals may alter, this thematic behavior seems to persist, almost as though it had a life of its own. This is particularly apparent in families where power relations are a controlling concern. Reversals and retributions of extraordinary dramatic force may occur as individuals rise to and fall from positions of power, without disturbing the thematic continuity that seems to govern the particular family. On the occasion of a family reunion it is the theme that will be apparent, not the drama, whose real events—those that led to and established a changed situation among the family members—will all have occurred offstage. As I mentioned earlier, one of the first rules of a family reunion is: Nothing must move.

This can be a hard rule both to learn and to keep. At my parents' anniversary my wife was more or less on display, since she and our baby were the newest additions to the central family, and she was meeting many of the clan for the first time. I asked her whether she had, in fact, enjoyed herself as much as she seemed to. Yes, she said, she had, except for Millie and Sam.

Millie and Sam were a married couple my parents' age—they, like my parents, are no longer living—who were members of our extended family, but who had also, accidentally, so to speak, known my wife since she was a child. She had not only a long and profound affection for them, they were important figures to her all her adult life, probably more than either of them knew. She saw them only very occasionally in those years, and much had happened since the last time they met. She had been looking forward particularly to seeing them again.

"I couldn't call off the party to be with them," she said, "so I had to be with them on the party's terms. There were no quiet empty corners we could slip into and talk in any real way, and those flying hugs and kisses and catching-up clatter just don't represent our relationship at all. We pressed each other's hands a lot, and looked into each other's eyes, and so on, but what all that amounted to was just a disagreeable cheapening of what I feel for them, which is serious, and very private and quiet, and doesn't, apparently, have a convenient public form. There I stood, with these people I loved, my arms around them, longing to say something that would be true, about me, about them, about our relation—and unable to speak a sensible word. It was painful."

Ironic though it may be, a family reunion is not an occasion that offers much scope to this major human concern, *love*, either as a personal emotion, pleasurable or not, or as a sacred duty, possible or not. Affection among members of this party may be commonplace and deep; it may also be virtually absent; these conditions will be reflected in differences in the quality, but not the necessity, of the occasion. Regardless of how instrumental affection is, or is not, in determining the shape and style of this family, it has no governing purpose—and has even a restricted place—on the occasion of a reunion. Affection may be felt; it may be expressed, for that can be handled symbolically; but it must not actually be exercised, for the exercise of love between people is an event that moves lives, and on the occasion of this collective portrait nothing must move; it would blur the picture. What is praised here is not persons, or the relationships between persons, whatever the nature of those relationships, but the state, the condition, of relatedness itself. What is honored is not the chosen connectedness that characterizes our friendships, and indeed may prevail our intimate families as well, but that connectedness whose reality lies entirely outside our inclination, and whose inescapability is, therefore, absolute.

So far as the occasion is concerned, I think some of the most deeply felt and cherished—and enjoyed—family reunions tend to occur at funerals. The pace of the event is slow, the mood reflective, intimate. People draw closer together to speak of the past, to frame that part of the story that holds the life that is gone. The young, especially, are instructed in the Chronicle, as their elders make fresh discoveries, new connections with their heritage. Death broods over the company, foretelling but also enhancing the lives of the living, whether they are harshly grieving or merely wondering at the eternal struggle between finality and endurance.

What, we are entitled to ask, does a family reunion have to tell us about ordinary life—life, and family life?

On the surface, very little, if we are looking for correspondences, references. Daily life within that irreducible unit of willed and unwilled connection that we have learned to call the "nuclear family" differs in every important way from the experience of a family reunion.

At a family reunion all is stasis; time stands still, so that an image of the structure that exists only in time may be convinced and grasped in that stilled moment. Family life, on the other hand, is all flow; living it is rather like a trip down a treacherous river in a small canoe; we spend a lot of time keeping the craft afloat, shooting the rapids. There are, of course, calmer passages as well, blessedly un-eventful, unexpected havens of simple routine—and in these quieter periods perhaps we will merely rest, perhaps we will look around, get our bearings, mark changes in the current, note the altered fea-tures of the countries we are passing through.

If the family reunion offers us a primer of birth and aging and death, family life constitutes the workbook, or the lab manual, for the same course.

Family life is much concerned with the passage of time: from now to next spring and graduation; from now to someone's birthday, next month; from now to the meeting this weekend; from now to lunch; and from all the nows that came before and pointed to this one.

The flow of family life, with its turbulence and calm, is actually a double current of time and activity. Now and then one or the other may predominate, at times they seem quite out of phase, even in conflict. Time may be experienced as boredom, or anticipation, or change. Activity may be simply an inertia of exertion on a single spot, or it may be felt as significant movement. In any case, this flow, in which time is always passing and we are sometimes truly moving—not with it, but within it—and sometimes still, "mark-ing time" it is said—this flow is very much part of our awareness of life together in a family. Events occur that punctuate and dramatize the flow itself. Children are born, they grow, they grow up, they go away from us toward their own lives, our own parents die, our friends die, it is growing late, it is years since we began.

What is it that we think of, when we think of ourselves and the time—and the times—that are gone? We want: to have lived hon-orably, to have mattered—to our time and to one another, to have had a meaning . . . we want, we want; meanwhile the potatoes are burning and the gas man is here to read the meter. What family life teaches us about time is that it goes—that what it brings or gives or permits, it also transforms or hardens or takes away. We learn that family life is a passionate daily traffic in perishables, and that what endures, in joy or grief, is seldom what we knew or chose.

Family life is personal life. The people within it play "roles" for one another, as we like to point out these days, but these roles are useful, flexible conventions (like everything else under the sun of course they can be abused); we can hide out inside them when we need relief, we can find a wealth of opportunity for expression and communication within them, and, we discover, we can transcend them altogether in moments when we reach one another deeply in one way or another. Family members talk a lot to one another and some of it is real talk. Family members move around and about in relation to one another, giving and taking their first—and thousandth —lessons in pride, anger, forgiveness, envy, betrayal, and love. A child growing up in a nuclear family learns that a human being is a creature who: is born into a family he did not choose, has needs and feelings and thoughts and ambitions—which are, or are not, filled, expressed, shared, and encouraged—and eventually becomes an independent individual, ready to address the world—and the family that nurtured him—on his own terms.

What endures for an individual is his individuality—his experience of his individuality—and that occurs in the now, connected, of course, to many other nows of personal consequence. An individual, inspired with subjectivity, spurred by the urgencies of personality, armed with self, single-handedly takes on time in mortal combat. Time wins, of course, but the battle may be glorious. We are all, needless to say, individuals, and most of us are the better for it.

But a human being is more than this, too. There are realities to his existence that seldom penetrate his consciousness because they are not directly perceived in experience, but may be brought to awareness through metaphor. At a family reunion a person may glimpse his own life in a way that does not belong to his ordinary perceptions.

As he looks from the oldest members at the gathering, many of whom may not be present at the next reunion, to the youngest, who were not here the last time, he can conceive an image of his own life as a trajectory in time, an arc that began at one point and will end at another, creating a tangible shape, and linking those points to a far huger but still tangible network of interconnecting arcs. That is, he sees his life as a whole, not as a series of experiences, but as a single act—a *thing*, real, objective, unique. He sees that his existence has a dimension in reality that is beyond his experience—almost, but perhaps not quite, beyond his comprehension.

He, who thought his existence was his own, belonged to him, is abruptly reeducated. His experience, which *is* his own, has taught him that living is a process of tracing on sand—that some patterns are deeper, or larger, or more beautiful than others, but that the wind and the water ultimately wash over all. Now, at this family reunion, as he beholds the great chain of generation (to which he belongs), threading its way through the present moment, linking the old to the young, the dead to the unborn, and as he sees that it contains—and is contained by—his own life, he imagines his life taking its particular place in a vast, organic, historical continuity.

In the same process by which time is constantly erasing its own surface, it is forming the deep structure that we never see—and that may be apprehended only through imagery—wherein our disappearing lives are set in stone. For, beneath the sand there is rock; the rock is shaped, is being shaped, will be shaped—by us, by our lives, by our tracings in the sand.

A human being, the family reunion teaches, is a creature who: is born into a family, lives without and within it, colors and shapes it with his being, brings to it his gifts, his acts, replenishes it with his children, and diminishes it—his final shaping—with his own death.

What do you say to people who think they are better than you because their ancestors were perhaps more illustrious than yours? May Natalie Tabak has an excellent possible solution in "My Grandmother Had Yichus." ("Yichus" is Yiddish for "family background.")

MY GRANDMOTHER HAD YICHUS

Aladdin had a lamp, the Rothschilds had money, someone's uncle had a candy store—my grandmother had *yichus*. It was as substantial as a stock of merchandise, yet magical and mysterious as the words "open sesame."

When I was very young, my mother died and her mother came to Chicago to live with us. It was from my grandmother that I learned Yiddish—and yichus. It was Big Bill Thompson's Chicago then. Our mayor had somehow destroyed or confused time for us, and we Chicagoans were desperately determined not to bow to the yoke of English tyranny. The watchword was: "All men are created free and equal." Every Chicago child was a defender of the weak, provider of the needy, and fighter for freedom. Our ancestors and our guide for living were the Minute Men, William Tell, and Sir Galahad. In the midst of all this my grandmother introduced yichus.

Yichus was everything. The possessor of yichus could see through false appearances, as Beauty saw beyond the Beast to the Beloved. In the face of any and all trials, poverty and riches, success or failure, yichus enabled you to conduct yourself with modesty, dignity, courage, and grace. It also imposed certain obligations: to behave with gentleness, courtesy, charity, and love toward everyone. Not for personal gain, that would be useless; the calculating older brothers were turned to stone by the King of the Golden River. Yichus, at the proper moment, revealed and rewarded the true worth of people and things.

My grandmother, I am sure, had never heard of Sindbad the Sailor, yet her tales convinced me that without yichus Sindbad would never have been "selected" for his adventures. Joan of Arc, Barbara Frietchie, Esther—all obviously had yichus. When a little later I read about Becky Sharp, I understood her behavior—no yichus. All the Knights of the Round Table, on the other hand, obviously had it. No one ever said so, and it was not necessary for me to think about it. I just understood it, as I understood that the world was round.

Other matters were also decided automatically by yichus. When my grandmother returned to New York with us, many people came to our house whom I had never met before; through the years, I was to hear their status discussed in detail. Some were considered undesirable. Pincus, for instance, was a *charm,* an illiterate, who had sneaked into the house through the back door by marrying a person of yichus. Such marriages were not unusual in this country where value had lost its meaning. Young Maxwell was a "shoester" and the son of shoesters. I already knew better than to point out to my grandmother that the unfortunate wretch had two college degrees. To my grandmother he was and would always remain simply a man who had no yichus.

Why? Quite simply: his father was no scholar, his grandfather was no scholar, his great-grandfather—the less said about him the better. It followed that even if Maxwell had gone to school, he had not done so because he was interested in learning for its own sake, but because he expected a profit from his investment in study. That made him a shoester.

Being a shoester—need I add?—had nothing to do with working on shoes. In this case the shoester taught French at Columbia. Conversely there had been famous rabbis who supported themselves and their families by cobbling. These men were not shoesters. Their thoughts were profound, their conversation learned and eloquent, their manners charming, and—they had yichus. In our house it never mattered, either for good or bad, how a man earned a living, or how much wealth he possessed. A doctor might sit in respectful silence while a buttonhole-maker held forth. Indeed, it is only now that I am very much older that I know he was a buttonhole-maker. In those days, all I gathered was that he was a learned man who had yichus, and was therefore listened to with respect.

Occasionally someone would show up who had plenty of yichus, but was nevertheless a fool. He aped the style of the learned and was said to be ignorant and pompous. Yet no one ever exposed him, and his inanities were never interrupted. His vain display was interpreted as an effort on his part to show respect for the scholarship of his ancestors by imitation. The company, therefore, showed its respect for that same scholarship by refraining from the Talmudic allusions and scholarly puns with which they would have hastened to put him in his place had he been lacking in yichus. In effect, the be-yichused dolt was treated with an almost tender tolerance, as if he had been the victim of an accident, say a twisted knee, or had a handicap, like a humped back. *Nebach a nahr.*

Recently my Uncle Hiram wrote a biography of my Uncle Barney. He dedicated it to my Uncle Sol, whose financial assistance made the publication possible. The dedication reads "To Kotin of California." Now "Kotin of California" is a trade name, well known in the dress industry. The dedication shocked me. Not only was my California uncle being addressed by a surname, but by a trade name. The book might as well have been dedicated to Coca-Cola or General Motors. In our house to introduce a man by his surname was equivalent to saying: here is a man who is nobody. A kind of John Doe or Joe Doaks. They call him Doaks or Levine because no one knows who his family is. (One can guess what they must be like.) Anyone who *was* someone, even if he were an old man, would be presented as Reb Tevyeh, son of Hershel, grandson of Michael. It was immediately apparent that here was a man of consequence. This eighty-year-old man had yichus. In mentioning his name one was remembering his grandfather. It was that simple.

Someone would pick up a child and ask: Whose child is this? No one thought to say, here are Hannah and Hank, the parents. Instead, it was always: he is the grandson of So-and-So, or even the great-grandson of So-and-So. My own grandfather had died in Europe long before I was born. Yet whenever we came to New York and met people at my grandmother's I was invariably identified as my Grandfather Michael's oldest grandchild.

Yichus was everything. My grandmother might grant that on rare occasions a man who appeared to have no distinguished rabbinical forebears had become an important scholar on his own. Trapped, she never went so far as to state flatly that appearances were deceitful and that *really* he was the descendant of a distinguished line. But by sighs and shrugs she did her best to intimate that if all could be told (sometimes the man might be dead three hundred years) yichus would be found not alien to him.

Gentiles, naturally, were foredoomed to a sort of second-class scholarship at best. With enough brains and application they might master a learned trade such as medicine or engineering. But *true* learning, the Talmud or philosophy, would forever remain incomprehensible to them. Of this my grandmother was convinced, and no amount of argument could alter her conviction. Triumphantly, I would confront her with the name of a great non-Jewish scientist, and give her an account of his accomplishments and of the honors and recognition he had received. My grandmother would respond by questioning the value of his contribution. If that could not be broken down, she would then attempt to prove that the scientist's discoveries were merely the restatement of the work of a Jew.

Take radio, for instance. Centuries ago the Talmud mentioned "radio" as a means by which one can hear voices from afar. My grandmother proved this by showing me an article to that effect in a Jewish newspaper. Don't ask me what it all meant, but there it actually was. If the claim of plagiarism failed, she would undertake to distort the great man's name to show that it was originally Jewish. Somehow this device filled me with particular fury, and the few times my grandmother proved to be right I refused to admit it. When every other explanation failed, my grandmother darkly hinted that for a long time people thought the child Moses was a goy—a nobody—child of a *shiksa* princess.

Sometimes, moreover, it seemed, the soul of a great rabbi might be returned for devious reasons to the world in order to teach him and mankind humility. This informed soul might appear sometimes in the child of a family lacking in yichus or even, though this was very rare, in a goy. It was never a mediocre scholar who was thus produced. He was always a *zaddik*, a genius—and easily recognizable. By this means certain individuals, who happened to have appeared in unlikely walks of life among the communicants of other religions, were granted a special exemption by my grandmother, since their origins were lost in mysteries known only to God and the angels.

Having dismissed everyone lacking in yichus, my grandmother could afford to be completely democratic. As I grew older I had friends of many groups and many religions. So far as I was ever able to see, it made no difference to my grandmother whether the girls I brought home to meals or to spend the night or a weekend were white, Negro or Chinese, Catholic or Mohammedan. Once she had mastered her disappointment at their lack of yichus, she treated them all with equal cordiality and hospitality. A Negro girl used to come with a Hindu boy. Both of them seemed too thin to my grandmother and she would worry about them. Whenever they visited our house she would provide in abundance the foods the Hindu permitted himself to eat, and she prepared special rich dishes for the Negro girl. To her all the races of the world, save one, were all the same—goyim. People—good, interesting, human—but not even Jews —and without yichus.

Her graciousness to these friends and her utter indifference to their financial or social position tended to lull my socialist-Jeffersonian militancy about the equality of all men, yichus or no yichus. And then I would bring home a well-dressed, brilliant Jewish classmate with excellent manners, only to note suddenly that my grandmother's thin lips had entirely disappeared and that her manner had become quite altered. I would become uneasy and at the first chance would rush her off into a corner. "What's wrong now?" I would demand belligerently.

"That I should live to see the day when Michael's grandchild associates with a vulgarian, the daughter of a *grobe yung.*"

"What do you know about her father?" I would cry. "He's a fine educated man, a lawyer."

"American education—a lawyer. A social climber, you'll see," and my grandmother would retire to her bedroom, bitter over the downfall of Michael's house.

Filled with rage, I would return to my friend, my innocent attachment spoiled. And sooner or later it would turn out the girl was affected, or her father told dirty jokes, or her grandfather was illiterate. In the end, no doubt, she married for money.

What a nose my grandmother had for yichus! A fine car would drive up and a boy in evening clothes would come in to take me to a prom. Before anything else, he had to be presented to my grandmother, who somehow or other could only be located on these occasions in the kitchen in an apron, peeling a token potato. We never discussed this, but the potato peeling was obviously some sort of test of the essential good breeding of a new rich friend—just as a new poor friend was somehow always greeted in the living room with great ceremony, and a new clean headkerchief. If the newcomer found favor in my grandmother's murderously critical eyes, she would rise and greet him.

"He has an *edele ponem*—a cultured face," she would say to me in Yiddish. "Ask him who his ancestors are." Blushing, I would ask the boy, who knew not one word of Yiddish, The Question. My grandmother confidently waited. Invariably, her judgment was vindicated: he would produce at least two rabbis.

My grandmother could even spot a kind of goyish variety of yichus—this never meant money or an old family, but an ancestor who was a poet, or a historian, or a scholar. In time, my friends learned to bring my grandmother the name of a worthy ancestor as one brings a box of candy.

My grandmother refused to speak English in the presence of a Jew. To me this was another grievance. She spoke Russian and German rather well and a couple of other languages adequately. (These she had learned in Europe in order to conduct a business to earn money to leave her rabbi husband free to study.) Our Anglo-

Saxon neighbors were all her friends. They exchanged roots and garden cuttings with her and always inquired about her respectfully when she failed to appear in the garden or street for a day or two. She could not have been so intimate with them had she not spoken some sort of English. But we in the family could never catch her at it. I am convinced that she regarded English and all other languages except Yiddish as good enough only for goyim and the mundane communications it was possible to exchange with them. Not for Jews. Slowly I came to realize that except in Yiddish she could not pepper her speech with the allusions and parables which her yichus and her responsibility to us demanded of her conversation with another Jew.

My father had become an atheist as a boy, when he had believed himself an anarchist. We grew up with the impression that religion was a matter of taste. But because my grandmother was the oldest and the most easily hurt, we observed at home all the most Orthodox practices. Every Seder my father conducted the services as if every detail were infinitely sacred to him. In restaurants he might eat pork regularly, but at home, even in my grandmother's absence, he would never put cream in his coffee after meat. In his later years, he has become a chain cigar-smoker, yet he has never smoked on the Sabbath in her presence. It became a custom for my grandmother to disappear after the Sabbath meals, presumably to take a nap. This is a silent acknowledgment that my father might be too tired to take a walk around the block while having his smoke. She never returns to the living room without a good many coughs or much loud talking. This gives my father the opportunity to get rid of his cigar butt. Thus his comfort is respected and her honor not impaired. I cannot say exactly what this has to do with yichus, yet this Sabbath ritual has always seemed to me to have some connection with it.

"What happened to the little girl with the dancing thievish eyes?" my grandmother once asked.

"She married a writer."

"A writer? Good. What does he write?"

"He has a successful play on Broadway. It's a comedy." Then I explained what a comedy was and how the plot of this one went.

"Very interesting," said my grandmother. "It sounds like an easy way to make a living. But you say he is a writer. Now tell me, what does he write?"

I tried to explain that plays, even such plays, had to be written, and that the people who wrote them were, in America, called writers. Impossible to make her see the point. This was not writing. Writing had to do with "learning," it was a serious, even a divine pursuit, and no man whose ancestors had devoted themselves to study would consider himself a writer because he manufactured trifles in order to earn some money.

That any cultivated household could conceivably not feel honored to welcome me, the granddaughter of Michael, her husband, never occurred to my grandmother. Thus I was trained to regard myself as a desirable member of any valid society. The possibility that I might be excluded or discriminated against because I was a Jew simply never entered my mind.

Instead of being concerned about the Jewish problem, I spent years insisting to my grandmother that *she* was intolerant, and that my Gentile friends were fully as good as I. I was so occupied with trying to get her to accept them that I never realized until very much later that perhaps they might have had similar difficulties trying to convince their parents that their own yichus was not compromised by me, a Jew.

As the years went by yichus assumed a new and unfortunate significance for my grandmother. It became a consolation, a protective mantle in which she could wrap herself and feel immune to the new ways and values that were freezing hers out. Many of the older people had died, and their children talked of strange things: how a business deal had been put over, how much their cars and fur coats cost, the poker hands they had held, the hotels and restaurants they had visited. Against all these wonders my grandmother could only assert the value of yichus, more and more desperately it seemed. Would she become the sole grim custodian and proprietor of yichus, like some ancient Southerner still treasuring his hoard of Confederate money, confident that some day it would recover its full value? Gone was the time when my grandmother dealt with the vulgar with light self-assurance. Now she fought them with bitterness and contempt, as if she sensed her inevitable defeat. Worse still, she now bragged of her yichus. It was pathetic, as if a king assured you that he really had a crown, and made of real fourteen-carat gold.

Came the summer's day in the country, when I broke the news to her that I was going to get married. My "friend" had gone for a walk and I was standing with my grandmother in the parlor of the old farmhouse we had been visiting for years.

"He's well educated," I explained. "A writer." My grandmother took on her most remote look and said nothing.

"He has no money," I went on, hunting around for likely references, "and will probably never earn any."

What more could she ask? Still no response. "He has contributed to a philosophical journal," I said hopefully.

Still silence. It was time to play my trump. "He reads and understands Hebrew."

"Who is his father?" my grandmother demanded in a dead and hopeless tone.

"A man who has taught his sons Hebrew," I said proudly. "And he goes to synagogue."

"Have you told his father who you are and what your yichus is?"

"Not altogether," I said evasively.

At this point the subject of our discussion walked in by the porch door.

Standing very erect, hands stiffly at her sides, eyes staring straight ahead, my grandmother launched into a recital of her yichus. She told him, without preliminaries, about my Grandfather Michael, about his father and his father's uncles and cousins, grandfathers and great grandfathers, where they had studied, who had ordained them. She did not ask whether he understood what she was talking about. Slowly and in orderly detail she went through the list as if she were replying to some immense questionnaire. Before she had finished I was faint with humiliation.

Then my friend spoke. In broken Yiddish, but with equal solemnity, though I detected an occasional glint, he began an account of his grandfathers *on both sides*, their uncles and cousins, his great-grandfathers and their uncles, the famous commentary of Rabbi So-and-So who was his maternal grandmother's first cousin. Casually he mentioned the celebrated interlineations of Rabbi Thus-and-So, who was simply his father's great-uncle. Surely, my grandmother must have known or at least heard of his maternal grandmother, familiar to everyone as Raisel of the Yeshiva. Yes, my grandmother had heard of her and of her accomplished uncles. Together, she and my friend pursued this line through a few centuries.

Then my friend switched to his paternal grandfather. These relatives were *really* interesting and important. Alas, they were also more numerous. In each generation they spread out over the yeshivas of Europe like a swarm of praying mantes, studying, writing, leading their communities, leaving a heritage of eternal wisdom. This uncle had a grandfather on his mother's side and an uncle on his father's side. That nephew—. The entire tribe of Jacob seemed caught in the net. All rabbis and all of the highest.

My friend had been cheerfully following the prolific and tireless branch into medieval Spain when I suddenly became aware that for a long time my grandmother had said not a word. I glanced quickly at her. She was still standing, looking out into the distance. But there was a slump in her figure. All at once I felt very sorry for her. The history of the Jews takes a long time to tell. "Perhaps," I interrupted, "we ought to sit down."

My grandmother awoke promptly to the opportunity I had offered her. She pulled herself together, and—rather severely, I thought—said to my friend: "Remember, my son," she said, "remember that yichus isn't everything. What really counts is what a man is, himself. Yichus is not everything."

When I first read Danny Siegel's poem "The Crippler," I experienced a chilling sensation. It seemed like a poem I would not like to read again. But I force myself to read it periodically, to remind myself that family history is not simply names, dates, and family legends. It is all quite real, which is something I too often forget.

THE CRIPPLER

I had always been told
my Zeyde cut his own finger off
to escape the 20+ years' exile in the Czar's army
but now I know the truth:
that there was this man in their community
in one-day-Poland next-day-Russia
called the Crippler
who obliged the Jews
by maiming the children
before the officers conscripted them.
And as the game developed
the Jews found
an index-finger was not sufficient—
the Czar would be a laughingstock.
So the cry arose for variety
to give appearance that everything
was from a natural accident.
And so the Crippler got new sticks and saws
and a holy sense of destiny
for it was he who said:
From this one I will take an eye
from that a leg
and those each shall be broken-backed.
Now I think that this
was how
his own Zeyde
came to be a deaf-mute tailor—
a stick in the ear,
acid in the mouth—
and he was free to stay home
bear children
and sail to America
before the last pogrom

robbed him
of his good fortune.
Here he could gesticulate his way
to old age
and pass on the tale
to his grandson
my Zeyde
who would tell me
in an Aleph-plus hotel
in Yerushalayim
how it was back then
                    back there
so that I might rise above
the shame
and promise my own children
that there are other ways
                    better ways
to be chosen.

Bertolt Brecht's poem, "A Worker Reads History," explains wonderfully why history was once my least favorite subject. As soon as I left school, it became an obsession.

A WORKER READS HISTORY

Who built the seven gates of Thebes?
The books are filled with names of kings.
Was it kings who hauled the craggy blocks of stone?
And Babylon, so many times destroyed,
Who built the city up each time? In which of Lima's houses,
That city glittering with gold, lived those who built it?
In the evening when the Chinese wall was finished
Where did the masons go? Imperial Rome
Is full of arcs of triumph. Who reared them up? Over whom
Did the Caesars triumph? Byzantium lives in song,
Were all her dwellings palaces? And even in Atlantis of the legend
The night the sea rushed in,
The drowning men still bellowed for their slaves.

Young Alexander conquered India.
He alone?
Caesar beat the Gauls.
Was there not even a cook in his army?
Philip of Spain wept as his fleet
Was sunk and destroyed. Were there no other tears?
Frederick the Great triumphed in the Seven Years War. Who
Triumphed with him?

Each page a victory,
At whose expense the victory ball?
Every ten years a great man,
Who paid the piper?

So many particulars.
So many questions.

Index